Architecture, Design and Construction Word Finder

David Kent Ballast

PRENTICE HALL
Englewood Cliffs, New Jersey 07632

Prentice-Hall International (UK) Limited, *London*
Prentice-Hall of Australia Pty. Limited, *Sydney*
Prentice-Hall Canada, Inc., *Toronto*
Prentice-Hall Hispanoamericana, S.A., *Mexico*
Prentice-Hall of India Private Limited, *New Delhi*
Prentice-Hall of Japan, Inc., *Tokyo*
Simon & Schuster Asia Pte. Ltd., *Singapore*
Editora Prentice-Hall do Brasil, Ltda., *Rio de Janeiro*

© 1991 *by*

PRENTICE-HALL, Inc.

Englewood Cliffs, NJ

10 9 8 7 6 5 4 3 2 1

Library of Congress Cataloging-in-Publication Data

Ballast, David Kent.
  Architecture, design, and construction word finder / David Kent
Ballast.
     p.   cm.
  ISBN 0-13-044397-2
  1. Architecture—Terminology. 2. Architectural design—
Terminology. 3. Building—Terminology.   I. Title.
NA31.B34 1991
720′.3—dc20   91–23356
                                                                    CIP

ISBN 0-13-044397-2

PRENTICE HALL
Business Information Publishing Division
Englewood Cliffs, NJ 07632

Simon & Schuster. A Paramount Communications Company

PRINTED IN THE UNITED STATES OF AMERICA

About the Author

David Ballast is a consultant and owner of Architectural Research Consulting, Denver, a firm offering applied research and information services to architects, interior designers, and others in the building industry. In addition to consulting, he is a contributing editor for *Architectural Record* magazine and teaches part time in the Interior Design Program at Arapahoe Community College.

As a licensed architect for over eighteen years, Mr. Ballast has worked in all phases of practice, including interior architecture. Before starting his own firm, he worked as a project manager for Gensler and Associates, Architects.

Mr. Ballast received a Bachelor of Architecture degree with special honors from the University of Colorado. He is a member of the American Institute of Architects and the Construction Specifications Institute. Mr. Ballast has written for *Architectural Record* and *The Construction Specifier*. He is the author of *The Architect's Handbook, Practical Guide to Computer Applications for Architecture and Design, Architect's Handbook of Formulas, Tables, and Mathematical Calculations*, and *Architect's Handbook of Construction Detailing*, all published by Prentice-Hall; *Guide to Quality Control for Design Professionals* and *Creative Records Management: A Guidebook for Architects, Engineers, and Interiors Designers*, both published by Practice Management Associates; and *Architecture Exam Review: Ballast's Guide to the A.R.E., Volume I, Structural Topics, Volume II, Non-structural Topics*, and *Sample Building and Site Design Exam Problem*, all published by Professional Publications.

Introduction

The *Architecture, Design and Construction Word Finder* provides a comprehensive, easy-to-use reference for anyone involved with architecture, interior design, and construction. When your work requires the accurate use of words this book will provide you with a fast, convenient way to pinpoint correct spelling, pronunciation, hyphenation, abbreviation use, and more. With it you can increase your efficiency, avoid mistakes, and stay current with the latest terminology. Because of its unique layout, you can find the answers to your word questions in seconds instead of wasting time searching through dozens of other references or fumbling with cumbersome, small-print dictionaries.

The main part of the *Word Finder* is an alphabetical list of over 12,500 words printed in easy-to-read type. With this list you can instantly and correctly spell nearly any word you use in your professional practice. This list also gives you the correct form of use for compound words and shows if the term should be capitalized. Accompanying each word is the same term divided for hyphenation and marked for correct pronunciation.

In addition to the indispensable main word list, there are several other reference sections you will find helpful. A separate list of abbreviations used in writing provides you with a table of terms often abbreviated in text and how they are shortened. There is also a cross reference list of the abbreviations. This is invaluable when you run across an abbreviation that is not familiar or when you need to check the preferred abbreviation.

Other lists give abbreviations commonly used on drawings. These are alphabetized both by term and by the abbreviation. The correct use of drawing abbreviations can help you avoid embarrassing and costly mistakes in addition to saving you drafting time and reducing the amount of space used on a drawing. They can be used on manually drafted construction documents as well as on CAD drawings.

Designed to work hand-in-hand with the abbreviation list is a glossary of preferred terminology for drawing notations. This list gives the generally accepted terms for calling out various items on construction documents. It includes many commonly-misused words and indicates what words should be used instead. Because precise usage is of utmost importance on drawings, architects, drafters, contractors, and others will find this an invaluable aid to communication.

An additional resource is the list of 300 trade associations arranged alphabetically with their address, phone number, and acronym. This section will help you locate these valuable sources of construction information.

Finally, there is a handy summary of the Construction Specifications Institute's *Masterformat* list of section numbers and titles for quick reference when you are writing specifications.

This book will give you immediate help with all your writing and communicating tasks. Whether you are writing letters, preparing specifications, issuing field reports, or completing construction drawings, the *Architecture, Design and Construction Word Finder* is an invaluable resource.

How to Use the *Word Finder*

The words and abbreviations in this book have been compiled from many sources, including dictionaries, trade association glossaries, standardized definitions, and technical reference books as well as recent periodicals which represent current terms and usage. There is a wide variety of words, ranging from common, often used terms to more obscure chemicals used in new building products, from architectural descriptors to those used by some specialty fields in interior design. Many historical terms are included when they may be used to describe contemporary construction or when they are used to describe existing buildings. However, some of the more arcane historical terms have been omitted. Commonly used (and misused) trade names and many well-known architect's names are also included.

Because the purpose of the *Word Finder* is to assist with correct spelling, hyphenation, and pronunciation not every derivative term with a unique definition is included. Instead, I have attempted to include the base word for correct spelling and any derived terms that may be unique based on being part of a compound word with a hyphen, a compound word without a hyphen, or two separate words. For example, there are over a dozen terms that begin with the word *mortise* but only four are included to indicate the basic spelling and hyphenation and to show variations like *mortise bolt* (a compound word with a space) and *mortise-and-tenon*, which is hyphenated when used as an adjective to the word *joint*. Other words, like *astragal* and *machine* that can be used with mortise can be looked up under their own listings if necessary.

The main word list is alphabetized according to a word-by-word format rather than a letter-by-letter system. This means that the blank space between two words counts. Thus, all second words in multi-word terms are alphabetized according to the first letter of the second word and precede a single word with a letter in the place of the blank space of the words preceding it. For example, *thermalized* is alphabetized <u>after</u> *thermal endurance, thermal lag, thermal mass* and *thermal shock* rather than being placed between *thermal endurance* and *thermal lag*. Hyphens are treated as spaces for the purpose of alphabetizing; other punctuation is ignored as is the difference between capital and lower case letters.

I have also included combinations of words that are commonly used which would assist someone not completely familiar with the term with its spelling. For example, a secretary needing the correct form of *in-line centrifugal fan* will find this under one listing rather than having to construct it from two or more words located in different parts of the book.

In some cases there are conflicting views about term usage, spelling, or how two or more words are compounded. There still seems to be no agreement about *calk* or *caulk*, for instance. In these situations, both words are listed and you may make the choice based on your preference or your organization's style. For architectural, design and construction use, however, I think brevity is preferable. Whichever form of word is used, be consistent.

Compound words present a particular problem. In many cases, different authoritative sources show compound words combined differently. The same term can be found written as solid, hyphenated, or open. When conflicting usages were encountered, the form shown in *The Random House Dictionary of the English Language, Unabridged, 2nd edition,* was used. Although the general trend in spelling compound words has been away from the use of hyphens (to spell as one solid word or with an open space) there are many times when a hyphen is the only logical choice. For example, a term like *machine-screw anchor* requires hyphenation of the first two terms to clearly describe it as an adjective of the noun it precedes. An open spelling might confuse some readers. This is the approach that is generally preferred when forming temporary compound terms.

The syllabic list accompanying the main word list shows how terms should be divided for hyphenation and gives a guide to pronunciation. Syllables given a heavy or primary accent are marked by a single accent mark (') while secondary accents are indicated by a double accent mark ("). The word division list can be used for a quick check on where words should be hyphenated at the end of lines. While most word processing programs have an automatic hyphenation feature, software algorithms do not always produce correct word divisions and these can be checked with this list.

As with the word list, the lists of text and drawing abbreviations were compiled from a variety of sources. Although there were some differences in the way abbreviations were shown in various sources, the ones included seem to represent the most commonly used forms. Most of the drawing abbreviations conform to ANSI standard Y1.1. Those that do not indicate the prevalent usage by architects.

Contents

A

A-frame	A' frame
A-labeled door	A la' beled
A-scale	A' scale
Aalto, Alvar	Aal' to, Al' var
Aalto stool	Aal' to stool"
Aaron's rod	Aar' on's rod'
abaca	a" ba ca'
abaciscus	a bac' is cus
abaculus	a bac' u lus
abacus	ab' a cus
abamurus	ab" a mur' us
abate	a bate'
abatement	a bate' ment
abatjour	a" bat jour'
abattant	a bat' tant
abattoir	ab' at toir"
abbatial	ab ba' tial
abbey	ab' bey
abbeystead	ab' bey stead
abbreviation	ab bre" vi a' tion
abeyance	a bey' ance
aboudikrou	a" bou dik' rou
abrading	a brad' ing
Abramovitz, Max	A bram' o vitz, Max'
Abrams' law	A' brams' law
abrasion	a bra' sion
abrasion resistance	a bra' sion re sis' tance
abrasive	a bra' sive
abrasive hardness	a bra' sive hard' ness
abrasive tile	a bra' sive tile
abreuvoir	a breu voir'
abrogate	ab' ro gate"
absolute	ab' so lute"
absolute humidity	ab' so lute" hu mid' i ty
absolute zero	ab' so lute" ze' ro
absorbance	ab sorb' ance
absorbed moisture	ab sorbed' mois' ture
absorber	ab sorb' er
absorptance	ab sorp' tance

1

absorption	ab sorp' tion
absorption field	ab sorp' tion field
absorption refrigerator	ab sorp' tion re frig' er a" tor
absorption system	ab sorp' tion sys' tem
absorptivity	ab' sorp tiv' i ty
abstract	ab stract'
abura	a bur' a
abut	a but'
abutment	a but' ment
acacia	a ca' cia
academy	a cad' e my
Academy Black	A cad' e my Black'
acajou moucheté	ac' a jou mou chete'
acanthine	a can' thine
acanthus leaf	a can' thus leaf
accelerated aging	ac cel' er at" ed ag' ing
accelerated depreciation	ac cel' er at" ed de pre" ci a' tion
accelerated weathering	ac cel' er at" ed weath' er ing
accelerating	ac cel' er at ing
acceleration	ac cel" er a' tion
acceleration rate	ac cel" er a' tion rate
accelerator	ac cel' er a" tor
accelerogram	ac cel' er o gram"
accelerometer	ac cel" er om' e ter
accent color	ac' cent col' or
accent lighting	ac' cent light' ing
accentuation	ac cen" tu a' tion
acceptable	ac cept' a ble
acceptance	ac cept' ance
acceptance test	ac cept' ance test
access	ac' cess
access door	ac' cess door
access flooring	ac' cess floor' ing
access panel	ac' cess pan' el
accessed	ac' cess ed
accessible	ac ces' si ble
accessing	ac' ces sing
accessories	ac ces' so ries
accessorize	ac ces' so rize"
accessory building	ac ces' so ry build' ing
accident	ac' ci dent
accidental	ac" ci den' tal

acclimatization	ac cli" ma ti za' tion
acclimatize	ac cli' ma tize"
accolade	ac' co lade"
accommodation	ac com" mo da' tion
accordion door	ac cor' di on door
accordion partition	ac cor' di on par ti' tion
accotoir	ac" co toir'
accounting	ac count' ing
accounts payable	ac counts' pay' a ble
accounts receivable	ac counts' re ceiv' a ble
accouple	ac cou' ple
accouplement	ac cou' ple ment
accra	ac' cra
accreditation	ac cred" i ta' tion
accretion	ac cre' tion
accrual accounting	accru' al ac count' ing
accumulated depreciation	ac cu' mu lat ed de pre" ci a' tion
accumulator	ac cu' mu la" tor
accuracy	ac' cu ra cy
acetal	ac' e tal'
acetate	ac' e tate"
acetic anhydride	ace' tic an hy' dride
acetone	ac' e tone"
acetoxic silicone	ac" e tox' ic sil' i con
acetylation	a cet" y la' tion
acetylene	a cet' y lene
achromatic	ach" ro mat' ic
achromatic color	ach" ro mat' ic col' or
acid copper chromate	ac' id cop' per chro' mate
acid-core solder	ac' id core sol' der
acid etched	ac' id etched
acid-etched nail	ac' id etched nail
acid etching	ac' id etch' ing
acid polishing	ac' id pol' ish ing
acid rain	ac' id rain
acid-resistant	ac' id re sist' ant
aciding	ac' id ing
acknowledgment	ac knowl' edg ment
acle	ac' le
acorn	a' corn
acoustic feedback	a cous' tic feed' back
acoustic impedance	a cous' tic im ped' ance

acoustic pressure	a cous' tic pres' sure
acoustic spectrometer	a cous' tic spec trom' e ter
acoustical ceiling	a cous' ti cal ceil' ing
acoustical door	a cous' ti cal door
acoustical tile	a cous' ti cal tile
acoustics	a cous' tics
acoustimeter	ac" ous tim' e ter
acquisition	ac" qui si' tion
acre	a' cre
Acrilan™	Ac' ri lan"
acropolis	a crop' o lis
across	a cross'
acroter	ac' ro ter
acroteria	ac" ro te' ri a
acroterion	ac" ro te' ri on
acroterium	ac" ro te' ri um
acrylate	ac' ry late"
acrylic	a cryl' ic
acrylic resin	a cryl' ic res' in
acrylic terpolymer	a cryl' ic ter pol' y mer
acrylonitrile	ac" ry lo ni' trile
acrylonitrile-butadiene-styrene	ac" ry lo ni' trile bu" ta di' ene sty' rene
Act of Parliament clock	Act' of Par' lia ment clock"
actinic	ac tin' ic
actinic glass	ac tin' ic glass"
activated carbon	ac' ti vat" ed car' bon
activator	ac' ti va" tor
active	ac' tive
active leaf	ac' tive leaf"
active mass damper	ac' tive mass damp' er
active solar energy	ac' tive so' lar en' er gy
activity	ac tiv' i ty
activity duration	ac tiv' i ty du ra' tion
actual damage	ac' tu al dam' age
actual size lumber	ac' tu al size lum' ber
actuate	ac' tu ate
actuating	ac' tu at ing
acuity	a cu' i ty
acute angle	a cute' an' gle
acute arch	a cute' arch"
acute-care	a cute' care"

ad valorem	ad va lo' em
Adair Marble	A dair' Mar' ble
adaptability	a dapt" a bil' i ty
adaptation	ad" ap ta' tion
adapter	a dapt' er
addenda	ad den' da
addendum	ad den' dum
addition	ad di' tion
additive	ad' di tive
additive alternate	ad' di tive al' ter nate
addorsed	ad dorsed'
adhere	ad here'
adherence	ad her' ence
adherend	ad her' end
adherend failure	ad her' end fail' ure
adhesion	ad he' sion
adhesive	ad he' sive
adhesive failure	ad he' sive fail' ure
adiabatic	ad" i a bat' ic
Adirondack chair	Ad" i ron' dack chair'
adjacencies	ad ja' cen cies
adjacent	ad ja' cent
adjudicate	ad ju' di cate"
adjustability	ad just" a bil' i ty
adjustable	ad just' a ble
adjustable base anchor	ad just' a ble base an' chor
adjustable clamp	ad just' a ble clamp"
adjustable-joint pliers	ad just' a ble joint pli' ers
adjustable shelving	ad just' a ble shelv' ing
adjustable wrench	ad just' a ble wrench'
adjuster	ad just' er
adjusting	ad just' ing
adjustment	ad just' ment
adjustment screw	ad just' ment screw"
adjuvant	ad' ju vant
administration	ad min" is tra' tion
administrator	ad min' is tra" tor
admiralty brass	ad' mi ral ty brass"
admittance	ad mit' tance
admittance ratio	ad mit' tance ra' tio
admixture	ad mix' ture
adobe	a do' be

5

adsorbed water	ad sorbed' wat' er
adsorbent	ad sorb' ent
adsorption	ad sorb' tion
adulterated	a dul' ter at ed
adulteration	a dul" ter a' tion
advanced decay	ad vanced' de cay'
advancing	ad vanc' ing
advertisement	ad" ver tise' ment
advertising	ad' ver tis" ing
adze	adze"
adze-eye hammer	adze' eye ham' mer
aediculae	ae dic' u lae"
aedicule	ae' di cule"
Aegean Crystal	Ae ge' an Crys' tal
aerate	aer' ate
aerated concrete	aer' at ed con' crete
aeration	aer a' tion
aeration equipment	aer a' tion e quip' ment
aerator	aer' a tor
aerial survey	aer' i al sur' vey
aerodrome	aer' o drome"
aerograph	aer' o graph"
aerosol	aer' o sol"
aesthetic	aes thet' ic
aesthetically	aes thet' i cal ly
affidavit	af" fi da' vit
affirmative action	af firm' a tive ac' tion
affront	af front'
affronted	af front' ed
African mahogany	Af' ri can ma hog' a ny
African rosewood	Af' ri can rose' wood
afrormosia	af" ror mo' si a
afterglow	af' ter glow"
aftershock	af' ter shock"
afwillite	af' wil lite"
agate	ag' ate
Agate	A' gate
agate ware	ag' ate ware"
agba	ag' ba
age hardening	age hard' en ing
aged accounts receivable	aged' ac counts' re ceiv' a ble
agency	a' gen cy

agent	a' gent
agglomeration	ag glom' er a' tion
aggregate	ag' gre gate
aging	ag' ing
aging time	ag' ing time
agitating speed	ag' i tat" ing speed
agitation	ag" i ta' tion
agitator	ag' i ta" tor
agora	ag' o ra
agreement	a gree' ment
agricultural building	ag" ri cul' tur al build' ing
aiguille	ai guille'
aileron	ai' ler on"
air brick	air brick"
air chamber	air" cham' ber
air change	air" change
air-condition	air" con di' tion
air conditioner	air" con di' tion er
air conditioning	air" con di' tion ing
air content	air" con' tent
air-cooled condenser	air" cooled con dens' er
air-cure	air" cure
air curtain	air" cur' tain
air diffuser	air" dif fus' er
air-dried	air" dried
air-driven nailer	air" driv' en nail' er
air-dry	air" dry"
air duct	air" duct
air-entrained concrete	air" en train' ed con' crete
air entraining	air" en train' ing
air-entraining admixture	air" en train' ing ad mix' ture
air entrainment	air" en train' ment
air-felting	air" felt' ing
air gap	air' gap"
air-handling	air" han' dling
air lock	air' lock
air rights	air" rights
air shaft	air" shaft
air-supported	air" sup port' ed
air-supported structure	air" sup port' ed struc' ture
air tightness	air" tight' ness
air-type solar system	air" type so' lar sys' tem

air-water system	air" wa' ter sys' tem
airboot	air" boot
airborne sound	air' borne" sound
airfield	air' field
airflow	air' flow
airfoam™	air' foam
airport	air' port
airway	air' way
aisle	aisle
aisleway	aisle' way
àjour	à' jour
ajouré	a" jou re'
akari lamp	a kar' i lamp
akroter	ak' ro ter
akroterion	ak ro ter' i on
Alabama marble	Al" a bam' a mar' ble
alabaster	al' a bas" ter
alabaster glass	al' a bas" ter glass"
albarium	al bar' i um
albedo	al be' do
Alberene Serpentine	Al' ber ene Ser' pen tine"
Albers, Josef	Al' bers, Jo' sef
Albert, Edouard	Al' bert, Ed' ouard
albertite	al' ber tite"
albronze	al' bronze"
alburnum	al bur' num
alclad	al' clad
alcove	al' cove
alder	al' der
aldol	al' dol
Alençon lace	A len' çon lace'
alette	a lette'
Alexander, Christopher	Al" ex an' der, Chris' to pher
aliasing	a' li as ing
alidade	al' i dade"
align	a lign'
alignment	a lign' ment
aliphatic	al" i phat' ic
alkali	al' ka li"
alkali-aggregate reaction	al' ka li" ag' gre gate" re ac' tion
alkali-silica reaction	al' ka li" sil' i ca re ac' tion
alkaline	al' ka line"

alkaline soil	al' ka line" soil
alkalinity	al" ka lin' i ty
alkoranes	al' ko ranes
alkyd	al' kyd
alkyd paint	al' kyd paint"
alkyd resin	al' kyd res' in
all-hair pad	all' hair" pad
all-risk policy	all' risk pol' i cy
all-veneer construction	all ve neer' con struc' tion
allée	al lee'
Allen wrench	Al' len wrench
alley	al' ley
alligatoring	al' li ga' tor ing
allotment	al lot' ment
allowable load	al low' a ble load"
allowable soil pressure	al low' a ble soil pres' sure
allowance	al low' ance
alloy	al' loy
alloy steel	al' loy steel"
alloyed zinc	al' loyed zinc"
allure	al lure'
alluvial	al lu' vi al
alluvium	al lu' vi um
allyl	al' lyl
allyl resin	al' lyl res' in
almemar	al me' mar
almery	alm' er y
almon	al' mon
almond	al' mond
almonry	al' mon ry
alodine	al' o dine
alpaca	al pac' a
alpha-beta brass	al' pha be' ta brass"
alpha gypsum	al' pha gyp' sum
altar	al' tar
altar rail	al' tar rail"
altar screen	al' tar screen"
altarpiece	al' tar piece"
altazimuth mounting	alt az' i muth mount' ing
alter	al' ter
alteration	al" ter a' tion
alternate	al' ter nate"

alternating current	al' ter nat" ing cur' rent
alternative	al ter' na tive
altimeter	al tim' e ter
altitude	al' ti tude"
alto-rilievo	al' to re lie' vo
alum	al' um
Alumilite™	A lu' mi lite"
alumina	a lu' mi na
alumina cement	a lu' mi na ce ment'
aluminate concrete	a lu' mi nate con' crete
aluminiferous	a lu" mi nif' er ous
aluminize	a lu' mi nize"
alumino-thermic welding	a lu" mi no ther' mic weld' ing
aluminum	a lu' mi num
aluminum bronze	a lu' mi num bronze"
aluminum oxide	a lu' mi num ox' ide
aluminum-silicone bronze	a lu' mi num sil' i cone bronze"
alure	al' ure
alveated	al' ve at" ed
amalgam	a mal' gam
amaranth	am' a ranth
Ambasz, Emilio	Am basz', E mil' io
ambe	am' be
amber	am' ber
ambiance	am' bi ance"
ambient	am' bi ent
ambient air	am' bi ent air"
ambient noise	am' bi ent noise"
ambient temperature	am' bi ent tem' per a ture
Ambiente	Am bien' te
ambo	am' bo
ambry	am' bry
ambulance	am' bu lance
ambulatory	am' bu la to" ry
ambusson	am bus' son
amenities	a men' i ties
amenity	a men' i ty
American black walnut	A mer' i can black wal' nut
American bond	A mer' i can bond
American Chippendale	A mer' i can Chip' pen dale"
American standard beam	A mer' i can stand' ard beam
American standard channel	A mer' i can stand' ard chan' nel

American standard pipe thread	A mer' i can stand' ard pipe" thread
American wire gauge	A mer' i can wire" gauge
amine	a' mine
amino resin	a mi' no res' in
ammeter	am' me ter
ammonia	am mo' nia
ammoniacal copper arsenite	am" mo ni' a cal cop' per ar' se nite"
ammonium phosphate	am mo' ni um phos' phate
amorphic silica	a mor' phic sil' i ca
amorphous	a mor' phous
amortization	am" or ti za' tion
amortize	am' or tize"
amp	amp'
ampacity	am pac' i ty
amperage	am' per age
ampere	am' pere
ampere-hour	am" pere hour"
ampere-hour meter	am' pere hour" me' ter
amphibolite	am phib' o lite"
amphiprostyle	am phip' ro style"
amphitheater	am' phi the" a ter
amphoteric	am" pho ter' ic
amplification	am" pli fi ca' tion
amplitude	am' pli tude"
amplitude decrement factor	am' pli tude" dec" re ment fac' tor
amugis	a mu' gis
amylaceous	am" y la' ceous
anaerobic	an" aer o' bic
anaesthetic system	an" aes thet' ic sys' tem
anaglyph	an' a glyph
anaglyphy	a nag' ly phy
anaglyptic	an" a glyp' tic
analogous colors	a nal' o gous col' ors
analysis	a nal' y sis
anchor	an' chor
anchor block	an' chor block"
anchor bolt	an' chor bolt"
anchorage	an' chor age
anchorage deformation	an' chor age de" for ma' tion
anchored	an' chored

ancillary	an' cil lar" y
ancon	an' con
ancona	an co' na
ancone	an co' ne
ancones	an co' nes
Andaman rosewood	An' da man rose' wood
andiroba	an" di ro' ba
andiron	and' i" on
Ando, Tadao	An' do, Ta da' o
Andrews, John	An' drews, John
anechoic	an" e cho' ic
anechoic chamber	an" e cho' ic cham' ber
anemometer	an" e mom' e ter
anemostat	a nem' o stat"
angel bed	an' gel bed"
angelique	an" ge lique'
angle	an' gle
angle bead	an' gle bead"
angle clip	an' gle clip"
angle closer	an' gle clos' er
angle fillet	an' gle fil' let
angle iron	an' gle i' ron
angle of incidence	an' gle of in' ci dence
angle of inclination	an' gle of in" cli na' tion
angle of reflection	an' gle of re flec' tion
angle of repose	an' gle of re pose'
angle paddle	an' gle pad' dle
angled stair	an' gled stair"
angora	an go' ra
angstrom	ang' strom
angular	an' gu lar
angularity	an" gu lar' i ty
angulated	an' gu lat" ed
anhydride	an hy' dride
anhydrite	an hy' drite
anhydrous calcium	an hy' drous cal' ci um
anhydrous gypsum plaster	an hy' drous gyp' sum plas' ter
anhydrous lime	an hy' drous lime"
anidex	an' i dex
aniline	an' i line
aniline-formaldehyde	an' i line form al' de hyde"
animal shelter	an' i mal shel' ter

anionic emulsion	an" i on' ic e mul' sion
anisometric perspective	an i" so met' ric per spec' tive
anisotropic	an i" so trop' ic
anisotropy	an" i sot' ro py
anneal	an neal'
annealed	an nealed'
annealing	an neal' ing
annex	an nex'
annotation	an" no ta' tion
annual	an' nu al
annuity	an nu' i ty
annular	an' nu lar
annular nail	an' nu lar nail"
annular thread	an' nu lar thread"
annulated column	an' nu lat" ed col' umn
annulet	an' nu let
annunciator	an nun' ci a" tor
anode	an' ode
anodic coating	an od' ic coat' ing
anodic protection	an od' ic pro tec' tion
anodize	an' o dize"
anodizing	an' o diz' ing
anolyte	an' o lyte"
anta	an' ta
antae	an' tae
ante-solarium	an' te so lar' i um
antechamber	an' te cham' ber
antechoir	an' te choir"
antefix	an' te fix"
antefixal	an" te fix' al
antemion	an tem' i on
antenna	an ten' na
antepagmenta	an' te pag' men ta
antependium	an" te pen' di um
anteportico	an" te por' ti co
anteroom	an' te room
anthropometric	an" thro po met' ric
anthropometrically	an" thro po met' ri cal ly
antibacterial	an" ti bac te' ri al
anticipation	an tic" i pa' tion
anticipatory breach	an tic' i pa to" ry breach"
anticlastic	an" ti clas' tic

anticline	an' ti cline"
anticorrosive	an" ti cor ro' sive
antiflooding	an" ti flood' ing
antifoam	an" ti foam
antifriction axle	an" ti fric' tion ax' le
antifriction latch bolt	an" ti fric' tion latch' bolt
anti-graffiti coating	an" ti graf fi' ti coat' ing
antimony	an' ti mo" ny
antimony oxide	an' ti mo" ny ox' ide
anti-Newton slide mount	an" ti New' ton slide mount"
antinode	an' ti node"
antioxidant	an' ti ox' i dant
antique	an tique'
antique finish	an tique' fin' ish
antiquing	an ti' quing
antiquity	an tiq' ui ty
antishort bushing	an' ti short bush' ing
antisiphon	an" ti si' phon
antiskinning	an' ti skin' ing
antislip	an' ti slip'
antismudge ring	an' ti smudge" ring"
antisotropic	an" ti so trop' ic
antistatic	an" ti stat' ic
antistatic agent	an" ti stat' ic
antitrust	an" ti trust"
anti-walk block	an" ti walk" block
Antron™	An' tron
anvil	an' vil
apa	a pa'
apartment	a part' ment
apartmentize	a part' ment ize"
aperture	ap' er ture
aperture card	ap' er ture card"
apex	a' pex
apitong	ap' i tong
apophyge	a poph' y ge"
apostilb	ap' o stilb"
apparent	ap par' ent
apparent authority	ap par' ent au thor' i ty
appeal	ap peal'
appendage	ap pend' age
appentice	ap pen' tice

applewood	ap' ple wood
appliance	ap pli' ance
application	ap" pli ca' tion
application for payment	ap" pli ca' tion for pay' ment
applicator	ap' pli ca" tor
applied molding	ap plied' mold' ing
appliqué	ap" pli que'
appliqué film	ap" pli que' film"
appraisal	ap prais' al
appraise	ap praise'
appreciation	ap pre" ci a' tion
apprentice	ap pren' tice
apprenticeship	ap pren' tice ship"
approach	ap proach'
approval	ap prov' al
approved	ap proved'
approved equal	ap proved" e' qual
approximate	ap prox' i mate
approximation	ap prox" i ma' tion
appurtenance	ap pur' te nance
apron	a' pron
apron flashing	a' pron flash' ing
apron stage	a' pron stage"
apse	apse
apsidal	ap' si dal
apsidiole	ap sid' i ole"
aquarium	a quar' i um
aquastat	aq' ua stat"
aqueduct	aq' ue duct"
aquiclude	aq' ui clude"
aquifer	aq' ui fer
aquitard	aq' ui tard"
Arabescato	Ar" a bes ca' to
Arabesco	Ar' a bes' co
arabesque	ar" a besque'
araca	a rac' a
aramid	ar' a mid
arbitration	ar" bi tra' tion
arbor	ar' bor
arboretum	ar" bo re' tum
arc	arc'
arc cutting	arc cut' ting

arc discharge	arc dis' charge
arc light	arc' light
arc welding	arc weld' ing
arcade	ar cade'
arcaded	ar cad' ed
arcading	ar cad' ing
arcature	ar' ca ture
arch	arch'
archaic	ar cha' ic
arched	arched
arched stretcher	arched stretch' er
archeology	ar" che ol' o gy
arching	arch' ing
architect	ar' chi tect
architect-engineer	ar' chi tect en" gi neer'
architectonic	ar" chi tec ton' ic
architectural	ar" chi tec' tur al
architectural bronze	ar" chi tec' tur al bronze'
architectural concrete	ar" chi tec' tur al con' crete
architectural volume	ar" chi tec' tur al vol' ume
architecturally	ar" chi tec' tur al ly
architecture	ar' chi tec" ture
architecture parlante	ar' chi tec ture par lan' te
architrave	ar' chi trave"
archival	ar chi' val
archive	ar' chive
archived	ar' chived
archives	ar' chives
archiving	ar' chiv ing
archivist	ar' chi vist
archivolt	ar' chi volt"
archway	arch' way"
arcograph	arc' o graph
arcuate	ar' cu ate
arcuated construction	ar' cu at" ed con struc' tion
ardish	ar' dish
area	ar' e a
area divider	ar' e a di vi' der
area drain	ar' e a drain"
area rug	ar' e a rug"
areaway	ar' e a way"
arena	a re' na

arenaceous	ar" e na' ceous
argillaceous	ar" gil la' ceous
argillite	ar' gil lite"
arid	ar' id
Arizona marble	Ar" i zo' na mar' ble
Arkansas marble	Ar' can sas mar' ble
arkose	ar' kose
arm pads	arm' pads
arm stump	arm' stump"
armature	ar' ma ture
armchair	arm' chair
armoire	ar moire'
armor	ar' mor
armor plate	ar' mor plate"
armored	ar' mored
armored cable	ar' mored ca' ble
armored front	ar' mored front"
armory	ar' mor y
armure	ar' mure
Arnel™	Ar nel'
aroclor	ar' o clor
aromatic	ar" o mat' ic
aromatic cedar	ar" o mat' ic ce' dar
aromatic polyester	ar" o mat' ic pol' y es" ter
aromilla	ar o mil' la
arras	ar' ras
array	ar ray'
arrester	ar rest' er
arris	ar' ris
arris fillet	ar' ris fil' let
arrissing	ar' riss ing
arriswise	ar' ris wise"
arrow	ar' row
art deco	art dec' o
art nouveau	art' nou veau'
art work	art' work"
artesian well	ar te' sian well'
articulate	ar tic' u late
articulation	ar tic" u la' tion
artifact	ar' ti fact"
artificial	ar" ti fi' cial
artificial bitumen	ar" ti fi' cial bi tu' men

artificial light	ar" ti fi' cial light"
artisan	ar' ti san
artist	art' ist
Arts and Crafts Movement	Arts' and Crafts' Move" men
Arup, Ove	Arup, Ove
as-built drawings	as' built draw' ing
as-fabricated	as' fab' ri cat ed
asbestine	as bes' tine
asbestos	as bes' tos
asbestos-base felt	as bes' tos base' felt
asbestos cement	as bes' tos ce ment'
aseismic	a seis' mic
ash	ash
ash dump	ash' dump
ashlar	ash' lar
ashlar masonry	ash' lar ma' son ry
ashlaring	ash' lar ing
ashpit	ash' pit"
askarel	as" ka rel'
aspect	as' pect
aspect ratio	as' pect ra' tio
aspen	as' pen
asphalt	as' phalt
asphalt-saturated	as' phalt sat' u rat" ed
asphaltene	as phal' tene
asphaltic	as phal' tic
asphaltic base course	as phal' tic base' course
asphaltic concrete	as phal' tic con crete'
asphalting	as' phalt ing
asphaltum	as phal' tum
aspiration	as" pi ra' tion
Asplund, Gunnar	Asp' lund, Gun' nar
assembly	as sem' bly
assembly drawing	as sem' bly draw' ing
assembly occupancy	as sem' bly oc' cu pan cy
assessed valuation	as sessed' val" u a' tion
assessment	as sess' ment
assigned	as signed'
assignment	as sign' ment
assize	as size'
associate	as so' ci ate"
association	as so" ci a' tion

associative dimensioning	as so' ci a" tive di men' sion ing
assumption	as sump' tion
Assyrian	As syr' i an
astragal	as' tra gal
astrakhan	as' tra khan
astronomical observatory	as" tro nom' i cal ob serv' a to" ry
asylum lock	a sy' lum lock"
asymmetric	a" sym met' ric
asymmetrical	a" sym met' ri cal
asymmetry	a sym' me try
asymptote	as' ymp tote"
asymptotic	as" ymp tot' ic
atactic	a tac' tic
atactic polypropylene	a tac' tic pol" y pro' pyl ene
atelier	at' el ier"
athletic	ath let' ic
atmosphere	at' mos phere"
atmospheric	at" mos pher' ic
atomization	at" om i za' tion
atomizer	at' om iz' er
atrium	a' tri um
attachment	at tach' ment
attenuation	at ten" u a' tion
attenuator	at ten' u a" tor
Atterberg test	At' ter berg" test
attic	at' tic
attic fan	at' tic fan
attic ventilator	at' tic ven' ti la" tor
attorney	at tor' ney
attorney-in-fact	at tor' ney in fact"
attribute	at trib' ute
attrition mill	at tri' tion mill"
Aubusson	Au' bus son
audible	au' di ble
audio	au' di o"
audio frequency	au' di o" fre' quen cy
audio-visual	au' di o" vis' u al
audiometric	au" di o met' ric
auditorium	au" di to' ri um
auger	au' ger
auger boring	au' ger bor' ing
auger flame	au' ger flame"

augered	au' gered
aumbry	aum' bry
aural	au' ral
aureole	au' re ole"
auricular	au ric' u lar
Aurisina	Au" ri si' na
austenite	aus' ten ite"
Austrian drape	Aus' trian drape
Austrian shade	Aus' trian shade
Austrian shade cloth	Aus' trian shade cloth
authentic	au then' tic
authentication	au then" ti ca' tion
authority	au thor' i ty
authorization	au" thor i za' tion
autoclave	au' to clave"
autoclaved	au' to claved
autoclaved cellular concrete	au' to claved cel' lu lar con' crete
autogenous healing	au tog' e nous heal' ing
automatic	au" to mat' ic
automatic door bottom	au" to mat' ic door bot' tom
automobile	au" to mo bile'
autonomy	au ton' o my
autopsy equipment	au' top sy e quip' ment
auxiliary	aux il' ia ry
aventurine	a ven' tu rine"
avenue	av' e nue"
average	av' er age
average grade	av' er age grade"
aviary	a' vi ar" y
avocado	av" o ca' do
avodire	av" o di re'
avoirdupois	av" oir du pois'
award	a ward'
awl	awl
awning	awn' ing
awning window	awn' ing win' dow
axe	axe
axial flow fan	ax' i al flow fan"
axial force	ax' i al force
axial stress	ax' i al stress"
axis	ax' is
axis of rotation	ax' is of ro ta' tion

axle steel	ax' le steel
Axminster carpet	Ax' min" ster car' pet
axonometric	ax" o no met' ric
ayan	ay' an
ayous	a yous'
azimuth	az' i muth
azion	a' zion
azlon	az' lon
azoic dye	azo' ic dye'

B

B-labeled door	B' la' beled door"
B-spline	B' spline"
babbitt metal	bab' bitt met' al
babbitted fastening	bat' bit ted fas' ten ing
babble	bab' ble
baccarat	bac' ca rat"
bachelor chest	bach' e lor chest"
back arch	back' arch"
back bed	back' bed"
back cut	back' cut"
back-draft damper	back' draft damp' er
back gutter	back' gut' ter
back lintel	back' lin' tel
back-nailing	back' nail' ing
back-paint	back' paint"
back plaster	back" plas' ter
back plate	back' plate"
back post	back' post"
back pressure	back' pres' sure
back putty	back' put' ty
back siphonage	back' si' phon age
back stool	back' stool"
back-to-back	back' to back'
back-up material	back' up ma te' ri al
back veneer	back" ve neer'
backband	back' band"
backbar	back' bar"
backbend	back' bend"
backboard	back' board"
backcharge	back' charge"

backcheck	back' check"
backdraft	back' draft"
backdrop	back' drop"
backed fabric	backed fab' ric
backer rod	back' er rod"
backerboard	back' er board"
backfill	back' fill"
backfilling	back' fill' ing
backflow	back' flow"
backflow valve	back' flow valve"
background noise	back' ground" noise
backhaul	back' haul'
backhoe	back' hoe"
backing	back' ing
backing board	back' ing board"
backing brick	back' ing brick"
backing out	back' ing out
backlighting	back' light" ing
backnailed	back' nailed
backnailing	back' nail" ing
backplate	back' plate"
backsaw	back' saw"
backset	back' set"
backsight	back' sight"
backsplash	back' splash"
backstage	back' stage'
backstop	back' stop"
backup	back' up"
backwash	back' wash"
backwrap	back' wrap"
Bacon, Edmund N.	Ba' con, Ed' mund N.
bacteria	bac te' ri a
bacteriological	bac te" ri o log' i cal
bacteriostat	bac te' ri o stat"
bacteriostatic	bac te" ri o stat' ic
badger	badg' er
badigeon	ba dig' eon
badminton court	bad' min ton court"
baffle	baf' fle
baffling	baf' fling
bag modeling	bag" mod' el ing
bagheera	bagh eer' a

bagtie	bag' tie
baguette	ba guette'
bahut	ba' hut
bail handle	bail' han' dle
bailey	bai' ley
bain-maries	bain' ma ries'
baize	baize
bake-out	bake' out
baked enamel finish	baked' e nam' el fin' ish
baked finish	baked fin' ish
baked-on finish	baked' on fin' ish
Bakelite™	Ba' ke lite
baker's table	bak' ers ta' ble
baking finish	bak' ing fin' ish
baku	ba ku'
balance	bal' ance
balance arm	bal' anced arm"
balanced construction	bal' anced con struc' tion
balanced door	bal' anced door"
balanced earthwork	bal' anced earth' work
balanced reinforcement	bal' anced re" in force' ment
balanced step	bal' anced step"
balancing	bal' anc ing
balconet	bal" co net'
balcony	bal' co ny
baldacchino	bal" dac chi' no
baldachin	bal' da chin
baline	ba' line
balk	balk
ball-and-claw foot	ball' and claw' foot"
ball-and-steeple finial	ball' and stee' ple fin' i al
ball-bearing hinge	ball' bear' ing hinge"
ball-burnishing	ball" bur' nish ing
ball-check	ball' check"
ball clay	ball' clay
ball cock	ball' cock"
ball flower	ball" flow' er
ball foot	ball' foot"
ball-peen hammer	ball' peen" ham' mer
ball penetration test	ball" pen" e tra' tion test
ball test	ball' test"
ball valve	ball' valve"

ballast	bal' last
balled-and-burlapped	balled' and bur' lapped
balloon	bal loon'
balloon back	bal loon' back"
balloon curtain	bal loon' cur' tain
balloon framing	bal loon' fram' ing
ballroom	ball' room
balsa	bal' sa
balsamo	bal sam' o
baluster	bal' us ter
balustrade	bal' us trade"
bamboo	bam boo'
bamboo shades	bam boo' shades"
bamboo-turned chair	bam boo' turned" chair
band	band
band joists	band' joists
band saw	band' saw"
band shell	band' shell"
bandage	band' age
banded column	band' ed col' umn
bandelet	ban' de let"
banderole	ban' de role"
banding	band' ing
bandwidth	band' width"
bandy style	ban' dy style"
bangtail	bang' tail
banister	ban' is ter
banister-back chair	ban' is ter back chair"
banjo taper	ban' jo ta' per
bank	bank
Bank of England chair	Bank' of Eng' land chair
bank-run gravel	bank' run grav' el
bank sand	bank' sand
banker	bank' er
bankruptcy	bank' rupt cy
banner screen	ban' ner screen"
banquet cart	ban' quet cart"
banquet hall	ban' quet hall"
banquette	ban quette'
baptistery	bap' tis ter y
bar	bar
bar back	bar' back"

bar chair	bar' chair"
bar handle	bar' hand' le
bar joist	bar' joist"
bar number	bar num' ber
bar sink	bar' sink"
bar-size section	bar' size sec' tion
bar spacing	bar' spac' ing
bar support	bar sup port'
bar tracery	bar' trac' er y
barathea	bar" a the' a
barbed	barbed
barbed wire	barbed" wire'
Barcelona chair™	Bar" ce lo' na chair
barchart	bar' chart
Bardiglio	Bar dig' li o
bare conductor	bare con duc' tor
barefaced tenon	bare' faced" ten' on
barefoot	bare' foot"
barège	ba rege'
barge course	barge' course"
barge rafter	barge' raft' er
barge tile	barge' tile
bargeboard	barge' board
bargello	bar gel' lo
barite	bar' ite
barium	bar' i um
barium sulfate	bar' i um sul' fate
bark	bark
bark extract	bark" ex' tract
barminutors	bar min' u tors
barn door hanger	barn' door hang' er
Barnes, Edward Larrabee	Barnes, Ed' ward Lar' ra bee
barometer	ba rom' e ter
barometric	bar o met' ric
barometric damper	bar o met' ric damp' er
Baroque	Ba roque'
barracks	bar' racks
Barragán, Luis	Bar ra gan', Luis
barrage	bar rage'
barré	bar re'
barred door	barred' door
barrel	bar' rel

barrel arch	bar' rel arch"
barrel bolt	bar' rel bolt"
barrel ceiling	bar' rel ceil' ing
barrel chair	bar' rel chair"
barrel vault	bar' rel vault"
barricade	bar' ri cade"
barrier-free	bar' ri er free"
bartizan	bar' ti zan
bas-relief	bas" re lief'
basal angle	ba' sal an' gle
basalt	ba salt'
base	base
base bid	base' bid"
base coat	base' coat"
base course	base' course"
base flashing	base' flash' ing
base map	base' map"
base metal	base' met' al
base molding	base' mold' ing
base ply	base' ply"
base shear	base' shear"
base sheet	base' sheet"
base shoe	base' shoe'
base stanchion	base' stan' chion
baseboard	base' board"
baseline	base' line"
basement	base' ment"
baseplate	base' plate"
basic services	ba' sic serv' ic es
basic stress	ba' sic stress"
basil	bas' il
basilica	ba sil' i ca
basin	ba' sin
basin stand	ba' sin stand"
basis weight	ba' sis weight"
basket chair	bas' ket chair"
basket weave	bas' ket weave"
basses	bass' es
basso-relievo	bas' so re lie' vo
basswood	bass" wood"
bast fiber	bast' fi' ber
bastard sawed	bas' tard sawed

bastion	bas' tion
bat	bat
batch	batch
batch mixer	batch mix' er
batch plant	batch' plant"
batched water	batched wa' ter
batcher	batch' er
batching	batch' ing
batement light	bate' ment light"
bath	bath
bath-shower module	bath' show' er mod' ule
bathhouse	bath' house"
bathroom	bath' room"
bathtub	bath' tub"
batik	ba tik'
batiste	ba tiste'
batt	batt
batt insulation	batt' in" su la' tion
batten	bat' ten
batten cap	bat' ten cap"
battening	bat' ten ing
batter	bat' ter
batter board	bat' ter board"
batter pile	bat' ter pile
battered wall	bat' tered wall"
battery	bat' ter y
batting	bat' ting
battlement	bat' tle ment
Bauhaus	Bau' haus"
bauxite	baux' ite
bay	bay
bay leaf garland	bay' leaf gar' land
bay window	bay' win' dow
bayadere	ba' ya dere"
bayeux tapestry	ba yeux' tap' es try
bayonet socket	bay' o net" sock' et
bazaar	ba zaar'
beach cloth	beach' cloth
beacon	bea' con
bead	bead
bead and butt	bead' and butt"
bead-and-reel molding	bead' and reel' mold' ing

bead glazing	bead" glaz' ing
bead molding	bead' mold' ing
bead plane	bead' plane"
beaded joint	bead' ed joint
beader	bead' er
beadflush	bead' flush
beading	bead' ing
beadwork	bead' work"
beak	beak
beaker dyeing	beak' er dye' ing
beakhead	beak' head
beaking joint	beak' ing joint"
beam	beam
beam-and-column	beam' and col' umn
beam-and-girder	beam' and gird' er
beam-and-slab	beam' and slab'
beam ceiling	beam' ceil' ing
beam clip	beam' clip"
beam compass	beam' com' pass
beam fireproofing	beam' fire' proof" ing
beam girder	beam' gird' er
beam pocket	beam' pock' et
beam saddle	beam' sad' dle
beam spread	beam' spread"
bear	bear
bearding	beard' ing
bearer	bear' er
bearing	bear' ing
bearing capacity	bear' ing ca pac' i ty
bearing partition	bear' ing par ti' tion
bearing plate	bear' ing plate"
bearing pressure	bear' ing pres' sure
bearing rail	bear' ing rail"
bearing-type connection	bear' ing type" con nec' tion
bearing wall	bear' ing wall"
bear's-claw foot	bears' claw foot"
Bears Den Quarry	Bears' Den Quar' ry
beating out	beat' ing out"
Beau Brummel	Beau' Brum' mel
beaumontage	beau' mon tage'
beauvais tapestry	beau vais' tap' es try
Beaux-Arts	Beaux Arts'

Becket, Welton	Beck' et, Wel' ton
bed	bed
bed frame	bed' frame"
bed joint	bed' joint"
bed molding	bed' mold' ing
bedding	bed' ding
bedding course	bed' ding course"
Bedford cord	Bed' ford cord'
bedplate	bed' plate"
bedrock	bed' rock"
bedroom	bed' room"
bedside screen	bed' side" screen"
bedspread	bed' spread"
bedstead	bed' stead"
Beeby, Thomas Hall	Beeb' y, Thom' as Hall
beech	beech
beechwood	beech' wood"
beeswax	bees' wax"
beetling	bee' tling
behavior	be hav' ior
behavioral	be hav' ior al
Behrens, Peter	Beh' rens, Pet' er
bel	bel
Belfast truss	Bel' fast truss"
belfry	bel' fry
Belgian Black	Bel' gian Black"
Belgian block	Bel gian block
bell	bell
bell-and-spigot	bell' and spi' got
bell roof	bell' roof"
bell seat	bell' seat"
bell tower	bell' tow' er
bell turning	bell' turn' ing
bell wire	bell' wire"
bella rosa	bel' la ros' a
bella rose	bel' la rose"
belled excavation	belled' ex" ca va' tion
bellflower	bell' flow er
belling	bel' ling
bellows expansion joint	bel' lows ex" pan' sion joint
Belluschi, Pietro	Bel lus' chi, Pi et' ro
belt course	belt' course"

belt loader	belt" load' er
belting	belt' ing
belvedere	bel' ve dere"
bema	be' ma
benatura	ben a tur' a
bench	bench
bench mark	bench' mark"
bench work	bench' work"
benching	bench' ing
benchstone	bench' stone
bend	bend
bending	bend' ing
bending moment	bend' ing mo' ment
bending radii	bend' ing ra' di i
bending schedule	bend' ing sched' ule
bending stress	bend' ing stress"
beneficial occupancy	ben" e fi' cal oc' cu pan cy
beneficiary	ben" e fi' ci ar y
beneficiation	ben" e fi" ci a' tion
benefit-cost analysis	ben' e fit cost a nal' y sis
benefit-to-cost ratio	ben' e fit to cost ra' tio
benefits	ben' e fits
bengaline	ben' ga line
Bennett, Ward	Ben' net, Ward"
benoto caisson	be no' to cais' son
bent	bent
bent glass	bent' glass"
bentonite	bent' ton ite
bentwood	bent' wood"
benzene	ben' zene
benzine	ben' zine
berber	ber' ber
Berea sandstone	Be re' a sand' stone
bergère	ber gere'
Berkeley	Berke' ley
berliner	ber lin' er
berm	berm
Bertoia, Harry	Ber toi a, Har' ry
beryllium	be ryl' li um
Bethel White	Bet' hel White"
Bethlehem Buff	Beth' le hem" Buff"
béton brut	be ton' brut"

Bettogli Vein	Bet tog' li Vein
bevel	bev' el
bevel cut	bev' el cut"
bevel joint	bev' el joint"
bevel siding	bev' el sid' ing
beveled edge	bev' el ed edge"
beveling	bev' el ing
bezel	bez' el
bezier curve	be zier' curve
Bianco de Nieve	Bian' co de Ni' eve
bias	bi' as
biaxial compression	bi ax' i al com pres' sion
biaxiality	bi ax" i al' i ty
bibb	bibb
bibcock	bib' cock
bicomponent fiber	bi" com po' nent fi' ber
biconstituent fiber	bi con stit' u ent fi' ber
bid	bid
bid bond	bid' bond"
bid date	bid' date"
bid form	bid' form"
bid opening	bid' open' ing
bid peddling	bid' ped' dling
bid shopping	bid' shop' ping
bidder	bid' der
bidding documents	bid' ding doc' u ments
bidet	bi' det
bidirectional	bi" di rec' tion al
Biedermeier cabinet	Bie' der mei' er cab' i net
bifold door	bi' fold door"
bifolding	bi' fold ing
bifurcated	bi' fur cat' ed
bifurcation	bi" fur ca' tion
bight	bight
bilinga	bi lin' ga
bill of materials	bill" of ma te' ri als
billet	bil' let
billing	bil' ing
bimorph	bi' morph
bin data	bin da' ta
binary	bi' nary
binder	bind' er

binder course	bind' er course"
binding agent	bind' er a' gent
binding joist	bind' ing joist"
biodegradable	bi" o de grad' a ble
biofuel	bi' o fuel
biomass	bi' o mass"
biparting	bi" part' ing
birch	birch
bird peck	bird' peck"
bird screen	bird' screen"
birdbath	bird' bath
bird's beak	bird's' beak"
bird's eye	bird's' eye"
bird's-eye maple	bird's' eye ma' ple
bird's mouth	bird's' mouth"
Birkerts, Gunnar	Bir' kerts, Gun' nar
biscuit tufting	bis' cuit tuft' ing
bisect	bi' sect
bisected vault	bi sec' ted vault
bishop	bish' op
bismuth	bis' muth"
bisque	bisque
bistro table	bis' tro tab' le
bit	bit
bit brace	bit' brace"
bit gage	bit' gage"
bit-key lock	bit' key' lock
bitch	bitch
bite	bite
bitting	bit' ting
bitumen	bi tu' men
bituminized	bi tu' mi nized
bituminous	bi tu' mi nous
bituminous emulsion	bi tu' mi nous e mul' sion
bituminous grout	bi tu' mi nous grout"
Bituthene™ waterproofing	Bit' u thene wa' ter proof" ing
black karuni	black' ka run' i
black knot	black' knot"
black pigment	black' pig' ment
blackbody	black' bod" y
blackbody radiation	black' bod" y ra" di a' tion
blackline	black' line

blackout curtain	black' out cur' tain
blacktop	black' top"
blade	blade
Blaine fineness	Blaine' fine' ness
Blake, Peter	Blake', Pe' ter
Blanco Macael	Blan' co Ma cael'
blank	blank
blank jamb	blank' jamb
blanket	blan' ket
blanket chests	blan' ket chests
blanket insulation	blan' ket in" sul a' tion
blanket policy	blan' ket pol' i cy
blanking	blank' ing
blast cleaning	blast' clean' ing
blast-furnace slag	blast' fur' nace slag
blast-resistant door	blast' re sist' ant door
Blau, Luigi	Blau", Lu i' gi
bleach	bleach
bleacher	bleach' er
bleaching	bleach' ing
bleb	bleb
bleed through	bleed' through"
bleeder	bleed' er
bleeding	bleed' ing
blemish	blem' ish
blend	blend
blender	blend' er
blending	blend' ing
blending-batch	blend' ing batch"
Blessing, Charles	Bless' ing, Charles"
blight	blight
blind	blind
blind arcade	blind' ar cade'
blind arch	blind' arch"
blind door	blind' door"
blind hoistway	blind' hoist' way
blind nailing	blind' nail' ing
blind stitching	blind' stitch' ing
blinding	blind' ing
blindstory	blind' sto" ry
blister	blis' ter
blistering	blis' ter ing

blistering resistance	blis' ter ing re sist' ance
blistery	blis' ter y
bloach	bloach
bloated	bloat' ed
block	block
block and tackle	block' and tack' le
block bridging	block' bridg' ing
block copolymer	block' co pol' y mer
block flooring	block' floor' ing
block foot	block' foot
block front	block' front"
block insulation	block' in" sul a' tion
block print	block' print"
blocked	blocked
blocking	block' ing
blockout	block' out"
blond woods	blond' woods"
bloom	bloom
blotch printing	blotch print' ing
blots	blots
blow count	blow' count
blow hole	blow' hole
blowback	blow' back"
blowdown	blow' down"
blower	blow' er
blowhole	blow' hole"
blown asphalt	blown' as' phalt
blown glass	blown' glass
blowpipe	blow' pipe"
blub	blub
blue stain	blue' stain"
blued	blued
blueline	blue' line
blueprint	blue' print"
blueprint match	blue' print" match"
blueprint matching	blue' print" match' ing
bluestone	blue' stone
blunt point	blunt' point"
blushing	blush' ing
board	board
board and batten	board' and bat' ten
board foot	board' foot"

board insulation	board' in" sul a' tion
board measure	board' meas' ure
board-type insulation	board' type in" sul a' tion
boarding	board' ing
boardwalk	board' walk"
boasted work	boast' ed work"
boaster	boast' er
boasting	boast' ing
boat-shaped table	boat' shaped ta' ble
boathouse	boat' house
bobbinet	bob" bi net
bodily injury	bod' i ly in' ju ry
body	bod' y
body coat	bod' y coat"
bodying in	bod' y ing in"
bog	bog
bog oak	bog' oak"
bog soil	bog' soil"
bogie	bo' gie
boil	boil
boil board	boil' board
boiler	boil' er
boiler blow-off	boil' er blow' off
boiler room	boil' er room
boiling	boil' ing
bois de spa	bois" de spa'
bolection molding	bo lec' tion mold' ing
boliden salts	bol' i den salts"
bollard	bol' lard
bolometer	bo lom' e ter
bolster	bol' ster
bolster arm	bol' ster arm"
bolt	bolt
boltel	bol' tel
bombé	bom be'
bona fide bid	bo' na fide bid'
bond	bond
bond beam	bond' beam"
bond-beam block	bond' beam' block"
bond breaker	bond' break' er
bond coat	bond' coat"
bond course	bond' course"

bond header	bond' head' er
bond stone	bond' stone"
bond strength	bond' strength"
bond stress	bond' stress"
bonded	bond' ed
bonded fabric	bond' ed fab' ric
bonded terrazzo	bond' ed ter raz' zo
bonder	bond' er
bonderize	bond' er ize
bonderized	bond" er ized
bonderizing	bond" er iz' ing
bonding	bond' ing
bonding capacity	bond' ing ca pac' i ty
bondstone	bond' stone"
Bonetto, Rodolfo	Bo net' to, Ro dol' fo
boning	bon' ing
bonnet	bon' net
bonnet top	bon' net top"
bonus	bo' nus
book-match veneer	book' match ve neer'
book matching	book' match' ing
bookcase	book' case"
booked	booked
booklift	book' lift
bookmatch	book' match"
bookstack	book' stack"
boolean	bool' e an
boom	boom
booster	boost' er
booster fan	boost' er fan"
booster heater	boost' er heat' er
booster pump	boost' er pump"
booth	booth
bootjack foot	boot' jack foot"
borate	bo' rate
borax	bo' rax
border stone	bor' der stone"
bore	bore
bored pile	bored' pile"
bored well	bored' well"
borehole	bore' hole"
borer hole	bor' er hole"

boring	bor' ing
boring jig	bor' ing jig"
borne	borne
boron	bo' ron
boron-loaded concrete	bo' ron load' ed con' crete
borrow	bor' row
borrowed light	bor' rowed light"
boss	boss
bossage	bos' sage
bosse	bosse
Boston ridge	Bos' ton ridge
Boston rocker	Bos' ton rock' er
Botta, Mario	Bot' ta, Mar' i o
Botticino	Bot" ti cin' o
bottle trap	bot' tle trap"
bottom arm	bot' tom arm"
bottom chord	bot' tom chord"
bottom rail	bot' tom rail"
bouclé	bou cle'
boulder	boul' der
bouldering	boul' der ing
boulevard	boul' e vard"
boundary	bound' a ry
boundary survey	bound' a ry sur' vey
bounding wall	bound' ing wall
bow	bow
bow back	bow' back"
bow-bay	bow' bay"
bow compass	bow' com' pass
bow front	bow' front"
bow top	bow' top"
bowling alley	bowl' ing al' ley
bowstring	bow' string"
bowstring truss	bow' string" truss"
bowtell	bow' tell
box beam	box' beam"
box bolt	box' bolt"
box casing	box' cas' ing
box lewis	box' lew' is
box match	box' match"
box nail	box' nail"
box out	box' out"

box pleating	box' pleat' ing
box pleats	box' pleats"
box stretcher	box' stretch' er
box system	box' sys' tem
box wrench	box' wrench"
boxed cornice	boxed' cor' nice
boxed eaves	boxed' eaves"
boxed pith	boxed' pith"
boxing	box' ing
boxing up	box' ing up"
boxwood	box' wood"
brace	brace
brace and bit	brace' and bit'
brace rails	brace' rails"
braced back	braced' back"
braced frame	braced' frame"
bracing	brac' ing
bracket	brack' et
bracket cornice	brack' et cor' nice
bracket foot	brack' et foot"
bracket plaques	brack' et plaques"
bracket scaffold	brack' et scaf' fold
bracketing	brack' et ing
brad	brad
bradawl	brad' awl"
braid	braid
braided	braid' ed
braided fabric	braid' ed fab' ric
braided rug	braid' ed rug"
brainstorming	brain' storm" ing
brake	brake
brake-metal	brake' me' tal
braking	brak' ing
branch	branch
branch circuit	branch' cir' cuit
branch drain	branch' drain"
branch duct	branch' duct"
branch knot	branch' knot"
branch vent	branch' vent"
brandering	bran' der ing
brandreth	bran' dreth
brandrith	bran' drith

brashness	brash' ness
brass	brass
brattishing	brat' tish ing
braze	braze
brazed joint	brazed' joint"
brazier	bra' zier
Brazilian rosewood	Bra zil' ian rose' wood
Brazilian White	Bra zil' ian White"
brazing	braz' ing
breach of contract	breach' of con' tract
break	break
break-in	break' in
breakfast-room	break' fast room"
breakfront	break' front"
breaking radius	break' ing ra' di us
breakwater	break' wat" ter
breast	breast
breast board	breast' board"
breast lining	breast' lin' ing
breast molding	breast' mold' ing
breastsummer	breast' sum" mer
breccia	brec' ci a
breccia marble	brec' ci a marble
brecciated	brec' ci at" ed
Breche Aurora	Breche' Au ro' ra
breeching	breech' ing
breezeway	breeze' way"
Breuer, Marcel	Breu' er, Mar cel'
Brewster chair	Brew' ster chair"
brick	brick
brick bond	brick' bond"
brick molding	brick' mold' ing
brick seat	brick' seat"
brick trimmer	brick' trim' mer
brick veneer	brick' ve neer'
brickbat	brick' bat"
bricklayer	brick' lay" er
brickwork	brick' work"
bridge	bridge
bridgeboard	bridge' board"
Bridgestone isolator	Bridge' stone i' so la" tor
bridging	bridg' ing

bridle joint	bri' dle joint"
Bright Blaze	Bright' Blaze"
bright dip	bright' dip"
Bright Red	Bright' Red"
bright-wood	bright' wood"
brightness	bright' ness
brightness ratio	bright' ness ra' tio
brindle iron	brin' dle i' ron
brine	brine
Brinell hardness	Brinell' hard' ness
briquette	bri quette'
brise-soleil	brise' so leil'
British Standard	Brit' ish stand' ard
British thermal unit	Brit' ish ther' mal u' nit
brittle	brit' tle
brittleness	brit' tle ness
broach	broach
broached work	broach' ed work
broadcast	broad' cast"
broadcloth	broad' cloth"
broadloom	broad' loom"
broadscope	broad' scope
brocade	bro cade'
brocatel	broc" a tel'
brocatelle	broc" a telle'
broché	bro che'
Brody, Samuel	Bro' dy, Sam' u el
broken arch	bro' ken arch"
broken bond	bro' ken bond"
broken joints	bro' ken joints"
broken pediment	bro' ken ped' i ment
broker	bro' ker
brokerage	bro' ker age
bromide	bro' mide
bromine	bro' mine
Bronceado	Bron" ce a' do
bronze	bronze
bronzing	bronz' ing
broom closet	broom' clos' et
broom finish	broom" fin' ish
brooming	broom' ing
Brown and Sharpe gage	Brown' and Sharpe' gage"

brown ash	brown' ash"
brown coat	brown' coat'
brown-line	brown' line"
brown rot	brown' rot'
Brown Terra	Brown' Ter' ra
browning brush	brown' ing brush"
brownstone	brown' stone"
brush	brush
brush finish	brush' fin' ish
brush mark	brush' mark"
brushability	brush" a bil' i ty
brushable	brush' a ble
brushed surface	brushed sur' face
brushout	brush' out"
Brussels carpet	Brus' sels car' pet
brutalism	bru' tal ism
bubbles	bub' bles
bubbling	bub' bling
bubinga	bu bin' ga
buck	buck
bucket	buck' et
bucket loader	buck' et load' er
Buckingham slate	Buck' ingham slate"
buckle	buck' le
buckling	buck' ling
buckram	buck' ram"
buckstay	buck' stay"
budget	bud' get
budgetary	budg' et ar" y
budgeting	budg' et ing
buff	buff
buffalo box	buf' fa lo box
buffer	buf' fer
buffet	buf fet'
buffing	buff' ing
bug holes	bug' holes"
buggy	bug' gy
bugle-head screw	bu' gle head screw"
build	build
build-up	build' up
buildable	build' a ble
builder	build' er

builders' hardware	build' ers hard' ware
builders' risk insurance	build' ers risk in sur' ance
building area	build' ing a' re a
building code	build' ing code"
building coverage	build' ing cov' er age
building drain	build' ing drain
building envelope	build' ing en' ve lope
building height	build' ing height
building inspector	build' ing in spec' tor
building line	build' ing line"
building paper	build' ing pap' er
building permit	build' ing per' mit
building sewer	build' ing sew' er
building stone	build' ing stone
building subdrain	build' ing sub' drain
built-in	built' in
built-up	built' up
built-up beam	built' up beam"
built-up roofing	built' up roof' ing
built-up timber	built' up tim' ber
bulb	bulb
bulb angle	bulb' an' gle
bulb edge	bulb' edge"
bulb pile	bulb' pile"
bulb-tee	bulb' tee'
bulge	bulge
bulk compound	bulk' com' pound"
bulk plane	bulk' plane"
bulkhead	bulk' head"
bulking	bulk' ing
bull float	bull' float"
bull floating	bull' float" ing
bull header	bull' head' er
bull-nose plane	bull' nose plane"
bull-nosed step	bull' nosed step"
bull stretcher	bull' stretch' er
bulldozer	bull' doz" er
bullet catch	bul' let catch"
bullet resistant	bul' let re sist' ant
bullet-resistant glazing	bul' let re sist' ant glaz' ing
bullet-resisting glass	bul' let re sist' ing glass"
bulletin	bul' le tin

bullhead tee	bull' head" tee"
bullion	bul' lion
bullnose	bull'nose"
bull's-eye	bulls' eye"
bulwark	bul' wark
bumper	bump' er
bumper hook	bump' er hook"
bumping	bump' ing
bun foot	bun' foot"
bundle pier	bun' dle pier"
bundled bars	bun' dled bars"
bungalow	bun' ga low"
bunk bed	bunk' bed"
Bunshaft, Gordon	Bun' shaft, Gor' don
burden	bur' den
bureau	bu' reau
Burgee, John	Bur' gee, John"
burl	burl
burl-dome shaped	burl' dome shaped"
burl veneer	burl" ve neer'
burlap	bur' lap
burling	burl' ing
burner	burn' er
burning rate	burn' ing rate"
burnish	bur' nish
burnisher	bur' nish er
burnishing	bur' nish ing
burnout	burn' out"
burr	burr
burring	burr' ing
Burton, Scott	Bur' ton, Scott"
bus bar	bus' bar"
bus way	bus' way"
bush hammer	bush' ham' mer
bush-hammer finish	bush' ham' mer fin' ish
bush-hammered concrete	bush' ham' mered con' crete
bush hammering	bush' ham' mer ing
bushing	bush' ing
business plan	busi' ness plan"
butadiene	bu" ta di' ene
butadiene-acrylonitrile	bu" ta di' ene ac" ry lo ni' trile
butcher block	butch' er block"

butsudan	but' su" dan
butt	butt
butt cut	butt' cut"
butt hinge	butt' hinge"
butt joint	butt' joint"
butt splice	butt' splice"
butt weld	butt' weld"
butted frame	but' ted frame"
butter	but' ter
butterflies	but' ter flies"
butterfly hinge	but' ter fly" hinge"
butterfly valve	but' ter fly" valve"
buttering	but' ter ing
butternut	but' ter nut"
button	but' ton
buttonhead	but' ton head"
buttoning	but' ton ing
buttress	but' tress
buttress cap	but' tress cap"
buttwood veneer	butt' wood" ve neer'
butyl rubber	bu' tyl rub' ber
butyl stearate	bu' tyl ste' a rate"
butylene	bu' tyl ene"
butylene plastic	bu' tyl ene" plas' tic
Buxy Ambre	Bux' y Am' bre
buzzer	buz' zer
BX cable	B X ca' ble
byatt	by' att"
bypass	by' pass"
bypass valve	by' pass" valve"
Byzantine	Byz' an tine"

C

C-labeled door	C la' beled door"
cab	cab
cabana	ca ban' a
cabildo	ca bil' do
cabin	cab' in
cabinet	cab' i net
cabinet filler	cab' i net fil' ler
cabinet vitrine	cab' i net vit' rine

cabinetmaker	cab' i net mak" er
cabinetwork	cab' i net work"
cable	ca' ble
cable fluting	ca' ble flut' ing
cable rack	ca' ble rack"
cable tray	ca' ble tray"
cabling	ca' bling
cabriole leg	cab' ri ole" leg"
cabriolet	cab" ri o let'
cadastral survey	ca das' tral sur' vey
cadaver lift	ca dav' er lift"
cadmium	cad' mi um
cadmium plating	cad' mi um plat' ing
Caen stone	Caen' stone"
cafe	ca fe'
cafe curtains	ca fe' cur' tains
cafeteria	caf" e te' ri a
Caffali process	Caf fal' i pro' cess
cage	cage
cairn	cairn
caisson	cais' son
cake	cake
Calacata	Cal" a cat' a
calcarenite	cal car' e nite"
calcareous	cal car' e ous
calcimine	cal' ci mine
calcimorphic soil	cal" ci morph' ic soil"
calcination	cal ci na' tion
calcine	cal' cine
calcining	cal' cin ing
calcite	cal' cite
calcite limestone	cal' cite lime' stone
calcite marble	cal' cite mar' ble
calcite streaks	cal' cite streaks"
calcium-aluminate cement	cal' ci um a lu' mi nate" ce' ment
calcium carbonate	cal' ci um car' bo nate
calcium chloride	cal' ci um chlo' ride
calcium hydroxide	cal' ci um hy drox' ide
calcium hypochlorite	cal' ci um hy" po chlo' rite
calcium silicate	cal' ci um sil' i cate"
calcium-silicate brick	cal' ci um sil' i cate brick"
calcium sulphate	cal' ci um sul' phate

calendar	cal' en dar
calender	cal' en der
calendering	cal' en der ing
calf's tongue molding	calfs' tongue" mold' ing
caliber	cal' i ber
calibrate	cal' i brate"
calibration	cal" i bra' tion
caliche	ca li' che
caliche base course	ca li' che base course"
calico	cal' i co"
caliduct	cal' i duct"
California bearing ratio	Cal' i for' nia bear' ing ra' tio
caliper	cal' i per
Caliza Capri	Ca liz' a Cap ri'
calk	calk
calked	calked
calking	calk' ing
call bell	call' bell"
callboard	call' board"
calligraphy	cal lig' ra phy
Callister, Charles Warren	Cal' lis ter", Charles' War' ren
calorie	cal' o rie
calorific value	cal" o rif' ic val' ue
calorimeter	cal" o rim' e ter
calotte	ca lotte'
calyon	cal' yon
calyx	ca' lyx
cam	cam
cam lock	cam' lock"
camarin	cam' a rin
camber	cam' ber
camber arch	cam' ber arch"
cambium	cam' bi um
cambric	cam' bric
came	came
camelback	cam' el back"
camel's hair	cam' els hair"
cameo	cam' e o
campaign chest	cam paign' chest"
campanile	cam" pa ni' le
camphorwood	cam' phor wood"
canal	ca nal'

canaletta	ca' na let' ta
canarywood	ca nar' y wood"
cancello	can cel' lo
candela	can de' la
Candela, Felix	Can de' la, Fe' lix
candle	can' dle
candlepower	can' dle pow" er
candlestick	can' dle stick"
cane	cane
cane bolt	cane' bolt"
caned-back chair	caned' back" chair
cannellated	can' nel lat" ed
canopy	can' o py
cant	cant
cant strip	cant' strip"
canted	cant' ed
canted beam	cant' ed beam"
cantilever	can' ti le" ver
cantilever footing	can' ti le" ver foot' ing
cantilevered joists	can' ti le" vered joists"
canting strip	cant' ing strip
cantling	can' tling
canton	can' ton
cantoria	can to' ri a
cantorial	can to' ri al
cantoris	can to' ris
canvas	can' vas
cap	cap
cap flashing	cap' flash' ing
cap molding	cap' mold' ing
cap sheet	cap' sheet"
capacitance	ca pac' i tance
capacitor	ca pac' i tor
capacity	ca pac' i ty
Cape Cod Colonial	Cape' Cod Co lon' i al
capillarity	cap" il lar' i ty
capillary	cap' il lar" y
capillary action	cap' il lar" y ac' tion
capillary migration	cap' il lar" y mi gra' tion
capillary water	cap' il lar" y wa' ter
capital	cap' i tal
capitalization	cap" i tal i za' tion

capitol	cap' i tol
capomo	ca po' mo
capped butt	capped' butt"
capping	cap' ping
capstone	cap' stone"
captain's chair	cap' tains chair"
captain's walk	cap' tains walk"
car	car
car enclosure	car' en clo' sure
car-leveling device	car' lev' el ing de vice'
car platform	car' plat' form"
caracole	car' a cole"
Caramela	Car a mel' a
carapa	ca ra' pa
carbene	car' bene
carbolineum	car" bo lin' e um
carbon-arc welding	car' bon arc weld' ing
carbon bisulfide	car' bon bi sul' fide
carbon dioxide	car' bon di ox' ide
carbon-electrode arc welding	car' bon e lec' trode arc weld' ing
carbon-equivalent	car' bon e quiv' a lent
carbon steel	car' bon steel"
carbon tetrachloride	car' bon tet" ra chlo' ride
carbonaceous	car" bo na' ceous
carbonate	car' bon ate"
carbonation	car' bon a' tion
Carborundum™	Car" bo run' dum
carburize	car' bu rize"
carcase	car' case
carcass	car' cass
carcassing	car' cass ing
carcinogen	car cin' o gen"
cardinal points	car' di nal points"
carding	card' ing
cardioid microphone	car' di oid' mi' cro phone"
Caribe Cream	Ca ri' be Cream"
carillon	car' il lon"
Carlton table	Carl' ton ta" ble
carnarvon arch	car nar' von arch
carnauba wax	car nau' ba wax"
carnelian	car nel' ian
carnival glass	car' ni val glass"

carol	car' ol
carpenter	car' pen ter
carpenter ant	car' pen ter ant"
carpenter's level	car' pen ters lev' el
carpenter's square	car' pen ters square"
carpentry	car' pen try
carpet	car' pet
carpet backing	car' pet back' ing
carpet cushion	car' pet cush' ion
carpet density	car' pet den' si ty
carpet fiber	car' pet fi' ber
carpet strip	car' pet strip"
carpet tile	car' pet tile"
carport	car' port"
Carrara White	Car ra' ra White"
carreau	car reau'
carrel	car' rel
carriage	car' riage
carriage bolt	car' riage bolt"
carriage house	car' riage house"
carrier angle	car' ri er an' gle
carrying channel	car' ry ing chan' nel
carton pierre	car ton' pierre'
cartoon	car' toon
cartouche	car touche'
cartridge	car' tridge
cartridge brass	car' tridge brass"
carve	carve
carving	carv' ing
caryatid	car" y at' id
cascading energy	cas cad' ing en' er gy
case	case
case-hardened	case' hard' ened
cased opening	cased' o' pen ing
casehardening	case" hard' en ing
casein	ca' sein
casein adhesive	ca' sein ad he' sive
casement	case' ment"
casement cloth	case' ment" cloth"
casement window	case' ment" win' dow
casework	case' work"
cash allowance	cash' al low' ance

cash flow	cash' flow"
cash-flow statement	cash' flow" state' ment
cashier window	cash ier' win' dow
cashmere	cash' mere
casing	cas' ing
casing bead	cas' ing bead"
casing-bead doorframe	cas' ing bead door' frame"
casing nail	cas' ing nail"
casino	ca si' no
cassapanca	cas" sa pan' ca
cassoon	cas soon'
cast	cast
cast-in-place concrete	cast' in place' con' crete
cast iron	cast' i' ron
cast stone	cast' stone"
castable	cast' a ble
castellated	cas' tel lat" ed
caster	cast' er
casting	cast' ing
casting copper	cast' ing cop' per
castle	cas' tle
cat	cat
catacombs	cat' a combs
Catalano, Eduardo	Cat' a lan" o, Ed uar' do
cataloging	cat' a log" ing
catalysis	ca tal' y sis
catalyst	cat' a lyst
catalytic	cat' a lyt' ic
catalytically	cat" a lyt' i cal ly
catalyzed metallic grout	cat' a lyzed me tal' lic grout"
catastrophe	ca tas' tro phe
catch	catch
catch basin	catch' ba" sin
catch drain	catch' drain"
catchment	catch' ment
catchment area	catch' ment ar' e a
catenary	cat' e nar" y
catenated	cat' e nat" ed
cathead	cat' head"
cathedral	ca the' dral
cathedral ceiling	ca the' dral ceil' ing
cathedral glass	ca the' dral glass"

catherine wheel	cath' er ine wheel"
cathode	cath' ode
cathode ray tube	cath' ode ray tube"
cathodic protection	ca thod' ic pro tec' tion
cationic emulsion	cat' i on" ic e mul' sion
cativo	ca ti' vo
cat's eye	cats' eye"
cat's-head molding	cats' head" mold' ing
catwalk	cat' walk"
caul	caul
caulking	caulk' ing
caustic	caus' tic
caustic dip	caus' tic dip"
caustic etch	caus' tic etch"
caution	cau' tion
cavetto	ca vet' to
cavil	cav' il
cavity batten	cav' i ty bat' ten
cavity flashing	cav' i ty flash' ing
cavity vent	cav' i ty vent"
cavity wall	cav' i ty wall"
cavo-rilievo	ca' vo ri lie' vo
cedar	ce' dar
cedar chest	ce' dar chest"
ceil	ceil
ceiling	ceil' ing
ceiling plenum	ceil' ing ple' num
ceiling strut	ceil' ing strut"
ceiling suspension system	ceil' ing sus pen' sion sys' tem
celature	cel' a ture"
cell	cell
cellar	cel' lar
cellular adhesive	cel' u lar ad he' sive
cellular concrete	cel' u lar con' crete
cellular glass	cel' u lar glass"
cellular raceway	cel' u lar race' way
celluloid	cel' lu loid"
cellulose	cel' u lose"
cellulosic	cel" lu lo' sic
cellulosic fiberboard	cel" lu lo' sic fi' ber board"
Celsius	Ce' si us
celure	cel' ure

cement	ce' ment
cement-coated nail	ce' ment coat' ed nail"
cement mortar	ce' ment mor' tar
cementation	ce" men ta' tion
cementing	ce ment' ing
cementitious	ce" men ti' tious
cenotaph	cen' o taph"
center	cen' ter
center bearing truss	cen' ter bear' ing truss"
center-hung door	cen' ter hung" door"
center-hung pivot	cen' ter hung" piv' ot
center match	cen' ter match"
center matched	cen' ter matched"
center of gravity	cen' ter of grav' i ty
center-opening door panels	cen' ter o' pen ing door" pan' els
center punch	cen' ter punch"
center-to-center	cen' ter to cen' ter
centerbulb	cen' ter bulb"
centering	cen' ter ing
centerline	cen' ter line"
centerpiece	cen' ter piece"
centigrade	cen' ti grade"
centimeter	cen' ti me" ter
centistoke	cen' ti stoke"
central air-conditioning	cen' tral air' con di' tion ing
central air-handling unit	cen' tral air' han' dling u' nit
central heating	cen' tral heat' ing
central station system	cen' tral sta' tion sys' tem
centrifugal	cen trif' u gal
centrifugal compressor	cen trif' u gal com pres' sor
centrifugal fan	cen trif' u gal fan"
centrifugal pump	cen trif' u gal pump"
centroid	cen' troid
centroid wavelength	cen' troid wave' length
centroidal axis	cen troi' dal ax' is
centrolinear projection	cen" tro lin' e ar pro jec' tion
ceramic	ce ram' ic
ceramic-faced glass	ce ram' ic faced" glass"
ceramic mosaic tile	ce ram' ic mo sa' ic
ceramic tile	ce ram' ic tile"
cerium	ce' ri um
certificate	cer tif' i cate

certificate for payment	cer tif' i cate for pay' ment
certificate of occupancy	cer tif' i cate of oc' cu pan cy
certification	cer' ti fi ca' tion
certified	cer' ti fied
Cesca chair	Ces' ca chair"
cesspool	cess' pool"
chafe	chafe
chafing strip	chaf' ing strip"
chain	chain
chain-link fence	chain' link fence"
chain-pipe vise	chain' pipe vise
chainblock	chain' block"
chaining	chain' ing
chair	chair
chair rail	chair' rail"
chaise longue	chaise" longue'
chaise lounge	chaise" lounge'
chalet	cha let'
chalk	chalk
chalk line	chalk' line"
chalkboard	chalk' board"
chalking	chalk' ing
chalking resistance	chalk' ing re sis' tance
challis	chal' lis
chamber	cham' ber
chamber test	cham' ber test"
chambranle	cham" bran le'
chambray	cham' bray
chamfer	cham' fer
chamfering	cham' fer ing
Champlain Black	Cham plain' Black"
chancel	chan' cel
chancery	chan' cer y
chandelier	chan" de lier'
change order	change' or' der
changeable letter board	change' a ble let' ter board"
channel	chan' nel
channel depth	chan' nel depth"
channel glazing	chan' nel glaz' ing
channel iron	chan' nel i' ron
channel runner	chan' nel run' ner
channel shear	chan' nel shear"

channeling	chan' nel ing
Chanteuil Bleu	Chan teuil' Bleu"
chantry chapel	chan' try chap' el
chapel	chap' el
chaplet	chap' let
chapter house	chap' ter house"
chaptrel	chap' trel
char	char'
characteristic	char" ac ter is' tic
characteristic impedance	char" ac ter is' tic im ped' ance
charcoal	char' coal
Charcoal Black	Char' coal Black
charge	charge
chargeable rate	charge' a ble rate"
charging	charg' ing
charging valve	charg' ing valve"
Charlie Brown	Char' lie Brown"
charmeuse	Char meuse'
Charpy test	Charp' y test
charrette	char rette'
charring	char' ring
chart of accounts	chart' of ac counts'
chase	chase
chase partition	chase' par ti' tion
chaser	chas' er
chasing	chas' ing
Chassagne Rose	Chas sagne' Ro se'
chassis	chas' sis
chat-sawed finish	chat' sawed" fin' ish
chat-sawn	chat' sawn"
chateau	cha teau'
chatter	chat' ter
check	check
check cracks	check' cracks"
check plot	check' plot"
check valve	check' valve
checker	check' er
checker plate	check' er plate"
checkerboard	check' er board"
checkered plate	check' ered plate"
checking	check' ing
checking floor hinge	check' ing floor' hinge

checking resistance	check' ing re sis' tance
checklist	check' list"
checkroom	check' room"
checks	checks
cheek	cheek
cheek pieces	cheek' pieces"
cheek wall	cheek' wall"
cheesy	chees' y
chelate	che' late
Chelmsford Gray	Chelms' ford Gray"
Chelmsford White	Chelms' ford White"
chemical conversion coating	chem' i cal con ver' sion coat' ing
chemical cure	chem' i cal cure"
chemical grout	chem' i cal grout"
chemical matrices	chem' i cal ma' tri ces"
chemical stabilization	chem' i cal sta" bi li za' tion
chemiluminescence	chem" i lum' i nes cence
chenchen	chen' chen"
cheneau	che neau'
chenille	che nille'
chenille carpet	che nille' car' pet
Chermayeff, Serge	Cher may' eff, Ser' ge"
Cherokee	Cher' o kee"
cherry	cher' ry
cherry picker	cher' ry pick' er
cherrywood	cher' ry wood"
chert	chert
cherub	cher' ub
chest	chest
chesterfield	ches' ter field"
chestnut	chest' nut
cheval mirror	che val' mir' ror
cheveret	cheve ret'
Cheviot	Chev' i ot
chevron	chev' ron
chiaroscuro	chi a" ro scu' ro
Chicago window	Chi ca' go win' dow
chiffon	chif fon'
chiller	chil' ler
chime	chime
chimera	chi me' ra
chimney	chim' ney

chimney arch	chim' ney arch"
chimney cap	chim' ney cap"
chimney effect	chim' ney ef fect'
chimney piece	chim' ney piece"
china cabinet	chi' na cab' i net
china closet	chi' na clos' et
Chinese wallpaper	Chi nese' wall' pap er
chink	chink
chinking	chink' ing
chinoiserie	chi noi" se rie'
chintz	chinz
chip	chip
chipboard	chip' board"
chipped grain	chipped' grain"
Chippendale	Chip' pen dale"
chipping	chip' ping
chipping resistance	chip' ping re sis' tance
chisel	chis' el
chlordane	chlor' dane
chloride	chlo' ride
chlorinated	chlo' ri nat" ed
chlorinated paraffin wax	chlo' ri nat" ed par' af fin wax
chlorinated polyethylene	chlo' ri nat" ed pol" y eth' yl ene
chlorinated polyvinyl chloride	chlo' ri nat" ed pol" y vi' nyl chlor' ide
chlorinated rubber	chlo' ri nat" ed rub' ber
chlorination	chlo" ri na' tion
chlorinator	chlo' ri na" tor
chlorine	chlo' rine
chlorofluorocarbon	chlo" ro fluor" o car' bon
chlorofluorohydrocarbon	chlo" ro fluor" o hy" dro car' bon
chloroprene rubber	chlo' ro prene" rub' ber
chlorosis	chlo ro' sis
chlorosulfonated polyethylene	chlo" ro sulf' o na ted pol" y eth'- y lene
choir	choir
choir screen	choir' screen"
choir stall	choir' stall"
choker	chok' er
chord	chord
chorometry	cho ro' met ry
chrismatory	chris' ma to" ry

chroma	chro' ma
chromacity	chro" ma' ci ty
chromate	chro' mate
chromated copper arsenate	chro' mated cop' per ar' se nate"
chromated zinc arsenate	chro' mated zinc ar' se nate
chromated zinc chloride	chro' mated zinc chlor' ide
chromatic	chro mat' ic
chromatic aberration	chro mat' ic ab" er ra' tion
chromaticity	chro" ma tic' i ty
chromatics	chro mat' ics
chromatography	chro" ma tog' ra phy
chrome plated	chrome' plat' ed
chrome steel	chrome' steel"
chrome-vanadium steel	chrome' va na' di um steel"
chromium	chro' mi um
chromium plating	chro' mi um plat' ing
chromochronology	chro" mo chro nol' o gy
chuck	chuck
chuffy brick	chuf' fy brick"
church	church
churn molding	churn' mold" ing
chute	chute
Ciampi, Mario J.	Ci am' pi, Mar' i o J.
ciborium	ci bo' ri um
cimelium	ci me' li um
cincture	cinc' ture
cinder block	cin' der block"
cinerarium	cin" e rar' i um
cinquefoil	cinque' foil
Cipollino Verde Apuano	Ci" pol lin' o Ver' de A pua' no
circassian walnut	cir cas' sian wal' nut
circuit	cir' cuit
circuit breaker	cir' cuit break' er
circuit vent	cir' cuit vent"
circular arch	cir' cu lar arch"
circular mil	cir' cu lar mil"
circular stair	cir' cu lar stair"
circulating water system	cir' cu lat" ing wat' er sys' tem
circulation	cir" cu la' tion
circumference	cir cum' fer ence
circumferential	cir' cum" fer en' tial
circumscribe	cir' cum scribe"

circumsolar	cir" cum so' lar
ciré	ci re'
cistern	cis' tern
citadel	cit' a del"
City Beautiful	Cit' y Beau' ti ful
city planning	cit' y plan' ning
cityscape	cit' y scape"
civic center	civ' ic cen' ter
civil engineering	civ' il en" gi neer' ing
cladding	clad' ding
claim	claim
clamp	clamp
clamping	clamp' ing
clamshell	clam' shell"
clapboard	clap' board
clapboard house	clap' board house"
clarification	clar" i fi ca' tion
clarifier	clar' i fi" er
clarity	clar' i ty
clarke beam	clarke' beam
class	class
class P ballast	class P' bal' last
classic	clas' sic
classic revival	clas' sic re vi' val
classical	clas' si cal
classical architecture	clas' si cal ar' chi tec" ture
classicism	clas' si cism"
classicist	clas' si cist
classification	clas" si fi ca' tion
classify	clas' si fy"
classroom	class' room"
clastics	clas' tics
clause	clause
claustrophobia	claus" tro pho' bi a
clavated	cla vat' ed
claw	claw
claw-and-ball foot	claw' and ball' foot
clay	clay
clay roofing tile	clay' roof' ing tile"
clayey	clay' ey
claypan	clay pan"
clean	clean

cleaner	clean' er
cleaning	clean' ing
cleanout	clean' out"
cleanup	clean' up"
clear	clear
clear all heart	clear' all" heart
clear face	clear' face"
clear span	clear' span"
clearance	clear' ance
clearing and grubbing	clear' ing and grub' bing
clearness number	clear' ness" num' ber
clearstory	clear' sto" ry
cleat	cleat
cleating	cleat' ing
cleavage	cleav' age
cleavage membrane	cleav' age mem' brane
cleavage plane	cleav' age plane"
clerestory	clere' sto" ry
clevice	cle' vice
clevis	clev' is
client	cli' ent
climate	cli' mate
climatic	cli mat' ic
climatology	cli" ma tol' o gy
climbing crane	climb' ing crane"
clinch bolt	clinch' bolt"
clinched	clinched
clinker	clink' er
clinker brick	clink' er brick"
clip	clip
clip angle	clip' an' gle
clipped gable	clipped ga' ble
clipper	clip' per
clo	clo
clo unit	clo' u' nit
cloakroom	cloak' room"
cloche	cloche
clockout	clock' out"
clockwise	clock' wise"
clod	clod
clogging	clog' ging
cloister	clois' ter

cloister garth	clois' ter garth"
close	close
close-cut	close' cut"
close-grained	close grained"
closed cell	closed' cell
closed-cell foam	closed' cell' foam
closed-circuit grouting	closed' cir' cuit grout' ing
closed-circuit television	closed' cir' cuit tel' e vi" sion
closed cornice	closed' cor' nice
closed shop	closed' shop"
closed traverse	closed' trav' erse
closeout	close' out
closer	clos' er
closet	clos' et
closet bend	clos' et bend"
closet rod	clos' et rod"
closet spindle	clos' et spin' dle
closing	clos' ing
closing device	clos' ing de vice'
closure	clo' sure
closure block	clo' sure block"
cloth	cloth
clothes chute	clothes' chute"
cloud cover	cloud' cov' er
cloudiness	cloud' i ness
clout nail	clout' nail
clowring	clowr' ing
club chair	club' chair"
club foot	club' foot"
cluster housing	clus' ter hous' ing
clustered column	clus' tered col' umn
clustering	clus' ter ing
coagulate	co ag' u late
coagulation	co ag" u la' tion
coak	coak
coal tar	coal' tar
coal-tar pitch	coal' tar' pitch"
coalescence	co" a les' cence
coaming	coam' ing
coarse aggregate	coarse' ag' gre gate"
coarse-grained	coarse' grained"
coarse sand	coarse' sand"

coarse sandy loam	coarse' sand' y loam"
coat	coat
coated base sheet	coat' ed base' sheet"
coated fabric	coat' ed fab' ric
coated nail	coat' ed nail"
coating	coat' ing
coatrack	coat' rack
coatroom	coat' room"
coaxial cable	co ax' i al ca' ble
cobble	cob' ble
cobblestone	cob' ble stone"
cobbly	cob' bly
cobwebbing	cob' web bing
cobwork	cob' work
cock	cock
cock beading	cock' bead' ing
cocoa fiber mat	co' coa fi' ber mat"
coconut oil	co' co nut' oil
code	code
coefficient of expansion	co" ef fi' cient of ex pan' sion
coefficient of performance	co" ef fi' cient of per for' mance
coefficient of utilization	co" ef fi' cient of u" til i za' tion
coffee table	cof' fee ta' ble
coffee urn	cof' fee urn"
coffer	cof' fer
cofferdam	cof' fer dam"
coffered	cof' fered
coffered ceiling	cof' fered ceil' ing
coffering	cof' fer ing
cog	cog
cogeneration	co" gen e ra' tion
cogging	cog' ging
cognition	cog ni' tion
cohered	co hered'
cohesion	co he' sion
cohesive failure	co he' sive fail' ure
coign	coign
coil	coil
coiled	coiled
coincident	co in' ci dent
coinsurance	co" in sur' ance
coir	coir

Colburn process	Col' burn" pro' cess
cold-air return	cold' air" re turn'
cold-cathode	cold' cath' ode
cold cathode lamp	cold' cath' ode lamp"
cold-finished	cold' fin' ished
cold-flow	cold' flow"
cold joint	cold' joint"
cold-laid asphalt	cold' laid" as' phalt
cold-process roofing	cold' pro' cess roof' ing
cold-rolled	cold' rolled"
cold-rolling	cold' rol' ling
cold roof	cold' roof
Cold Spring Green	Cold' Spring' Green"
cold-storage door	cold' stor' age door"
colinear	co lin' e ar
colinear force	co lin' e ar force"
coliseum	col" i se' um
collapse	col lapse'
collar	col' lar
collar beam	col' lar beam"
collar joint	col' lar joint"
collate	col' late
collated	col' lat ed
collateral	col lat' er al
collect	col lect'
collection	col lec' tion
collective bargaining	col lec' tive bar' gain ing
collector	col lec' tor
college	col' lege
collimated	col' li mat" ed
collinear	col lin' e ar
collision insurance	col li' sion in sur' ance
colloid	col' loid
colloidal	col loi' dal
colloidal grout	col loi' dal grout"
colloidal solution	col loi' dal so lu' tion
collusion	col lu' sion
cologne earth	co logne' earth
colonial	co lo' ni al
colonial casing	co lo' ni al cas' ing
Colonial Revival	Co lo' ni al Re vi' val
colonnade	col" on nade'

colonnette	col on nette'
color	col' or
color-correcting	col' or cor rect' ing
color matching	col' or match' ing
color temperature	col' or tem' per a ture"
color washing	col' or wash' ing
colorant	col' or ant
colored aggregate	col' ored ag' gre gate
colorfast	col' or fast"
colorimeter	col" or im' e ter
colorimetric photometer	col" or i met' ric pho tom' e ter
colorimetric value	col" or i met' ric val' ue
colorimetry	col" or im' e try
Colosseum	Col" os se' um
columbarium	col" um bar' i um
Columbia	Co lum' bi a
columbium	co lum' bi um
column	col' umn
column schedule	col' umn sched' ule
columniation	co lum" ni a' tion
comb	comb
comb grain	comb' grain"
Combe Brun	Combe' Brun"
combed plywood	combed' ply' wood"
combination	com" bi na' tion
combination lock	com" bi na' tion lock"
combination mirror/shelf	com" bi na' tion mir' ror shelf"
combined load	com bined' load"
combined stress	com bined' stress"
combing	comb' ing
Comblanchien	com blanch' ien
combplate	comb' plate"
combustible	com bus' ti ble
combustion	com bus' tion
combustion air	com bus' tion air"
comfort	com' fort
comfort chart	com' fort chart"
comfort zone	com' fort zone"
commercial	com mer' cial
commercial bronze	com mer' cial bronze"
commercial marble	com mer' cial mar' ble"
commission	com mis' sion

commode	com mode'
commode step	com mode' step"
common bond	com' mon bond"
common brick	com' mon brick"
common nail	com' mon nail"
common trap	com' mon trap"
common wall	com' mon wall"
communal	com mu' nal
communicating door	com mu' ni cat" ing door"
communicating frame	com mu' ni cat" ing frame"
communication	com mu" ni ca' tion
communion rail	com mun' ion rail"
community	com mu' ni ty
compact	com pact'
compact section	com pact' sec' tion
compacted	com pac' ted
compacting	com pac' ting
compaction	com pac' tion
compartment	com part' ment
compartmentation	com part" men ta' tion
compass	com' pass
compatibility	com pat" i bil' i ty
compensating	com' pen sat" ing
compensating hub	com' pen sat" ing hub"
compensation	com" pen sa' tion
competition	com" pe ti' tion
competitive	com pet' i tive
competitive bidding	com pet' i tive bid' ding
complementary	com" ple men' ta ry
complementary angle	com" ple men' ta ry an' gle
complementary colors	com" ple men' ta ry col' ors
completed	com plet' ed
completion	com ple' tion
component	com po' nent
composite	com pos' ite
composite arch	com pos' ite arch"
composite beam	com pos' ite beam"
composite construction	com pos' ite con struc' tion
composite door	com pos' ite door"
composite order	com pos' ite or' der
composition	com" po si' tion
composition shingles	com" po si' tion shin' gles

compost	com' post
compound	com' pound
compound arch	com' pound arch"
compregnated	com preg' nat ed
comprehensive	com" pre hen' sive
compressed	com pressed'
compressed lead head nail	com pressed' lead' head nail"
compressibility	com pres" si bil' i ty
compression	com pres' sion
compression flange	com pres' sion flange"
compression glazing	com pres' sion glaz' ing
compression seal	com pres' sion seal
compressional	com pres' sion al
compressive strength	com pres' sive strength"
compressometer	com" press o' met er
compressor	com pres' sor
compressor-condenser unit	com pres' sor con dens' er u' nit
compromise	com' pro mise
computer	com put' er
computer-aided	com put' er aid' ed
computer-aided design	com put' er aid' ed de sign'
computer-aided drafting	com put' er aid' ed draft' ing
computerized	com put' er ized"
concave	con cave'
concave bead	con cave' bead"
concave joint	con cave joint"
concavity	con cav' i ty
concealed cleat	con cealed" cleat"
concealed closer	con cealed clos' er
concealed hinge	con cealed hinge"
concealed-type purlin hanger	con cealed type pur' lin hang' er
concentrated load	con' cen trat" ed load
concentrating	con' cen trat" ing
concentrating collector	con' cen trat" ing col lec' tor
concentration	con" cen tra' tion
concentrator	con" cen tra" tor
concentric	con cen' tric
concentric load	con cen' tric load"
concentricity	con" cen tric' i ty
concept	con' cept
conceptual	con cep' tu al
conch	conch'

concha	con' cha
concrete	con' crete
concrete block	con' crete block"
concrete pumping	con' crete pump' ing
concurrent force	con cur' rent force"
condemn	con demn'
condemnation	con" dem na' tion
condensate	con' den sate
condensation	con" den sa' tion
condensation gutter	con" den sa' tion gut' ter
condensation polymer	con" den sa' tion pol' y mer
condense	con dense'
condenser	con dens' er
condensing unit	con dens' ing u' nit
conditioning	con di' tion ing
conditions	con di' tions
conditions of the contract	con di' tions of the con' tract
condominium	con" do min' i um
conductance	con duct' ance
conduction	con duc' tion
conductive flooring	con duc' tive floor' ing
conductive mortar	con duc' tive mor' tar
conductive terrazzo	con duc' tive ter raz' zo
conductive tile	con duc' tive tile
conductivity	con" duc tiv' i ty
conductor	con duc' tor
conduit	con' duit
conduit box	con' duit box"
cone-cut veneer	cone' cut ve neer'
cone-nut tie	cone' nut tie"
cone penetrometer	cone' pen" e trom' e ter
confessional	con fes' sion al
configurated glass	con fig' u rat" ed glass"
configuration	con fig" u ra' tion
confined concrete	con fined' con' crete
conflagration	con" fla gra' tion
conflict of interest	con' flict of in' ter est
conformance	con form' ance
conformed set	con formed' set"
congé	con' ge
conglomerate	con glom' er ate
congruence	con gru' ence

conical	con' i cal
conifer	con' i fer
connected load	con nect' ed load"
connecting door lock	con nect' ing door' lock"
connector	con nec' tor
conoid	co' noid
consensus	con sen' sus
consent of surety	con sent' of sur' e ty
consequential loss	con" se quen' tial loss"
conservation	con" ser va' tion
conservatory	con serv' a to" ry
consideration	con sid" er a' tion
consignment	con sign' ment
consistency	con sist' en cy
consistometer	con" sis tom' e ter
consistory	con sis' to ry
console	con' sole
console directory	con' sole di rec' to ry
console table	con' sole ta' ble
consolidating	con sol' i dat" ing
consolidation	con sol" i da' tion
consonance	con' so nance
constant	con' stant
construct	con struct'
constructed	con struct' ed
constructible	con struct' i ble
construction	con struc' tion
construction classification	con struc' tion clas" si fi ca' tion
construction documents	con struc' tion doc' u ments
construction estimate	con struc' tion es' ti mate
construction joint	con struc' tion joint"
construction management	con struc' tion man' age ment
constructivist	con struc' tiv ist
constuctivism	con struc' tiv ism
consulate	con' su late
consultant	con sult' ant
consulting	con sult' ing
consumer	con sum' er
contact	con' tact
contact adhesive	con' tact ad he' sive
contact cement	con' tact ce ment'
contaminant	con tam' i nant

contemporary	con tem' po rar" y
contextual	con tex' tu al
contextualism	con tex' tu al ism"
continental seating	con" ti nen' tal seat' ing
contingency	con tin' gen cy
contingent	con tin' gent
continuity	con" ti nu' i ty
continuous	con tin' u ous
continuous beam	con tin' u ous beam"
continuous filament	con tin' u ous fil' a ment
continuous hinge	con tin' u ous hinge"
continuous slab	con tin' u ous slab"
continuous tone	con tin' u ous tone"
continuous vent	con tin' u ous vent"
contour	con' tour
contour interval	con' tour in' ter val
contour line	con' tour line"
contour map	con' tour map"
contract	con' tract
contract design	con' tract des sign'
contract documents	con' tract doc' u ments
contract furniture	con' tract fur' ni ture
contraction	con trac' tion
contraction joint	con trac' tion joint"
contraction-joint grouting	con trac' tion joint grout' ing
contractor	con' trac tor
contractor's liability insurance	con' trac tors li a bil' i ty in sur'- ance
contractual	con trac' tu al
contraflexure point	con" tra flex' ure point"
contrast	con' trast
contrast ratio	con' trast ra' tio
contrast rendition factor	con' trast ren di' tion fac' tor
contribution	con" tri bu' tion
contributory negligence	con trib' u to" ry neg' li gence
control	con trol'
control damper	con trol' damp' er
control joint	con trol' joint"
control-joint grouting	con trol' joint grout' ing
controlled fill	con trolled' fill"
controller	con trol' ler
conurbation	con" ur ba' tion

convalescent home	con" va les' cent home"
convection	con vec' tion
convection oven	con vec' tion ov' en
convector	con vec' tor
convenience outlet	con ven' ience out' let
convent	con' vent
conventional	con ven' tion al
conventional design	con ven' tion al de sign'
convergence	con ver' gence
convergence zone	con ver' gence zone"
conversion factor	con ver' sion fac' tor
converter	con vert' er
convex bead	con vex' bead"
convexity	con vex' i ty
conveyance	con vey' ance
conveyor	con vey' or
convolute	con' vo lute"
Cook, Peter	Cook, Pet' er
coolant	cool' ant
cooling degree-day	cool' ing de gree' day"
cooling pond	cool' ing pond"
cooling tower	cool' ling tow' er
cooperative	co op' er a' tive
coopered joint	coop' ered joint
coordinated	co or' di nat ed
coordinates	co or' di nates
coordination	co or" di na' tion
coordinator	co or' di na" tor
copal	co' pal"
cope	cope
coped	coped
coped joint	coped' joint"
coping	cop' ing
coping stone	cop' ing stone"
coplanar force	co pla' nar force"
copolymer	co pol' y mer
copper	cop' per
copper-asphalt composite	cop' per as' phalt com pos' ite
copper-clad stainless steel	cop' per clad" stain' less steel"
copper ounce-weight thickness	cop' per ounce' weight" thick'-ness
copperplate	cop' per plate"

copperplating	cop' per plat" ing
copyright	cop' y right"
coquillage	co" quil lage'
coquina	co qui' na
coralwood	cor' al wood"
Corati Rose	Co rat' i Rose"
corbel	cor' bel
corbeled arch	cor beled arch"
corbelling	cor' bel ing
corbiestep	cor' bie step"
cord	cord
cording	cord' ing
corduroy	cor' du roy"
core	core
core blister	core' blis' ter
core block	core' block"
core boring	core' bor' ing
core drill	core' drill"
core stock	core' stock"
core test	core' test"
coreboard	core' board"
cored brick	cored' brick"
coring	cor' ing
Corinthian order	Co rin' thi an or' der
cork	cork
corkstone	cork' stone"
corner angle	cor' ner angle
corner bead	cor' ner bead"
corner block	cor' ner block"
corner pole	cor' ner pole"
corner post	cor' ner post"
cornerstone	cor' ner stone"
cornice	cor' nice
cornice return	cor' nice re turn'
coro	co' ro
corolitic	co' ro lit" ic
corona	co ro' na
coronizing	cor' o niz" ing
corporation	cor" po ra' tion
corporation cock	cor" po ra' tion cock"
corpuscular theory	cor pus' cular the' o ry
correction	cor rec' tion

correlation	cor" re la' tion
correlational	cor" re la' tion al
corridor	cor' ri dor
Corrigan, Peter	Cor' ri gan, Pet' er
corrosion	cor ro' sion
corrosion-resistant	cor ro' sion re sist' ant
corrosive	cor ro' sive
corrugated	cor' ru gat" ed
corrugated key	cor' ru gat" ed key"
corrugated metal	cor' ru gat" ed met' al
corundum	co run' dum
cosigner	co' sign" er
cosine	co' sine
cosine law	co' sine law"
cost benefit analysis	cost' ben' e fit a nal' y sis
cost-plus contract	cost' plus" con' tract
cottage	cot' tage
cottage-set curtain	cot' tage set cur' tain
cotton	cot' ton
cottoning	cot' ton ing
couch	couch
coulisse	cou lisse'
coulomb	cou' lomb
counter	count' er
counterbalance	coun' ter bal" ance
counterclockwise	coun" ter clock' wise
counterflashing	coun' ter flash" ing
counterfort	coun' ter fort"
counteroffer	coun' ter of" fer
countersink	coun' ter sink"
countersunk	coun' ter sunk"
countertop	count' er top"
countertorque	count' er torque"
counterweight	count' er weight"
coupled columns	cou' pled col' umns
coupler	cou' pler
coupling	cou' pling
course	course
coursed rubble	coursed' rub' ble
coursed veneer	coursed' ve neer'
court	court
courthouse	court' house"

courtroom	court' room"
courtyard	court' yard"
cove	cove
cove lighting	cove' light' ing
cove molding	cove' mold' ing
coved base	coved' base"
covenant	cov' e nant
cover	cov' er
coverage	cov' er age
covert	co' vert
coving	cov' ing
cowl	cowl
Cox, Warren J.	Cox, War' ren J.
crab	crab
crack	crack
crack-control reinforcement	crack' con trol' re" in force' ment
crack length	crack' length"
cracking	crack' ing
cracking resistance	crack' ing re sist' ance
crackle	crack' le
crackle glaze	crack' le glaze"
cradling	cra' dling
craft	craft
craftsman	crafts' man
craftsperson	crafts' per" son
cramming	cram' ming
cramp	cramp
crane	crane
crane boom	crane' boom"
crash bar	crash' bar"
crater	cra' ter
cratering	cra' ter ing
crawl	crawl
crawl space	crawl' space
crawl-space plenum	crawl' space plen' um
crawl-space ventilation	crawl' space ven" ti la' tion
crawler	crawl' er
crawler crane	crawl' er crane"
crawling	crawl' ing
crawlway	crawl' way"
craze cracks	craze' cracks"
crazing	craz' ing

Cream Kasota	Cream' Ka so' ta
Cream Mankato	Cream' Man ka' to
Cream Mansota	Cream' Man so' ta
Cream Wombeyan	Cream' Wom bey' an
creativity	cre" a tiv' i ty
credence	cre' dence
credenza	cre den' za
credit	cred' it
creditor	cred' i tor
creep	creep
crematorium	cre" ma to' ri um
crematory	cre' ma to" ry
cremorne bolt	cre morne' bolt"
crenel	cren' el
crenelated	cren' el at ed
Creole	Cre' ole
creosote	cre' o sote"
creosoting	cre' o sot" ing
crepe	crepe
crescent	cres' cent
crest	crest
crest rail	crest' rail"
cresting	crest' ing
cretonne	cre tonne'
crevice corrosion	crev' ice cor ro' sion
crewel	crew' el
crib	crib
cribbing	crib' bing
cricket	crick' et
crimp	crimp
crimped	crimped
crimper	crimp' er
crimping	crimp' ing
cripple rafter	crip' ple raft' er
cripple stud	crip' ple stud"
criteria	cri te' ri a
criterion	cri ter' i on
critical path method	crit' i cal path" meth' od
critical slope	crit' i cal slope"
critique	cri tique'
crizzle	criz' zle
crocket	crock' et

crocking	crock' ing
croft	croft
crook	crook
croquet court	cro quet' court"
cross	cross
cross aisle	cross' aisle"
cross-bedding	cross' bed' ding
cross break	cross' beak"
cross-connection	cross' con nec' tion
cross-cultural	cross' cul' tur al
cross-dyeing	cross' dye' ing
cross-garnet	cross' gar' net
cross grain	cross' grain"
cross-laminated	cross' lam' i nat ed
cross-linking	cross' link' ing
cross section	cross' sec' tion
cross-sectional area	cross' sec' tion al area
cross talk	cross' talk"
cross tees	cross' tees"
cross valve	cross' valve"
crossband	cross'band"
crossbanding	cross' band" ing
crosscut	cross' cut"
crosscutting	cross' cut" ing
crossette	cross ette'
crosshatching	cross' hatch" ing
crossing	cros' sing
crosslap	cross' lap
crossover	cross' o" ver
crossrail	cross' rail"
crotch	crotch
crotch swirl	crotch' swirl
crotch veneer	crotch' ve neer"
crotchwood	crotch' wood
crow-stepped	crow' stepped"
crowbar	crow' bar"
crowding	crowd' ing
crowfoot	crow' foot"
crown	crown
crown bed	crown' bed
crown glass	crown' glass"
crown molding	crown' mold' ing

crowning	crown' ing
crowstep	crow' step
crucifix	cru' ci fix
cruciform	cru' ci form
crucks	crucks
crumb	crumb
crumber	crumb' er
crush	crush
crush plate	crush' plate"
crushed gravel	crushed' grav' el
crusher-run	crush' er run"
crushing	crush' ing
cryogenic	cry" o gen' ic
cryolite	cry' o lite"
cryology	cry" ol' o gy
crypt	crypt
cryptomeria	cryp" to mer' i a
crystalline limestone	crys' tal line" lime' stone
cubage	cub' age
cube strength	cube' strength"
cubic foot	cu' bic foot"
cubic marble	cu' bic mar' ble
cubic measure	cu' bic meas' ure
cubicle	cu' bi cle
cul-de-sac	cul' de sac'
cull	cull
cullet	cul' let
culls	culls
cultivate	cul' ti vate"
cultured marble	cul' tured mar' ble
culvert	cul' vert
cumulative	cu' mu la" tive
cumulus	cu' mu lus
cup	cup
cup-up	cup' up"
cupboard	cup' board
cupellation	cu" pel la' tion
cupola	cu' po la
cuprammonium rayon	cu" pram mo' ni um ray' on
cupronickel	cu' pro nick" el
curb	curb
curb cock	curb' cock"

curb joint	curb' joint"
curdling	cur' dling
cure	cure
curia	cu' ri a
curing	cur' ing
curing agent	cur' ing a' gent
curing membrane	cur' ing mem' brane
curl	curl
curling	curl' ing
curls	curls
curly grain	curl' y grain"
current	cur' rent
current amplification	cur' rent am" pli fi ca' tion
current assets	cur' rent as' sets
current dollars	cur' rent dol' lars
current liabilities	cur' rent li" a bil' i ties
current ratio	cur' rent ra' tio
curstable	curst' a ble
curtail step	cur tail' step"
curtain	cur' tain
curtain track	cur' tain track"
curtain wall	cur' tain wall"
curtaining	cur' tain ing
curule chair	cu' rule chair
curvature friction	cur' va ture fric' tion
curvatures	cur' va tures
curve	curve
curved	curved
curvilinear	cur" vi lin' e ar
cushion	cush' ion
cushion edge	cush' ion edge"
cushion tank	cush' ion tank"
cushioned	cush' ioned
cushioned frieze	cush' ioned frieze"
cushioned vinyl flooring	cush' ioned vi' nyl floor' ing
cusp	cusp
cusping	cusp' ing
custom	cus' tom
custom-built	cus' tom built"
customary	cus' tom ar" y
cut	cut
cut and fill	cut' and fill'

cut-in brace	cut' in brace"
cut-loop pile	cut' loop' pile"
cut-off stop	cut' off stop
cut-pile	cut' pile"
cut pile	cut' pile'
cut stone	cut' stone"
cut-to-order	cut' to ord' er
cut washer	cut' wash' er
cutback	cut' back"
cutback asphalt	cut' back" as' phalt
cutoff	cut' off
cutoff angle	cut' off an' gle
cutoff stop	cut' off stop"
cutout	cut' out"
cutter	cut' ter
cutting	cut' ting
cutting torch	cut' ting torch"
cutwork	cut' work"
cyan	cy' an
cyanuric acid	cy' anu' ric ac' id
cybermedia	cy' ber me" di a
cycle	cy' cle
cycling	cy' cling
cycloid	cy' cloid
cycloidal arch	cy cloi' dal arch"
cyclopean aggregate	cy' clope' an ag' gre gate
cyclorama	cy" clo ram' a
cyclostyle	cy' clo style"
cylinder	cyl' in der
cylinder lock	cyl' in der lock"
cylinder strength	cyl' in der strength"
cylinder test	cyl' in der test"
cylindrical	cy lin' dri cal
cyma recta	cy' ma rec' ta
cyma reversa	cy' ma re ver' sa
cymatium	cy ma' ti um
cymbia	cym' bi a
cymograph	cy' mo graph"
cypress	cy' press

D

dab	dab
dabbing	dab' bing
dacite	da' cite
dado	da' do
dairy	dair' y
dais	da' is
Dakota Mahogany	Da ko' ta Ma hog' a ny
damages	dam' ages
damask	dam' ask
dammar	dam' mar
damp	damp
damp course	damp' course"
damper	damp' er
damping	damp' ing
dampness	damp' ness
dampproof course	damp' proof" course"
dampproofing	damp' proof ing
dancing step	danc' ing step"
dangerous	dan' ger ous
danta	dan' ta
dap	dap
dapped	dapped
dapping	dap' ping
darby	dar' by
darbying	dar' by ing
Dark Pearl	Dark' Pearl"
darkroom	dark' room"
darkroom equipment	dark" room" e quip' ment
dash-bond coat	dash' bond' coat"
dash coat	dash' coat"
data	da' ta
database	da' ta base
datum	da' tum
datum point	da' tum point"
daub	daub
daubing	daub' ing
davenport	dav' en port"
davit	dav' it
daybed	day' bed"
daylight factor	day' light" fac' tor

daylighting	day' light ing
dbA	d b A
de-icing	de ic' ing
de Stijl	de Stijl'
dead-air space	dead" air' space
dead blow hammer	dead' blow" ham' mer
dead end	dead' end'
dead level	dead' lev' el
dead-level asphalt	dead lev' el as' phalt
dead load	dead' load"
deadbolt	dead' bolt"
deadening	dead' en ing
deadlatch	dead' latch
deadline	dead' line"
deadlock	dead' lock"
deadman	dead' man"
deaerator	de aer' a tor
dealkalization	de al" ka li za' tion
debit	deb' it
debris	de bris'
debt-equity ratio	debt' eq' ui ty ra' tio
debug	de bug'
deburring	de burr' ing
decade	dec' ade
decating	dec' at ing
decatizing	dec' a tiz" ing
decay	de cay'
decay rate	de cay' rate"
decayed knot	de cayed' knot"
decentralization	de cen" tral i za' tion
dechlorinator	de chlo' ri na" tor
decibel	dec' i bel
deciduous	de cid' u ous
decimal equivalent	dec' i mal e quiv' a lent
deck	deck
deck chair	deck' chair"
deck-on-hip	deck' on hip'
decking	deck' ing
declination	dec" li na' tion
decolorizer	de col' or i" zer
decolorizing	de col' or iz' ing
deconstructionism	de" con struc' tion ism

deconstructionist	de" con struc' tion ist
deconstructivism	de" con struc' tiv ism
deconstructivist	de" con struct' tiv ist
decor	de cor'
decorated	dec' o rat" ed
decoration	dec" o ra' tion
decorative	dec' o ra tive
decorative laminate	dec' o ra tive lam' i nate
decorator	dec' o ra" tor
decrement factor	dec' re ment fac' tor
dedicate	ded' i cate
deductible	de duct' i ble
deduction	de duc' tion
deductive alternate	de duc' tive al' ter nate
deducts	de' ducts
deed	deed
deemphasis	de em' pha sis
deep-buttoning	deep' but' ton ing
deeping	deep' ing
Deer Island	Deer' Is' land
default	de fault'
defect	de' fect
defective work	de fec' tive work"
deferred	de ferred'
deficit	def' i cit
deflection	de flec' tion
deflects	de flects'
deflocculate	de floc' cu late"
deflocculating agent	de floc' cu lat" ing a' gent
defoliate	de fo' li ate"
deform	de form'
deformability	de form" a bil' i ty
deformation	de" for ma' tion
deformed bar	de formed' bar"
degradation	deg" ra da' tion
degrade	de grade'
degreaser	de greas' er
degree	de gree'
degree-day	de gree' day"
degree-day heating	de gree' day" heat' ing
degumming	de gum' ming
dehumidification	de" hu mid" i fi ca' tion

dehumidifier	de" hu mid' i fi er
dehumidify	de" hu mid' i fy
dehydrate	de hy' drate
dehydration	de" hy dra' tion
dehydrator	de hy' dra tor
deionized	de i' on ized"
delamination	de lam" in a' tion
delay	de lay'
delay damages	de lay' dam' ages
delayed-action fuse	de layed' ac' tion fuse"
deletion	de le' tion
delineated	de lin' e at ed
deliquescence	del" i ques' cence
deliquescent	del" i ques' cent
delta connection	del' ta con nec' tion
deluge system	del' uge sys' tem
delusterant	de lus' ter ant
delustered nylon	de lust' ered ny' lon
delustering	de lust' er ing
demand	de mand'
demand factor	de mand' fac' tor
demarcation	de" mar ca' tion
demi-column	dem" i col' umn
demineralization	de min" er al i za' tion
demising wall	de mis' ing wall"
demographic	dem" o graph' ic
demolding	de mold' ing
demolition	dem" o li' tion
demountability	de mount' a bil' i ty
demountable	de mount' a ble
denier	de nier'
denim	den' im
dense-grain	dense' grain"
densification	den" si fi ca' tion
densifier	den' si fi" er
densitometer	den" si tom' e ter
densitometry	den" si tom' e try
density	den' si ty
denticular	den tic' u lar
denticulate	den tic' u late"
denticulation	den tic" u la' tion
dentil	den' til

dentil course	den' til course"
dentiled	den' tiled
deoxidized copper	de ox' i dized" cop' per
depletion	de ple' tion
depolished glass	de pol' ished glass"
depolymerization	de" po lym" er i za' tion
deposited metal	de pos' it ed met' al
depositories	de pos' i to ries
depository	de pos' i to ry
depot	de' pot
depreciation	de pre" ci a' tion
depressed panel	de pressed' pan' el
depth factor	depth' fac' tor
depth of fusion	depth' of fu' sion
depth perception	depth' per cep' tion
derrick	der' rick
describe	de scribe'
descriptive specification	de scrip' tive spec" i fi ca' tion
descriptor	de scrip' tor
desiccant	des' ic cant
desiccate	des' ic cate
desiccated	des' ic cat" ed
desiccation	des" sic ca' tion
design	de sign'
design-build	de sign' build"
design development	de sign' de vel' op ment
design load	de sign' load"
design span	de sign' span"
design temperature	de sign' tem' per a ture
designer	de sign' er
desk	desk
desocialization	de so" cial i za' tion
destruction	de struc' tion
detachable pole	de tach' a ble pole"
detached house	de tached' house"
detail	de' tail
detailer	de' tail er
detailing	de' tail ing
detection system	de tec' tion sys' tem
detector	de tec' tor
detention equipment	de ten' tion e quip' ment
detention screen	de ten' tion screen"

detention window	de ten' tion win' dow
deterioration	de te" ri o ra' tion
determine	de ter' mine
detonator	det' o na tor
detritus	de tri' tus
developed length	de vel' oped length"
developer	de vel' o per
development	de vel' op ment
development length	de vel' op ment length"
deviling	dev' il ing
devitrification	de vit" ri fi ca' tion
dew point	dew' point"
dewater	de wa' ter
dewatering	de wa' ter ing
dezincification	de zinc" i fi ca' tion
diagonal brace	di ag' o nal brace"
diagonal cracking	di ag o nal crack' ing
diagram	di' a gram
diagrammatically	di" a gram mat' i cal ly
dial	di' al
diamagnetic	di" a mag net' ic
diameter	di am' e ter
diamond matching	dia' mond match' ing
diamond-mesh lath	dia' mond mesh" lath
Diamond Pearl	Dia' mond Pearl"
Diamond Pink	Dia' mond Pink"
diamond-sawn	dia' mond sawn"
diamonding	dia' mond ing
diaper	dia' per
diaper work	dia' per work"
diaphragm	di' a phragm
diaspore clay	di' a spore" clay"
diastyle	di' a style"
diatomaceous	di" a to ma' ceous
diatomite	di" a to mite'
diazo	di az' o
diazonium salts	di" a zo' ni um salts"
diazotype	di az' o type"
dicalcium silicate	di cal' ci um si' li cate
dice	dice
dichlorodifluoromethane	di chlo" ro di fluor" o meth' ane
dichroic	di chro' ic

dichromate treatment	di chro' mate treat' ment
die	die
die-cast	die' cast"
die casting	die' cast' ing
die-embossed sign	die' em bossed' sign
dielectric	di" e lec' tric
diene	di' ene
diesel	die' sel
differential settlement	dif" fer en' tial set' tle ment
diffraction	dif frac' tion
diffuse	dif fuse'
diffuse porous wood	dif fuse' por' ous wood"
diffuse radiation	dif fuse' ra" di a' tion
diffused lighting	dif fused' light' ing
diffuser	dif fus' er
diffusion	dif fus' ion
diffusivity	dif" fu siv' i ty
digging line	dig' ging line"
digital	dig' it al
digital indicator	dig' it al in' di ca" tor
digitizer	dig' i tiz" er
diglyph	di' glyph
digs	digs
dihedral cut	di he' dral cut"
dilatancy	di la' tan cy
dilation	di la' tion
diluent	dil' u ent
dilutability	di lut" a bil' i ty
dilution air	di lu' tion air"
dimension	di men' sion
dimension lumber	di men' sion lum' ber
dimension stone	di men' sion stone"
dimensional	di men' sion al
dimensioned	di men' sioned
diminution	dim" i nu' tion
dimmer	dim' mer
dimple	dim' ple
dinette	di nette'
dinette table	di nette' table
dinging	ding' ing
dining room	din' ing room"
Dinkeloo, John	Dink' e loo, John"

diode	di' ode
diorama	di" o ram' a
dip-grained wood	dip' grained' wood"
diplexer	di plex' er
dipole antenna	di' pole" an ten' na
dipped	dipped
dipping	dipp' ing
dipylon	di py' lon
direct current	di rect' cur' rent
direct expense	di rect' ex pense'
direct glare	di rect' glare"
direct glue-down	di rect' glue' down"
direct-indirect lighting	di rect' in di' rect light' ing
direct lighting	di rect' light' ing
direct personnel expense	di rect' per" son nel' ex pense'
direction	di rec' tion
directional	di rec' tion al
directional arrow sign	di rec' tion al ar' row sign"
directional lighting	di rec' tion al light' ing
directionality	di rec" tion al' i ty
directories	di rec' to ries
directory	di rec' to ry
director's chair	di rec' tors chair"
dirt	dirt
dirt-depreciation factor	dirt' de pre" ci a' tion fac' tor
disability	dis" a bil' i ty
disabled	dis a' bled
disappearing stairs	dis" ap pear' ing stairs"
disc sander	disc' sand' er
discharge	dis' charge
discharge head	dis' charge head"
disclosure	dis clo' sure
discoloration	dis col" or a' tion
discomfort glare	dis com' fort glare"
disconnect	dis" con nect'
disconnecting switch	dis" con nect' ing switch
discontinuity	dis" con ti nu' i ty
discontinuous	dis" con tin' u ous
discount	dis' count
discount rate	dis' count rate"
discounting	dis' count ing
discovery	dis cov' er y

discrete	dis crete'
discrimination	dis crim" i na' tion
dished	dished
dishwasher	dish' wash" er
disintegration	dis in" te gra' tion
dispensary	dis pen' sa ry
dispenser	dis pens' er
dispersal	dis per' sal
dispersant	dis per' sant
dispersed	dis persed'
dispersing	dis pers' ing
dispersion	dis per' sion
displacement	dis place' ment
display	dis play'
display casework	dis play' case' work"
disposable	dis pos' a ble
disposal	dis pos' al
disposer	dis pos' er
disputes	dis putes'
disqualification	dis qual" i fi ca' tion
dissipation	dis" si pa' tion
dissolve	dis solve'
dissonance	dis' so nance
distance	dis' tance
distemper	dis tem' per
distortion	dis tor' tion
distressing	dis tress' ing
distributed load	dis trib' ut ed load"
distribution box	dis" tri bu' tion box
distribution field	dis" tri bu' tion field
distribution panel	dis" tri bu' tion pan' el
district	dis' trict
district heating	dis' trict heat' ing
distyle	dis' tyle
ditch	ditch
ditching	ditch' ing
diurnal	di ur' nal
diurnal temperature	di ur' nal tem' per a ture
divergence	di ver' gence
diversion	di ver' sion
diverter	di vert' er
divided	di vid' ed

dividend	div' i dend
divider strip	di vid' er strip"
dividing strip	di vid' ing strip"
diving platform	div' ing plat' form
divisibility	di vis" i bil' i ty
division	di vi' sion
dobby weave	dob' by weave"
dobie	do' bie
document	doc' u ment
document glass	doc' u ment glass"
dog anchor	dog' an' chor
dog-leg stair	dog' leg stair'
dogging device	dog' ging de vice'
dogleg	dog' leg"
dogtooth molding	dog' tooth" mold' ing
dolly	dol' ly
Dolly Varden siding	Dol' ly Var' den sid' ing
dolomite	do' lo mite"
dolomite marble	do' lo mite" mar' ble
dolomitic limestone	dol" o mit' ic lime' stone"
dome	dome
domical vault	dom' i cal vault"
domicile	dom' i cile"
Dominion Red	Do min' ion Red
door	door
door bevel	door' bev' el
door bumper	door' bump' er
door closer	door' clos' er
door pull	door' pull"
door schedule	door sched' ule
doorbell	door' bell"
doorframe	door' frame"
doorframe anchor	door' frame an' chor
doorjamb	door' jamb"
doorstop	door' stop"
doorway	door' way"
dooryard	door' yard"
dope	dope
doping	dop' ing
doppler effect	dop' pler ef fect'
dore silver	dore' sil' ver
Doric cyma	Dor' ic cy' ma

Doric order	Dor' ic or' der
dormer	dor' mer
dormer window	dor' mer win' dow
dormitory	dor' mi to" ry
dosing chamber	dos' ing cham' ber
dosing pump	dos' ing pump"
dot	dot
dot matrix	dot' ma' trix
dote	dote
dotted	dot' ted
doty	dot' y
double-acting door	dou' ble act' ing door
double-acting hinge	dou' ble act' ing hinge
double angle	dou' ble an' gle
double bridging	dou' ble bridg' ing
double door	dou' ble door"
double egress frame	dou' ble e gress frame"
double-extra-strong pipe	dou' ble ex' tra strong" pipe
double-faced	dou' ble faced"
double-glazed	dou' ble glazed"
double glazing	dou' ble glaz' ing
double header	dou' ble head' er
double hem edge	dou' ble hem' edge"
double-hung window	dou' ble hung" win' dow
double-knit	dou' ble knit'
double L stair	dou' ble L stair"
double-lock seam	dou' ble lock" seam
double-margin door	dou' ble mar' gin door
double-pitched skylight	dou' ble pitched" sky' light
double rabbet frame	dou' ble rab' bet frame'
double return stair	dou' ble re turn' stair"
double strength	dou' ble strength"
double-strength glass	dou' ble strength" glass
double-sweep tee	dou' ble sweep" tee
double-throw bolt	dou' ble throw" bolt
double-throw switch	dou' ble throw" switch
double trimmer	dou' ble trim' mer
double wall	dou' ble wall"
doublet	dou' blet
doubly reinforced concrete	dou' bly re" in forced' con' crete
Douglas fir	Doug' las fir'
douppioni	doup" pi o' ni

dovecote	dove' cote"
dovetail	dove' tail"
dovetailing	dove' tail ing
dowel	dow' el
dowel-bar reinforcement	dow' el bar re" in force' ment
doweling	dow' el ing
dowicide G	dow' i cide G
down-feed system	down' feed" sys' tem
downdraft	down' draft"
downlight	down' light"
downspout	down' spout"
downstairs	down' stairs"
downtime	down' time"
Doxiades, Constantinos	Dox" i a' des, Con" stan tin' os
doze	doze
draft	draft
draft curtain	draft' cur' tain
draft diverter	draft' di vert' er
draft hood	draft' hood
draft regulator	draft' reg' u la" tor
draft stop	draft' stop
drafter	draft' er
drafting machine	draft' ing ma chine'
draftsman	drafts' man
draftsperson	drafts' per" son
draftstop	draft' stop"
drag	drag
dragging	drag' ging
dragline	drag' line"
dragon beam	drag' on beam
dragon tie	drag' on tie
dragon wagon	drag' on wag' on
drain	drain
drain cock	drain' cock
drain tile	drain' tile
drain-waste-vent system	drain' waste' vent' sys' tem
drainage	drain' age
drainboard	drain' board"
drainpipe	drain' pipe"
drapery	dra' per y
drapery track	dra' per y track"
draw curtain	draw' cur" tain

draw-leaf table	draw' leaf ta' ble
drawboard	draw' board"
drawbore pin	draw' bore" pin
drawdown	draw' down"
drawer	draw' er
drawer pull	draw' er pull"
drawer runner	draw' er run' ner
drawer slide	draw' er slide
drawfile	draw' file"
drawing	draw' ing
drawing board	draw' ing board
drawing room	draw' ing room
drawknife	draw' knife
drawn finish	drawn' fin' ish
drawn glass	drawn' glass
dredge	dredge
drench shower	drench' show' er
dress	dress
dress circle	dress' cir' cle
dressed	dressed
dressed size	dressed' size"
dressed stone	dressed stone"
dresser	dress' er
dressing	dress' ing
dressing room	dress' ing room"
drier	dri' er
drift	drift
driftbolt	drift' bolt"
driftpin	drift' pin"
drill	drill
drillability	drill" a bil' i ty
drillable	drill' a ble
drilled	drilled
drilled-in caisson	drilled' in cais' son
drilling	drill' ing
drinking fountain	drink' ing foun' tain
drip	drip
drip cap	drip' cap"
drip edge	drip' edge"
drip line	drip' line"
drip mold	drip' mold"
drip sink	drip' sink"

dripstone	drip' stone"
drive-in	drive' in"
drive screw	drive' screw"
driven pile	driv' en pile"
drivers	driv' ers
drivescrew nail	drive' screw" nail
driveway	drive' way"
driving-rain index	driv' ing rain in' dex
drop	drop
drop chute	drop' chute"
drop elbow	drop' el' bow
drop hammer	drop' ham' mer
drop-in beam	drop' in' beam
drop-leaf table	drop' leaf' ta' ble
drop molding	drop' mold' ing
drop panel	drop' pan' el
drop siding	drop' sid' ing
drop tee	drop' tee"
dropback	drop' back"
dropchute	drop' chute"
droplight	drop' light"
dropped ceiling	dropped' ceil' ing
dropped panel	dropped' pan' el
dropping	drop' ping
drought	drought
drove	drove
drugget	drug' get
drum	drum
drum table	drum' tab' le
drum trap	drum' trap"
dry	dry
dry-batch weight	dry' batch' weight
dry-blend	dry' blend"
dry-bulb temperature	dry' bulb tem' per a ture
dry cleaning	dry' clean' ing
dry film thickness	dry' film thick' ness
dry glazing	dry' glaz' ing
dry joint	dry' joint"
dry-mix shotcrete	dry' mix shot' crete"
dry-out	dry' out"
dry-pack	dry' pack"
dry-packed concrete	dry' packed con' crete

dry packing	dry' pack' ing
dry pipe sprinkler	dry' pipe' sprink' ler
dry-pipe sprinkler system	dry' pipe sprin' kler sys' tem
dry-press brick	dry' press' brick
dry-rodded volume	dry' rod' ded vol' ume
dry rot	dry' rot'
dry-rotted	dry' rot' ted
dry sample	dry' sam' ple
dry-set	dry' set"
dry-shake hardener	dry" shake hard' en er
dry sheet	dry' sheet"
dry tack	dry' tack"
dry-type transformer	dry' type" trans' form er
dry well	dry' well"
dry wood	dry' wood"
dryer	dry' er
drying	dry' ing
drying in	dry' ing in
drying shrinkage	dry' ing shrink' age
dryout	dry' out"
dryseal	dry' seal"
drywall	dry' wall"
dual-duct system	dual' duct' sys' tem
dub	dub
dubbing out	dub' bing out"
duck	duck
duckbill pliers	duck' bill" pli' ers
duckboard	duck' board"
duct	duct
duct fan	duct' fan
duct furnace	duct' fur' nace
duct lining	duct' lin' ing
ductile	duc' tile
ductility	duc til' i ty
ductwork	duct' work"
due care	due' care"
dumbwaiter	dumb' wait" er
dummy	dum' my
dummy cylinder	dum' my cyl' in der
dummy trim	dum' my trim
dummying	dum' my ing
dumpy level	dump' y lev" el

Duncan Phyfe	Dun' can Phyfe'
dune	dune
dunnage	dun' nage
duomo	duo' mo
duplex	du' plex
duplex dwelling	du' plex dwel' ling
duplex head nail	du' plex head nail"
duplex receptacle	du' plex re cep' ta cle
duplication	du" pli ca' tion
durability	du" ra bil' i ty
durable	du" ra ble
duralumin	du ral' u min
duraluminum	du" ra lum' i num
duranodic	dur" a nod' ic
duration	du ra' tion
duress	du ress'
durometer	du rom' e ter
D'Urso, Joseph	DUr' so, Jo' seph
dust	dust
dust board	dust' board"
dust control	dust' con trol'
dust-free time	dust' free' time
dust-press process	dust' press' pro' cess
dustfree	dust' free"
dusting	dust' ing
dustpressed	dust' pressed
dustproof	dust' proof"
dustproof strike	dust' proof" strike
dusttight	dust' tight"
dutch	dutch
Dutch bond	Dutch' bond'
Dutch door	Dutch' door'
dutchman	dutch' man
duty	du' ty
duvetyn	du' ve tyn"
dwang	dwang
dwarf partition	dwarf' par ti' tion
dwelling	dwell' ing
dye	dye
dymaxion	dy max' i on
dynamic	dy nam' ic
dynamic analysis	dy nam' ic a nal' y sis

dynamic creep	dy nam' ic creep
dynamic load	dy nam' ic load
dynamic loading	dy nam' ic load' ing
dynamic range	dy nam' ic range
dynamite	dy' na mite"
dynamometer	dy" na mom' e ter
dyne	dyne

E

Eames chair	Eames' chair"
Eames, Charles	Eames', Char' les
ear	ear
Early English	Ear' ly Eng' lish
early strength	ear' ly strength
early wood	ear' ly wood"
earth	earth
earth flow	earth' flow"
earth pressure	earth' pres' sure
earth-sheltered	earth' shel' tered
earthenware	earth' en ware"
earthing	earth' ing
earthquake	earth' quake"
earthwork	earth' work"
eased edge	eased' edge"
easement	ease' ment
easing	eas' ing
East Indian laurel	East In' di an lau' rel
eastern hemlock	east' ern hem' lock
eastern red cedar	east' ern red ce' dar
eaves	eaves
eaves course	eaves' course"
eaves fascia	eaves' fas' ci a
ebonite	eb' on ite"
ebonize	eb' on ize"
ebony	eb' on y
eccentric	ec cen' tric
eccentric force	ec cen' tric force"
eccentric loading	ec cen' tric load' ing
eccentrically	ec cen' tri cal ly
ecclesiastical	ec cle" si as' ti cal
echinus	e chi' nus

echo	ech' o
eclectic	ec lec' tic
eclecticism	ec lec' ti cism"
École des Beaux-Arts	E cole' des Beaux' Arts
ecological	ec" o log' i cal
ecologist	e col' o gist
ecology	e col' o gy
economic	ec" o nom' ic
economizer	e con' o miz" er
economy	e con' o my
ecosystem	ec' o sys" tem
edge beam	edge' beam"
edge clearance	edge' clear' ance
edge-grained	edge' grained"
edge joint	edge' joint"
edge molding	edge' mold' ing
edge pull	edge' pull"
edge-tracking	edge' track' ing
edge venting	edge' vent' ing
edger	edg' er
edgestone	edge' stone"
edgestrip	edge' strip"
edging	edg' ing
edifice	ed' i fice
effective	ef fec' tive
effective area	ef fec' tive ar' e a
effective depth	ef fec' tive depth"
effective length	ef fec' tive length"
effective span	ef fec' tive span"
effective temperature	ef fec' tive tem' per a ture
efficacy	ef' fi ca cy
efficiency	ef fi' cien cy
efflorescence	ef" flo res' cence
effluent	ef' fluent
egg-and-dart	egg' and dart'
egg crate	egg' crate"
egg crate louver	egg' crate" lou' ver
eggshell	egg' shell"
eggshelling	egg' shell" ing
egress	e gress
egresses	e gres ses
Egyptian	E gyp' tian

Ehrenkrantz, Ezra	Eh' ren krantz, Ez' ra
eight-cut finish	eight' cut fin' ish
ejector	e jec' tor
elastic	e las' tic
elastic deformation	e las' tic de" for ma' tion
elastic limit	e las' tic lim' it
elastic shortening	e las' tic short' en ing
elasticity	e las tic' i ty
elasto-plastic	e las' to plas' tic
elastomer	e las' to mer
elastomeric	e las" to mer' ic
elastoplastic	e las' to plas' tic
elbow	el' bow
elbow catch	el' bow catch"
electric	e lec' tric
electric-arc welding	e lec' tric arc weld' ing
electric-discharge lamp	e lec' tric dis' charge lamp"
electric elevator	e lec' tric el' e va" tor
electric lock	e lec' tric lock"
electric strike	e lec' tric strike"
electrical	e lec' tri cal
electrical code	e lec' tri cal code"
electrical metallic tubing	e lec' tri cal me tal' lic tub' ing
electrician	e lec tri' cian
electricity	e lec tric' i ty
electrified	e lec' tri fied"
electro-magnetic	e lec" tro mag net' ic
electroacoustic	e lec" tro a cous' tic
electrochemical	e lec" tro chem' i cal
electrochemistry	e lec" tro chem' is try
electrochromic coating	e lec" tro chrom' ic coat' ing
electrode	e lec' trode
electrodeposition	e lec" tro dep" o si' tion
electroendosmosis	e lec" tro end" os mo' sis
electroforming	e lec' tro form" ing
electrogalvanizing	e lec" tro gal' va niz" ing
electrohydraulic	e lec" tro hy drau' lic
electrokinetics	e lec" tro ki net' ics
electroless plating	e lec' tro less plat' ing
electrolier switch	e lec' tro lier" switch"
electroluminescence	e lec" tro lu" mi nes' cence
electroluminescent	e lec" tro lu" mi nes' cent

electrolysis	e lec trol' y sis
electrolyte	e lec' tro lyte"
electrolytic	e lec" tro ly' tic
electrolytically	e lec" tro lyt' i cal ly
electromagnet	e lec" tro mag' net
electromagnetic	e lec" tro mag net' ic
electrometer	e lec trom' e ter
electron	e lec' tron
electronic	e lec tron' ic
electroosmosis	e lec' tro os mo' sis
electrophoresis	e lec" tro pho re' sis
electrophotographic	e lec" tro pho" to graph' ic
electroplated	e lec' tro plat" ed
electroplating	e lec' tro plat" ing
electropolish	e lec' tro pol' ish
electrostatic	e lec" tro stat' ic
electrostatic filter	e lec" tro stat' ic fil' ter
electrostatic plotter	e lec" tro stat' ic plot' ter
electrostatic precipitator	e lec" tro stat' ic pre cip' i ta tor
element	el' e ment
elephant trunk	el' e phant trunk"
elevation	el" e va' tion
elevator	el' e va" tor
elevator cab	el' e va" tor cab"
elevator car-frame sling	el' e va" tor car' frame sling"
elevator car platform	el' e va" tor car plat' form
eliminator	e lim' i na" tor
Elizabethan	E liz" a bet' than
ell	ell
ellipse	el lipse'
ellipsoid	el lip' soid
elliptical	el lip' ti cal
Ellwood, Craig	Ell' wood", Craig
elm	elm
elongated	e lon' gat ed
elongation	e lon ga' tion
embalming table	em balm' ing ta' ble
embankment	em bank' ment
embassy	em' bas sy
embattled	em bat' tled
embattlement	em bat' tle ment
embedded column	em bed' ded col' umn

embedment	em bed' ment
embedment length	em bed' ment length
embellish	em bel' lish
embellishment	em bel' lish ment
emblem	em' blem
emboss	em boss'
embossed	em bossed'
embossing	em bos' sing
embrasure	em bra' sure
embrittlement	em brit' tle ment
embroidery	em broi' der y
emergency	e mer' gen cy
emergency-exit lighting	e mer' gen cy ex' it light' ing
emergency lighting	e mer' gen cy light' ing
emery	em' er y
eminent domain	em' i nent do main'
emissivity	em" is siv' i ty
emittance	e mit' tance
emitted radiant exitance	e mit' ted ra' di ant ex' i tance
Empire	Em' pire
empirical	em pir' i cal
employee	em ploy' ee
employer	em ploy' er
employer's	em ploy' ers
employment	em ploy' ment
emulsifier	e mul' si fi" er
emulsifying agent	e mul' si fy" ing a' gent
emulsion	e mul' sion
enamel	e nam' el
encarpus	en car' pus
encase	en case'
encased knot	en cased' knot'
encaustic tile	en caus' tic tile
enceinte wall	en ceinte' wall"
enclosed	en closed'
enclosure	en clo' sure
encroachment	en croach' ment
encumbrance	en cum' brance
end-bearing pile	end' bear' ing pile
end block	end' block
end channel	end' chan' nel
end-cutting nippers	end' cut' ting nip' pers

end distance	end' dis' tance
end grain	end' grain
end joint	end' joint
end-lap joint	end' lap' joint
end match	end' match
end-matched	end' matched"
end restraint	end' re straint'
end table	end' ta' ble
endive scroll	en' dive scroll"
endorsement	en dorse' ment
endothermic	en" do ther' mic
endurance test	en dur' ance test
energy	en' er gy
enfilade	en" fi lade'
engage	en gage'
engaged column	en gaged' col' umn
engineer	en" gi neer'
engineer-in-training	en" gi neer' in train' ing
engineered	en gi neered'
engineering	en gi neer' ing
engineering officer	en gi neer' ing of' fi cer
engineer's scale	en gi neers' scale"
engleman spruce	en' gle man spruce"
English bond	Eng' lish bond"
English brown oak	Eng' lish brown" oak
engrailed	en grailed'
engrailment	en grail' ment
engraving	en grav' ing
enrichment	en rich' ment
ensemble	en sem' ble
entablature	en tab' la ture
entail	en tail'
entasis	en' ta sis
entering temperature	en' ter ing tem' per a ture
enthalpy	en' thal py
entity	en' ti ty
entourage	en" tou rage'
entrained air	en trained' air"
entrance	en' trance
entrapped air	en trapped' air
entresol	en' tre sol"
entropy	en' tro py

entry	en' try
entryway	en' try way"
envelope	en' ve lope"
environment	en vi' ron ment
environmental	en vi" ron men' tal
environmental impact statement	en vi" ron men' tal im' pact state'- ment
enzymes	en' zymes
epi	ep' i
epicenter	ep' i cen" ter
epigraph	ep' i graph"
epistle side	e pis' tle side"
epistyle	ep' i style
epoxy	ep ox' y
epoxy adhesive	ep ox' y ad he' sive
epoxy-catalyzed	ep ox' y cat' a lyzed"
epoxy paint	ep ox' y paint"
epoxyamide	ep ox' y a" mide
equalizer	e' qual iz" er
equalizing	e' qual iz" ing
equi-energy source	e" qui en' er gy source"
equilateral	e" qui lat' er al
equilibrium	e" qui lib' ri um
equilibrium moisture content	e" qui lib' ri um mois' ture con'- tent
equinox	e' qui nox"
equipment ground	e quip' ment ground"
equitable	eq' ui ta ble
equity	eq' ui ty
equivalent	e quiv' a lent
equivalent direct radiation	e quiv' a lent di rect' ra" di a' tion
equivalent friction loss	e quiv' a lent fric' tion loss
equivalent sphere illumination	e quiv' a lent sphere il lu" mi na'- tion
equiviscous	eq ui vis' cous
eradicator	e rad' i ca" tor
eraser	e ras' er
erasing shield	e ras' ing shield
erdalith	erd' a lith
erect	e rect'
erecting	e rect' ing
erection	e rec' tion

erection drawing	e rec' tion draw' ing
ergonometric	er" go no met' ric
ergonomic	er" go nom' ic
ergonomically	er" go nom' i cal ly
ergonomist	er gon' o mist
Erickson, Arthur	Er' ick son, Ar' thur
erosion	e ro' sion
erosion resistance	e ro' sion re sist' ance
errata	er ra' ta
erratum	er ra' tum
errors and omissions	er' rors and o mis' sions
escalation	es" ca la' tion
escalator	es' ca la" tor
escape chute	es cape' chute"
escarpment	es carp' ment
esconson	es con' son
escrow	es' crow
escutcheon	es cutch' eon
Esherick, Joseph	Esh' er ick, Jo' seph
esonarthex	es" o nar' thex
espagnolette bolt	es pa' gno lette" bolt
esplanade	es' pla nade
essex board measure	es' sex board meas' ure
estate	es tate'
ester	es' ter
ester gum	es' ter gum"
estimate	es' ti mate
estimating	es' ti mat" ing
estimator	es' ti ma" tor
estrade	es trade'
Estremoz Branco	Es' tre moz Bran' co
Estremoz Vergado	Es' tre moz Ver ga' do
étagère	e" ta gere'
etch	etch
etched	etched
etching	etch' ing
ethylene glycol	eth' yl ene" gly' col
ethylene plastic	eth' yl ene" plas' tic
ethylene propylene diene monomer	eth' yl ene" pro' pyl ene" di' ene mon' o mer
Etowah Fleuri	Et' o wah Fleu' ri
Etowah Pink	Et' o wah Pink"

101

Etruscan order	E trus' can or' der
Euler's equation	Eu' lers e qua' tion
Eureka Danby	Eu re' ka Dan' by
eurhythmy	eu rhyth' my
eustyle	eu' style
eutectic alloy	eu tec' tic al' loy
eutectic salt	eu tec' tic salt
evacuated tube collector	e vac' u at ed tube col lec' tor
evaluation	e val" u a' tion
evaporable water	e vap' o ra ble wa' ter
evaporate	e vap' o rate"
evaporation	e vap" o ra' tion
evaporative	e vap' o ra" tive
evaporative cooling	e vap' o ra" tive cool' ing
evaporator	e vap' o ra tor
even-textured	e' ven tex' tured
event	e vent'
evergreen	ev' er green"
eviction	e vic' tion
evidence	ev' i dence
evolute	ev' o lute
examination	ex am" i na' tion
excavate	ex' ca vate
excavating	ex' ca vat ing
excavation	ex" ca va' tion
excavator	ex' ca va" tor
excess air	ex cess' air
exchange	ex change'
excitation	ex" ci ta' tion
exclusionary zoning	ex clu' sion ar" y zon' ing
exculpation	ex" cul pa' tion
exculpatory	ex cul' pa to" ry
exedra	ex' e dra
exfoliation	ex fo" li a' tion
exhaust fan	ex haust' fan
existing building	ex ist' ing build' ing
existing conditions	ex ist' ing con di' tions
exit	ex' it
exit corridor	ex' it cor' ri dor
exit device	ex' it de vice'
exit light	ex' it light"
exit passageway	ex' it pas' sage way

exitance	ex' i tance
exitway	ex' it way"
exonarthex	ex" o nar' thex
exothermic	ex" o therm' ic
exothermic welding	ex' o therm ic weld' ing
expanded metal	ex pand' ed me' tal
expanded-metal partition	ex pand' ed me' tal par ti' tion
expanded polystyrene	ex pand' ed poy" y sty' rene
expanding cement	ex pand' ing ce ment'
expansion	ex pan' sion
expansion bearing	ex pan' sion bear' ing
expansion bolt	ex pan' sion bolt"
expansion joint	ex pan' sion joint"
expansion loop	ex pan' sion loop"
expansion strip	ex pan' sion strip"
expansion tank	ex pan' sion tank"
expansive	ex pan' sive
expediter	ex' pe dit" er
expendable	ex pend' a ble
expenses	ex penses
experimental	ex per' i men' tal
expert witness	ex' pert wit' ness
expletive	ex' ple tive
exploded view	ex plod' ed view
explosion-proof	ex plo' sion proof
explosive	ex plo' sive
explosive-driven fastener	ex plo' sive driv' en fas' ten er
exponential	ex" po nen' tial
exporter	ex' port er
exposed	ex posed'
exposed aggregate	ex posed' ag' gre gate
exposed-aggregate finish	ex posed' ag' gre gate fin' ish
exposed suspension system	ex posed' sus pen' sion sys' tem
exposure	ex po' sure
exposure hazard	ex po' sure haz' ard
express warranty	ex press' war' ran ty
extended-care facility	ex tend' ed care fa ci' i ty
extender	ex tend' er
extensibility	ex ten" si bil' i ty
extension	ex ten' sion
extension bolt	ex ten' sion bolt"
extension ladder	ex ten' sion lad' der

extensions of time	ex ten' sions of time
exterior	ex te' ri or
exterior finish	ex te' ri or fin' ish
exterior plywood	ex te' ri or ply' wood
exterior-type plywood	ex te' ri or type ply' wood
externally operated disconnect	ex ter' nal ly op' er at" ed dis'- con nect
extinction	ex tinc' tion
extinguish	ex tin' guish
extinguisher	ex tin' guish er
extra	ex' tra
extra-strong pipe	ex' tra strong pipe"
extractives	ex trac' tives
extrados	ex' tra dos
extreme fiber stress	ex treme' fib' er stress
extreme tension fiber	ex treme' ten' sion fib' er
extrude	ex trude'
extruded	ex trud' ed
extruded polystyrene	ex trud' ed pol" y sty' rene
extruding	ex trud' ing
extrusion	ex tru' sion
exudation	ex" u da' tion
eye	eye
eyebolt	eye' bolt"
eyebrow	eye' brow"
Eyring formula	Ey' ring for' mu la

F

fabric	fab' ric
fabric roof-system	fab' ric roof sys' tem
fabric wall covering	fab' ric wall cov' er ing
fabricated	fab' ri cat" ed
fabricating	fab' ri cat" ing
fabrication	fab" ri ca' tion
fabricator	fab' ri ca" tor
facade	fa cade'
face	face
face-bedded	face' bed' ded
face brick	face' brick
face glazing	face' glaz' ing
face layer	face' lay' er

face weight	face' weight"
faced block	faced' block"
faced plywood	faced' ply' wood
faced wall	faced' wall"
faceplate	face' plate"
facete	fac' ete
faceted	fac' et ed
facing	fac' ing
facing tile	fac' ing tile"
facsimile	fac sim' i le
factor of safety	fac' tor of safe' ty
factory	fac' to ry
factory-built	fac' to ry built"
Factory Mutual	Fac' to ry Mu' tu al
factory square	fac' to ry square"
facture	fac' ture
fadeometer	fade om' e ter
fading	fad' ing
Fahrenheit	Fahr' en heit"
faience	fa ience'
faience tile	fa ience' tile"
fail-safe	fail' safe"
faille	faille
failure	fail' ure
fair	fair
fall	fall
fall-front desk	fall' front' desk
fallback	fall' back"
fallout shelter	fall' out" shel' ter
false ceiling	false' ceil' ing
false joint	false' joint"
false set	false' set"
falsework	false' work"
family	fam' i ly
fan	fan
fan coil	fan' coil"
fan-coil unit	fan' coil" u' nit
fan Fink truss	fan' Fink' truss
fan truss	fan' truss"
fanback chair	fan' back" chair"
fanlight	fan' light"
fantail	fan' tail

fanwork	fan' work
farad	far' ad
farmhouse	farm' house"
fascia	fas' ci a
fascia board	fas' ci a board
fast-pin butt	fast' pin' butt"
fast-pin hinge	fast' pin' hinge"
fast track	fast' track'
fast-track construction	fast' track' con struc' tion
fastener	fas' ten er
fastness	fast' ness
fat mix	fat' mix"
fat mortar	fat' mor' tar
fatigue	fa tigue'
fattening	fat' ten ing
faucet	fau' cet
fault	fault
fault breccia	fault' brec' cia
faulting	fault' ing
faux-bamboo	faux' bam boo'
faux bois	faux' bois"
faux marbre	faux' mar' bre
favus	fa' vus
faying surface	fay' ing sur' face
feasibility study	fea" si bil' i ty stud' y
feather	feath' er
feather grain	feath' er grain"
feather joint	feath' er joint"
feather tips	feath' er tips"
featheredge	feath' er edge"
feathering	feath' er ing
featherrock	feath' er rock"
feature strip	fea' ture strip"
featured edge	fea' tured edge"
fee	fee
feedback	feed' back"
feeder	feed' er
feedpump	feed' pump"
feedwater	feed' wa" ter
feint	feint
feldspar	feld' spar"
felt	felt

felt-tip marker board	felt' tip mark' er board"
felting	felt' ting
female thread	fe' male thread"
femerell	fem' e rell
fence	fence
fencing	fenc' ing
fender	fend' er
fenestra method	fe nes' tra met' hod
fenestration	fen" es tra' tion
feretory	fer' e to ry
ferrocement	fer" ro ce ment'
ferroconcrete	fer" ro con' crete
ferrous metal	fer' rous met' al
ferruginous	fer ru' gi nous
ferrule	fer' rule
fertilize	fer' ti lize"
festoon	fes toon'
festoon drape	fes toon' drape"
fiber-asphalt laminate	fi' ber as' phalt lam' i nate
fiber cabling	fi' ber ca' bling
fiber-metal laminate	fi' ber met' al lam' i nate
fiber optics	fi' ber op' tics
fiber-reinforced concrete	fi' ber re" in forced' con' crete
fiber-resin	fi' ber res' in
fiber saturation point	fi' ber sat" u ra' tion point
fiber stress	fi' ber stress
fiberboard	fi' ber board"
fiberfill	fi' ber fill"
fiberglass	fi' ber glass"
Fiberglas™	Fi' ber glas"
fiberplug	fi' ber plug"
fibrous	fi' brous
fibrous concrete	fi' brous con' crete
fibrous-felted board	fi' brous felt' ed board
fictile	fic' tile
fiddle back chair	fid' dle back" chair
fiddleback veneer	fid' dle back ve neer'
fidelity	fi del' i ty
fiduciary	fi du' ci ar" y
field	field
field bending	field' bend' ing
field check	field' check"

field house	field' house"
field-molded sealant	field' mold' ed seal' ant
field order	field' or' der
field representative	field' rep" re sent' a tive
fielded panel	field' pan' el
fieldstone	field' stone"
figure	fig' ure
figured	fig' ured
figured glass	fig' ured glass"
figuring	fig' ur ing
filament	fil' a ment
file	file
filiform	fil' i form
filigree	fil' i gree"
filigreed	fil' i greed"
fill	fill
fill insulation	fill' in" sul a' tion
filler	fil' ler
filler strip	fil' ler strip"
fillet	fil' let
fillet weld	fil' let weld"
filling	fill' ing
fillister	fil' lis ter
film	film
filter	fil' ter
filtration	fil tra' tion
fin	fin
fin tube radiation	fin' tube' ra" di a' tion
final acceptance	fi' nal ac cept' ance
final completion	fi' nal com ple' tion
final payment	fi' nal pay' ment
final set	fi' nal set"
financial	fi nan' cial
financial management	fi nan' cial man' age ment
fine aggregate	fine' ag gre gate
fine grading	fine' grad' ing
fine sand	fine' sand"
fine sandy loam	fine' sand' y loam"
fine-textured	fine' tex' tured
fineness	fine' ness
fines	fines
finger blisters	fin' ger blis' ters

finger guard	fin' ger guard"
finger joint	fin' ger joint"
finger pull	fin' ger pull"
finial	fin' i al
finish	fin' ish
finish carpentry	fin' ish car' pen try
finish coat	fin' ish coat"
finish compound	fin' ish com' pound
finish floor	fin' ish floor
finish flooring	fin' ish floor' ing
finish grade	fin' ish grade"
finish hardware	fin' ish hard' ware"
finishing	fin' ish ing
finite element	fi' nite el' e ment
Fink truss	Fink' truss"
Finn weave	Finn' weave"
fins	fins
fir	fir
fire	fire
fire assembly	fire' as sem' bly
fire canopy	fire' can' o py
fire clay	fire' clay"
fire cut	fire' cut"
fire damper	fire' damp' er
fire detection system	fire' de tec' tion sys' tem
fire district	fire' dis' trict
fire door	fire' door"
fire-door latch	fire' door' latch
fire-door rating	fire' door' rat' ing
fire escape	fire' es cape'
fire exposure	fire' ex po' sure
fire extinguisher	fire' ex tin' guish er
fire-extinguishing	fire' ex tin' guish ing
fire hazard	fire' haz' ard
fire-hazard classification	fire' haz' ard clas" si fi ca' tion
fire hose cabinet	fire' hose' cab' i net
fire-polish	fire' pol' ish
fire protection	fire' pro tec' tion
fire-protection rating	fire' pro tec' tion rat' ing
fire-rated door	fire' rat' ed door"
fire resistance	fire' re sis' tance
fire resistance rating	fire' re sist' tance rat' ing

109

fire-resistant	fire' re sist' ant
fire-resistive	fire' re sis' tive
fire-retardant	fire' re tard' ant
fire-retardant barrier	fire' re tard' ant bar' ri er
fire-retardant coating	fire' re tard' ant coat' ing
fire-retardant finish	fire' re tard' ant fin' ish
fire-retardant lumber	fire' re tard' ant lum' ber
fire safety	fire' safe' ty
fire safing	fire' saf' ing
fire separation	fire' sep" ar a' tion
fire window	fire' win' dow
fireback	fire' back"
firebox	fire' box"
firebrick	fire' brick"
firecut	fire' cut"
fired bond	fired' bond"
fireplace	fire' place"
fireplace insert	fire' place in' sert
fireproof	fire' proof"
fireproofed	fire' proofed"
fireproofing	fire' proof" ing
firestat	fire' stat"
firestop	fire' stop"
firestopped	fire' stopped"
firestopping	fire' stop" ping
firewall	fire' wall"
firing	fir' ing
firm knot	firm' knot"
first floor	first' floor'
fiscal year	fis' cal year'
fish-bellied	fish' bel' lied
fish joint	fish' joint"
fish tape	fish' tape"
fished	fished
fisheye	fish' eye"
fishing wire	fish' ing wire"
fishmouth	fish' mouth"
fishnet	fish' net"
fishplate	fish' plate"
fishtail	fish' tail"
fishtail bolt	fish' tail" bolt
fissility	fis sil' i ty

110

fission	fis' sion
fissure	fis' sure
fista	fis' ta
fitting	fit' ting
fitting-up	fit' ting up"
fixed-bar grille	fixed' bar' grille
fixed beam	fixed' beam"
fixed carbon	fixed' car' bon
fixed end	fixed' end"
fixed-feature space	fixed' fea' ture space
fixed light	fixed' light"
fixed-place collector	fixed' place' col lec' tor
fixed-price contract	fixed' price' con' tract
fixed sash	fixed' sash"
fixing	fix' ing
fixture	fix' ture
fixture branch	fix' ture branch"
fixture drain	fix' ture drain"
fixture unit	fix' ture u' nit
fixture-unit flow rate	fix' ture u' nit flow' rate"
fixture vent	fix' ture vent"
flag	flag
flagger	flag' ger
flagging	flag' ging
flagpole	flag' pole"
flagstone	flag' stone"
flake	flake
flakeboard	flake' board"
flaked	flaked
flaking	flak' ing
flaking resistance	flak' ing re sist' ance
flambeau	flam' beau
flamboyant	flam boy' ant
flame	flame
flame cutting	flame' cut' ting
flame finish	flame' fin' ish
flame front	flame' front"
flame gun	flame' gun"
flame photometer	flame' pho tom' e ter
flame-resistant	flame' re sist' ant
flame retardant	flame' re tard' ant
flame-retardant fabric	flame' re tard' ant fab' ric

flame spread	flame' spread"
flame-spread index	flame' spread in' dex
flame-spread rating	flame' spread rat' ing
flame stitch	flame' stitch"
flameproof	flame' proof"
flammability	flam" ma bil' i ty
flammable	flam' ma ble
flanch	flanch
flange	flange
flange form	flange' form"
flange plate	flange' plate"
flanged pipe	flanged' pipe'
flanging	flang' ing
flank	flank
flanking	flank' ing
flanking path	flank' ing path"
flanking transmission	flank' ing trans mis' sion
flannel	flan' nel
flanning	flan' ning
flap valve	flap' valve"
flare	flare
flare fitting	flare' fit' ting
flaring tool	flar' ing tool
flash	flash
flash coat	flash' coat
flash point	flash' point"
flashback	flash' back"
flasher	flash' er
flashing	flash' ing
flashing condition index	flash' ing con di' tion in' dex
flashover	flash' o" ver
flat	flat
flat arch	flat' arch"
flat-chord truss	flat' chord' truss
flat cut	flat' cut"
flat glass	flat' glass"
flat grain	flat' grain"
flat-grained	flat' grained"
flat plate	flat' plate"
flat-plate collector	flat' plate col lec' tor
flat-platen pressed	flat' plat' en pressed
flat-sawn	flat' sawn"

flat slab	flat' slab"
flat-stock anchor	flat' stock an' chor
flatness	flat' ness"
flatting agent	flat' ting a' gent
flatwise	flat' wise"
flatwork	flat' work"
flaw	flaw
flax	flax
flax board	flax' board
flèche	fleche
fleck	fleck
fleece	fleece
Flemish bond	Flem' ish bond
fleur-de-lis	fleur" de lis'
fleuri	fleu ri'
flex	flex
flexibility	flex" i bil' i ty
flexible	flex' i ble
flexible conduit	flex' i ble con' du it
flexible connector	flex' i ble con nec' tor
flexible tubing	flex' i ble tub' ing
flexural bond	flex' ur al bond"
flexural strength	flex' ur al strength"
flexure	flex' ure
flier	fli' er
flight	flight
flint	flint
flitch	flitch
flitch beam	flitch' beam"
flitchplate	flitch' plate"
float	float
float finish	float' fin' ish
float glass	float' glass"
float switch	float' switch"
float time	float' time"
float valve	float' valve"
floated coat	float' ed coat"
floater	float' er
floating	float' ing
floating end joints	float' ing end" joints
floating floor	float' ing floor"
floating point	float' ing point"

floatstone	float' stone"
floc	floc
floccing	floc' cing
flocculate	floc' cu late"
flocculation	floc" cu la' tion
flocculator	floc' cu la" tor
flocked	flocked
flocking	flock' ing
flood coat	flood' coat"
flood plain	flood' plain"
floodlight	flood' light"
floodlighting	flood' light" ing
floor	floor
floor anchor clip	floor' an' chor clip
floor area	floor' ar' e a
floor-area ratio	floor' ar' e a ra' tio
floor closer	floor' clos' er
floor drain	floor' drain"
floor joist	floor' joist"
floor load	floor' load"
floor plan	floor' plan"
floor plate	floor' plate"
floor receptacle	floor' re cep' ta cle
floor runner track	floor' run' ner track
floor stop	floor' stop"
floor tile	floor' tile"
floorboard	floor' board"
flooring	floor' ing
floptical disk	flop' ti cal disk"
floral	flo' ral
floriated	flo' ri at" ed
floss	floss
flounce	flounce
floury	flour' y
flow	flow
flow capacity	flow' ca pac' i ty
flow chart	flow' chart"
flow-out	flow' out"
flow point	flow' point"
floweret	flow' er et
flowmeter	flow' me" ter
flowrate	flow' rate"

fluctuating noise	fluc' tu at" ing noise
fluctuation	fluc" tu a' tion
flue	flue
flue lining	flue' lin' ing
flueway	flue' way"
fluffing	fluff' ing
fluid	flu' id
fluid-applied	flu' id ap plied'
fluid-type solar system	flu' id type so' lar sys' tem
fluidifier	flu id' i fi er
fluidity	flu id' i ty
fluing	flu' ing
flume	flume
fluor-chrome-arsenate- phenol	fluor' chrome" ar' se nate" phe'- nol
fluoresce	fluo resce'
fluorescence	fluo res' cence
fluorescent	fluo res' cent
fluoridation	fluor" i da' tion
fluorocarbon	fluor' o car" bon
fluorocarbon paint	fluor' o car" bon paint
fluorocarbon plastic	fluor' o car" bon plas' tic
fluorohydrocarbon	fluor" o hy" dro car' bon
fluoroplastic	fluor" o plas' tic
fluoropolymer	fluor" o pol' y mer
fluorspar	flu' or spar"
fluosilicate	flu" o sil' i cate
flush	flush
flush bolt	flush' bolt"
flush door	flush' door"
flush glazing	flush' glaz' ing
flush panel	flush' pan' el
flush plate	flush' plate"
flush tank	flush' tank"
flush valve	flush' valve"
flushing	flush' ing
flushometer	flush" om' e ter
flute	flute
fluted	flut' ed
fluting	flut' ing
flutter	flut' ter
flutter echo	flut' ter ec' ho

flutter fatigue	flut' ter fa tigue'
flux	flux
fluxstone	flux' stone"
fly ash	fly' ash"
fly curtain	fly' cur' tain
fly gallery	fly' gal' ler y
fly loft	fly' loft"
fly rafter	fly' raft' er
fly wheel effect	fly' wheel ef fect'
flying buttress	fly' ing but' tress
flying form	fly' ing form
flying scaffold	fly' ing scaf' fold
flywheel	fly' wheel"
foam core	foam' core"
foam glass	foam' glass"
foam in place	foam' in place"
foam plastic insulation	foam' plas' tic in" su la' tion
foamable	foam' a ble
foamed adhesive	foamed' ad he' sive
foamed-in-place insulation	foamed' in place in" su la' tion
foamed plastic	foamed' plas' tic
foaming agent	foam' ing a' gent
focusing	fo' cus ing
fog curing	fog' cur' ing
fogging	fog' ging
foil	foil
foil-backed insulation	foil' backed' in" su la' tion
foil-faced fiberglass	foil' faced' fiber' glass
folded plate	fold' ed plate
folded-plate roof	fold' ed plate roof
folding door	fold' ing door'
folding table	fold' ing ta' ble
foldstir mixer	fold' stir" mix' er
foliage	fo' li age
foliated	fo' li at" ed
foliation	fo" li a' tion
follower	fol' low er
folly	fol' ly
font	font
food service equipment	food' ser' vice e quip' ment
food tray rail	food' tray" rail
foot	foot

foot bolt	foot' bolt
foot-operated	foot' op' er a ted
foot-pound	foot' pound'
foot scraper	foot' scrap' er
footage	foot' age
footboard	foot' board"
footcandle	foot' can' dle
footing	foot' ing
footing forms	foot' ing forms
footlambert	foot' lam" bert
footlight	foot' light"
footpace	foot' pace"
footpieces	foot' pieces"
footplate	foot' plate"
footstall	foot' stall"
footstool	foot' stool"
forb	forb
force	force
forced-air furnace	forced' air fur' nace
forced circulation	forced' cir" cu la' tion
forced convection	forced' con vec' tion
forced fit	forced' fit
forced hot-water heating	forced' hot" wa' ter heat' ing
forced warm-air heating	forced' warm" air heat' ing
forechoir	fore' choir"
forecourt	fore' court"
foreman	fore' man
forepole	fore' pole"
forepoling	fore' pol" ing
foreshocks	fore' shocks"
foresight	fore' sight"
forestage	fore' stage"
forged	forged
forged metal	forged' met' al
forging	forg' ing
form	form
form board insulation	form' board in" su la' tion
form coating	form' coat' ing
form insulation	form' in" su la' tion
form liner	form' lin' er
form oil	form' oil
form scabbing	form' scab' bing

form tie	form' tie
formability	form" a bil' i ty
formal	for' mal
formal garden	for' mal gar' den
formaldehyde	form al' de hyde"
format	for' mat
formboard	form' board"
former	form' er
Formica™	For mi' ca
forming	form' img
Formosa White	For mo' sa White"
formula	for' mu la
formwork	form' work"
fort	fort
fortress	for' tress
forum	fo' rum
fossil fuel	fos' sil fuel"
Foster, Norman	Fos' ter, Nor' man
foundation	foun da' tion
foundry	found' ry
fountain	foun' tain
four-centered arch	four' cen' tered arch
4-phenylcyclohexene	4 phen' yl cy" clo hex' ene
four-way switch	four' way" switch"
Fourcoult process	Four' coult" pro' cess
fourposter	four' post' er
foxiness	fox' i ness
foxing	fox' ing
foxtail wedge	fox' tail" wedge
foyer	foy' er
frac-shot	frac' shot"
fractable	frac' ta ble
fraction	frac' tion
fracture	frac' ture
fracture toughness	frac' ture tough' ness
fracturing	frac' tur ing
fragmentation	frag" men ta' tion
frame	frame
frame clearance	frame' clear' ance
frame-high	frame' high"
frame pulley	frame' pul' ley
frame wall	frame' wall"

framed building	framed' build' ing
frameless	frame' less"
framework	frame' work"
framing	fram' ing
framing anchor	fram' ing an' chor
framing clip	fram' ing clip"
framing plan	fram' ing plan"
framing square	fram' ing square"
frank	frank
franking	frank' ing
Franklin	Frank' lin
Franzen, Ulrich	Franz' en, Ul' rich
fraternity house	fra ter' ni ty house"
fraud	fraud
free area	free' ar' e a
free-body diagram	free' bod' y di' a gram
free fall	free' fall'
free field	free' field"
free float	free' float"
free-floating	free' float' ing
free form	free' form'
free moisture	free' mois' ture
free oscillation	free' os" cil la' tion
free water	free' wa' ter
freehand drawing	free' hand" draw' ing
freestanding	free' stand' ing
freestone	free' stone"
freeway	free' way"
freeze-thaw cycle	freeze' thaw cy' cle
freezeback	freeze' back"
freezer	freez' er
freezestat	freeze' stat"
freezing	freez' ing
freight elevator	freight' el' e va" tor
French	French
French bed	French' bed"
French curve	French' curve"
French door	French' door"
French drain	French' drain"
French Normandy	French' Nor' man dy
French Provincial	French' Pro vin' cial
Freon™	Fre' on

frequency	fre' quen cy
frequency distribution	fre' quen cy dis" tri bu' tion
fresco	fres' co
fresh-air inlet	fresh' air in' let
fresnel	fres nel'
Fresnel lens	Fres nel' lens
Fresnel reflection	Fres nel' re flec' tion
Fresnel-reflector system	Fres nel' re flec' tor sys' tem
fret	fret
fretwork	fret' work"
friable	fri' a ble
friction	fric' tion
friction catch	fric' tion catch"
friction head	fric' tion head"
friction hinge	fric' tion hinge"
friction loss	fric' tion loss"
friction pile	fric' tion pile"
friction-type connection	fric' tion type con nec' tion
Friedberg, M. Paul	Fried' berg, M. Paul"
frieze	frieze
frilled	frilled
fringe	fringe
fritfront	frit' front"
frog	frog
front	front
front putty	front' put' ty
front yard	front' yard"
frontage	front' age
frontal	fron' tal
frontispiece	fron' tis piece"
frost	frost
frost heave	frost' heave"
frostat	fros' tat
frosted	frost' ed
frosted finish	frost' ed fin' ish
frosting	frost' ing
frostline	frost' line"
frustum	frus' tum
fuel	fu' el
fueling depot	fu' el ing de' pot
fulcrum	ful' crum
full-bound	full' bound"

full coat	full' coat'
full-flush door	full' flush' door
full mortise hinge	full' mor' tise hinge
full-penetration butt weld	full' pen e tra' tion butt weld
full radiator	full' ra' di a tor
full size	full' size"
full-surface hinge	full' sur' face hinge
Fuller, Buckminster	Ful' ler, Buck' mins" ter
fuller's earth	fu' lers earth'
fulling	ful' ling
fume	fume
fume hood	fume' hood"
fumed oak	fumed' oak"
fumigant	fu' mi gant
fumigation	fu" mi ga' tion
fumigation chamber	fu" mi ga' tion cham' ber
functionalism	func' tion al ism"
fundamental frequency	fun" da men' tal fre' quen cy
fundamental period	fun" da men' tal pe' ri od
fungi	fun' gi
fungicide	fun' gi cide
fungus	fun' gus
funicular	fu nic' u lar
funicular shape	fu nic' u lar shape"
fur	fur
furan	fu' ran
furan mortar	fu' ran mor' tar
furan resin	fu' ran res' in
furnace	fur' nace
furnish	fur' nish
furnishings	fur' nish' ings
furniture	fur' ni ture
furred	furred
furring	fur' ring
furring channel	fur' ring chan' nel
fuse	fuse
fusestat	fuse' stat"
fusetron	fuse' tron"
fuseway	fuse' way"
fusible	fu' si ble
fusible link	fu' si ble link"
fusion	fu' sion

fusion welding	fu' sion weld' ing
fust	fust
fustian	fus' tian
future value	fu' ture val' ue
fuzzing	fuz' zing

G

gabardine	gab' ar dine"
gabion	ga' bi on
gable	ga' ble
gable end	ga' ble end"
gable wall	ga' ble wall"
gable window	ga' ble win' dow
gable-windowed	ga' ble win' dowed
gableboard	ga' ble board"
gablet	gab' let"
gadroon	ga droon'
gadrooning	ga droon' ing
gage	gage
gage line	gage' line"
gain	gain
gaine	gaine
galilee	gal' i lee
gallery	gal' ler y
gallet	gal' let
galleting	gal' let ing
gallon	gal' lon
galloon	gal loon'
gallows bracket	gal' lows brack' et
galvanic corrosion	gal van' ic cor ro' sion
galvanic series	gal van' ic se' ries
galvanize	gal' va nize
galvanized iron	gal' va nized i' ron
galvanizing	gal' va niz ing
gambrel	gam' brel
gamma radiography	gam' ma ra" di og' ra phy
gamma ray	gam' ma ray
gang forming	gang' form' ing
gang saw	gang' saw"
gang sawn	gang' sawn"
ganged forms	ganged' forms"

gangnail	gang' nail"
gangway	gang' way"
ganosis	ga no' sis
gantry	gan' try
gantry crane	gan' try crane
gantt chart	gantt' chart"
gap-graded aggregate	gap' grad' ed ag' gre gate
gap grading	gap' grad' ing
garage	ga rage'
garbage	gar' bage
garbage-disposal unit	gar' bage dis pos' al u' nit
garden	gar' den
garden city	gar' den cit' y
gargoyle	gar' goyle
garland	gar' land
garnet	gar' net
garnishment	gar' nish ment
garret	gar' ret
garreting	gar' ret ing
garth	garth
gas	gas
gas drip	gas' drip"
gas-filled lamp	gas' filled lamp
gas-fired	gas' fired
gas furnace	gas' fur' nace
gas main	gas' main
gas metal-arc welding	gas" me' tal arc" weld' ing
gas meter	gas' me' ter
gas-shielded arc welding	gas" shield' ed arc" weld' ing
gas tungsten-arc welding	gas" tung' sten arc" weld' ing
gas welding	gas' weld' ing
gaseous discharge	gas' e ous dis' charge
gaseous inclusions	gas' e ous in clu' sions
gasket	gas' ket
gasket glazing	gas' ket glaz' ing
gasoline	gas" o line'
gassing	gas' sing
gate	gate
gate posts	gate' posts"
gate tower	gate' tow' er
gate valve	gate' valve
gatehouse	gate' house"

gateleg table	gate' leg" ta' ble
gatepost	gate' post"
gathering	gath' er ing
gating	gat' ing
gauge	gauge
gauge board	gauge' board"
gauge rod	gauge' rod"
gauged	gauged
gauged arch	gauged' arch"
gauged mortar	gauged' mor' tar
gauging	gaug' ing
gauging plaster	gaug' ing plas' ter
gaul	gaul
gauze	gauze
gazebo	ga ze' bo
geared traction machine	geared' trac' tion ma chine'
gearless traction machine	gear' less" trac' tion ma chine'
Geddes, Norman Bel	Ged' des, Nor' man Bel
Gehry, Frank O.	Geh' ry, Frank" O.
gel	gel
gel-coated fiberglass	gel' coat' ed fi' ber glass"
gel permeation chromatography	gel' per" me a' tion chro" ma tog'- ra phy
gelation	ge la' tin
gelling	gel' ling
gemel	gem' el
gemel window	gem' el win' dow
general conditions	gen' er al con di' tions
general contract	gen' er al con' tract
general contractor	gen' er al con' trac tor
general diffuse lighting	gen' er al dif' fuse light' ing
generator	gen' er a" tor
Genessee Valley bluestone	Gen" es see' Val' ley blue' stone"
geodesic	ge' o des" ic
geodesic dome	ge' o des" ic dome"
geodesy	ge od' e sy
geodetic survey	ge" o det' ic sur' vey
geology	ge ol' o gy
geomembrane	ge" o mem' brane
geometric	ge" o met' ric
geometrical	ge" o met' ri cal
geometry	ge om' e try

georgette	geor gette'
Georgia marble	Geor' gia mar' ble
Georgian	Geor' gian
geosynthetic	ge" o syn the' tic
geotechnical	ge" o tech' ni cal
geotechnics	ge" o tech' nics
geotextile	ge" o tex' tile
geothermal energy	ge" o ther' mal en' er gy
German	Ger' man
Germanic	Ger man' ic
gesso	ges' so
gestalt	ge stalt'
ghetto	ghet' to
ghosting	ghost' ing
gib	gib
Gibbs surround	Gibbs' sur round'
gig stick	gig' stick"
gilding	gild' ing
gillmore needle	gill' more nee' dle
gilsonite	gil' son ite"
gimlet	gim' let
gimp	gimp
gimp pin	gimp' pin
gin poles	gin' poles"
gingerbread style	gin' ger bread" style
gingham	ging' ham
Gioia Vein	Gi o' i a Vein"
girder	gird' er
girt	girt
girth	girth
Giurgola, Romaldo	Giur' go la, Ro mal' do
glacial	gla' cial
glacial till	gla' cial till"
glacier	gla' cier
gland	gland
glare	glare
glare-reducing glass	glare' re duc' ing glass
glass	glass
glass block	glass' block"
glass-ceramic	glass ce ram' ic
glass fiber	glass' fi' ber
glass mesh mortar unit	glass' mesh' mor' tar u' nit

glass-reinforced	glass' re" in forced'
glass stop	glass' stop"
glassy slag	glass' y slag
glaze	glaze
glaze coat	glaze' coat"
glazed brick	glazed' brick"
glazed tile	glazed tile"
glazement	glaze' ment
glazier	gla' zier
glazier's putty	gla' zier's put' ty
glazing	glaz' ing
glazing bead	glaz' ing bead"
glazing gasket	glaz' ing gas' ket
glitter	glit' ter
globe valve	globe' valve
gloss	gloss
glow	glow
glue	glue
glue block	glue' block"
glue line	glue' line
glue nailed	glue' nailed"
glue nailing	glue' nail' ing
glued buildup	glued' build' up
glued laminated	glued' lam' i nat" ed
glued-laminated timber	glued' lam' i nat" ed tim' ber
glued-up stock	glued' up' stock"
glulam	glu' lam"
glycerin	glyc' er in
glyceryl phthalate resin	glyc' er yl phthal' ate res' in
glycol	gly' col
glyph	glyph
glyptal	glyp' tal
glyptic	glyp' tic
gneiss	gneiss
goals	goals
Goff, Bruce	Goff', Bruce"
goggles	gog' gles
gold	gold
gold leaf	gold' leaf'
Gold Mist	Gold' Mist"
Goldberg, Bertrand	Gold' berg, Ber' trand
Golden Gray	Gold' en Gray

goniophotometer	go" ni o pho tom' e ter
gooseneck	goose' neck"
gorgerin	gor' ger in
gospel side	gos' pel side"
Gothic arch	Goth' ic arch"
Gothic revival	Goth' ic re viv' al
gouache	gouache
gouge	gouge
gouging	goug' ing
governor	gov' er nor
gow caisson	gow' cais' son
grab bar	grab' bar"
gradation	gra da' tion
grade	grade
grade beam	grade' beam"
grade line	grade' line"
grade mark	grade' mark"
grade trademark	grade' trade' mark
graded aggregate	grade' ag' gre gate
grader	grad' er
gradient	gra' di ent
gradient height	gra' di ent height"
gradine	gra' dine
grading	grad' ing
graduate	grad' u ate"
graduated roof	grad' u at ed roof"
graduation	grad" u a' tion
graffiti	graf fi' ti
graffito	graf fi' to
graft copolymer	graft' co pol' y mer
Graham, Bruce	Graham', Bruce"
grain	grain
grain raise	grain' raise"
grain size	grain' size"
graining	grain' ing
gram	gram
granary	gra' na ry
grandfather clock	grand' fa" ther clock"
grandmaster key	grand" mas' ter key
grandstand	grand' stand"
grange	grange
granite	gran' ite

granolithic concrete	gran" o lith' ic con' crete
granular	gran' u lar
granular-fill insulation	gran' u lar fill in" sul a' tion
granulated	gran' u lat" ed
granules	gran' ules
graph	graph
graphic	graph' ic
graphite	graph' ite
grapple	grap' ple
grass	grass
grass cloth	grass' cloth"
grate	grate
grate area	grate' ar' e a
graticulate	gra" tic' u late
grating	grat' ing
gravel	grav' el
gravel basin	grav' el ba' sin
gravel stop	grav' el stop"
graveled roof	grav' eled roof
Graves, Michael	Graves', Mi' chael
gravity	grav' i ty
gravity-sand filter	grav' i ty sand fil' ter
gravity ventilator	grav' i ty ven' ti la" tor
gravity wall	grav' i ty wall"
gray body	gray' bod" y
Gray Canyon sandstone	Gray' Can' yon sand' stone"
Gray, Eileen	Gray,' Ei leen'
Gray Mist	Gray' Mist'
Gray St. Anne Basque	Gray' St. Anne' Basque"
gray water	gray' wa' ter
grease interceptor	grease' in" ter cep' tor
grease trap	grease' trap"
great grandmaster key	great' grand" mas' ter key
Greco-Roman	Gre" co Ro' man
Greek cross	Greek' cross'
Greek revival	Greek' re viv' al
green	green
green concrete	green' con' crete
Green County sandstone	Green' Coun' ty sand' stone"
green lumber	green' lum' ber
greenbelt	green' belt"
Greene, Charles Sumner	Greene', Charles' Sum' ner

Greene, Henry Mather	Greene', Hen' ry Math' er
greenfield	green' field"
greenhouse	green' house"
greenhouse effect	green' house" ef fect'
greenroom	green' room"
greenstone	green' stone"
Gregotti, Vittorio	Gre got' ti, Vit tor' io
greige	greige
grid	grid
grid ceiling	grid' ceil' ing
grid line	grid' line"
griddle	grid' dle
gridiron	grid' i" ron
griffe	griffe
griffin	grif' fin
grill	grill
grillage	gril' lage
grille	grille
grillwork	grill' work"
grin	grin
grind	grind
grinder	grind' er
grindstone	grind' stone
grinning	grin' ning
griotte	gri otte'
grip	grip
Gris Antique	Gris' An tique'
Gris Duquesa	Gris' Du ques' a
Gris Lilas	Gris' Li' las
grisaille	gri saille'
grit	grit
grit number	grit' num' ber
grizzly	griz' zly
grog fire clay mortar	grog' fire' clay" mor' tar
groin	groin
groined	groined
groined vault	groined' vault"
groining	groin' ing
grommet	grom' met
groove	groove
grooved plywood	grooved' ply' wood
groover	groov' er

grooving	groov' ing
Gropius, Walter	Grop' i us, Wal' ter
grosgrain	gros' grain"
grospoint	gros' point"
gross area	gross' ar' e a
grotesque	gro tesque'
grotto	grot' to
ground	ground
ground acceleration	ground' ac cel" er a' tion
ground cover	ground' cov" er
ground-fault circuit interrupter	ground' fault cir' cuit in" ter-rupt' er
ground floor	ground' floor'
ground joint	ground' joint"
ground light	ground' light"
ground motion	ground' mo' tion
ground table	ground' ta' ble
ground water	ground' wa' ter
ground-water barrier	ground' wa" ter bar' ri er
ground wire	ground' wire"
groundbreaking	ground' break" ing
grounded	ground' ed
grounding electrode	ground' ing e lec' trode
groundings	ground' ings
groundsill	ground' sill"
groundwork	ground' work"
group	group
group knot	group' knot"
group vent	group' vent"
grouped columns	grouped' col' umns
grout	grout
grouted	grout' ed
grouting	grout' ing
growth ring	growth' ring"
grozing iron	groz' ing i" ron
grub	grub
grubbing	grub' bing
Gruen, Victor	Gru' en, Vic' tor
guarantee	guar" an tee'
guaranteed maximum	guar" an teed' max' i mum
guaranty	guar' an ty"
guard	guard

guard bar	guard' bar"
guarded	guard' ed
guardrail	guard' rail"
guarea	gua re' a
Guastavino	Guas ta vin' o
Guatemala Extra White	Gua" te ma' la Ex' tra White
gudgeon	gudg' eon
guest room	guest' room"
guesthouse	guest' house"
guide rail	guide' rail"
guide roller	guide' rol' ler
guideline	guide' line"
guildhall	guild' hall"
guilloche	guil loche'
Guimard, Hector	Gui mard', Hec' tor
gullet	gul' let
gully	gul' ly
gum	gum
gumbo	gum' bo
gumwood	gum' wood"
gun	gun
gun grade	gun' grade"
gunite	gun' ite
gunmetal	gun' met" al
gunning	gun' ning
gunny sack	gun' ny sack"
gusset	gus' set
gusset plate	gus' set plate"
gutta	gut' ta
guttae	gut' tae
gutter	gut' ter
guy	guy
guy derrick	guy' der' rick
Gwathmey, Charles	Gwath' mey, Charles'
gymnasium	gym na' si um
gymstand	gym' stand"
gypsum	gyp' sum
gypsum backerboard	gyp' sum back' er board"
gypsum board	gyp' sum board"
gypsum concrete	gyp' sum con' crete
gypsum fiberboard	gyp' sum fi' ber board"
gypsum lath	gyp' sum lath"

gypsum plaster	gyp' sum plas' ter
gypsum wallboard	gyp' sum wall' board"
gyration	gy ra' tion

H

H-bar	H' bar
H molding	H' mold' ing
H-pile	H' pile
H stretcher	H' stretch' er
habitable	hab' it a ble
hachure	ha chure'
hacienda	ha" ci en' da
hack	hack
hackberry	hack' ber" ry
hacking	hack' ing
hackle	hack' le
hackling	hack' ling
hacksaw	hack' saw"
haft	haft
hagioscope	hag' i o scope"
hairline	hair' line"
hairline cracking	hair' line crack' ing
hairline joint	hair' line joint"
hairpin	hair' pin"
halation	ha la' tion
half bat	half' bat'
half header	half" head' er
half landing	half" land' ing
half-lap joint	half' lap' joint
half-mortise hinge	half" mor' tise hinge"
half-rabbeted lock	half" rab' bet ed lock"
half-round	half' round"
half section	half" sec' tion
half story	half' sto' ry
half-surface hinge	half" sur' face hinge"
half-timber	half' tim' ber
half-timbered	half" tim' bered
halfpace	half' pace"
halftone	half' tone"
halide	hal' ide
hall	hall

hall button	hall' but' ton
hall lantern	hall' lan' tern
hallway	hall' way"
halocarbon plastic	hal" o car' bon plas' tic
halogen	hal' o gen
halogen agent	hal' o gen a' gent
Halprin, Lawrence	Hal' prin, Law' rence
halved joint	halved' joint"
halving	halv' ing
hammer	ham' mer
hammer beam	ham' mer beam"
hammer-beam roof	ham' mer beam" roof
hammer brace	ham' mer brace"
hammer-head key	ham' mer head" key
hammered glass	ham' mered glass"
hammerhead crane	ham' mer head crane"
hammering	ham' mer ing
hand	hand
hand-blocked	hand' blocked
hand-cut	hand' cut"
hand of door	hand' of door"
hand-screw clamp	hand' screw" clamp"
hand split	hand' split"
hand-split shakes	hand' split' shakes"
handed	hand' ed
handgrip	hand' grip"
handhole	hand' hole"
handicapped	hand' i capped"
handle	han' dle
handling	han' dling
handrail	hand' rail"
handsaw	hand' saw"
handset	hand' set"
hang	hang
hangar	hang' ar
hangar door	hang' ar door"
hanger	hang' er
hanging	hang' ing
hanging hardware	hang' ing hard' ware
hanging rail	hang' ing rail"
hanging stair	hang' ing stair"
hanging stile	hang' ing stile"

Hankinson formula	Hank' in son form' u la
hard burned	hard' burned"
hard-burnt	hard' burnt"
hard water	hard' wa' ter
hardboard	hard' board"
harden	hard' en
hardened concrete	hard' ened con' crete
hardener	hard' en er
hardening	hard' en ing
hardness	hard' ness
hardpan	hard' pan"
hardware	hard' ware"
hardwood	hard' wood"
hardwood strip flooring	hard' wood" strip" floor' ing
Hardy, Hugh	Har' dy, Hugh'
harmonic	har mon' ic
harmonic distortion	har mon' ic dis tor' tion
harmonic motion	har mon' ic mo' tion
harmonize	har' mo nize"
Harrison, Wallace K.	Har' ri son, Wal lace K.
harsh	harsh
hasp	hasp
hassock	has' sock
hatch	hatch
hatchet	hatch' et
hatching	hatch' ing
hatchway	hatch' way"
hatrack	hat' rack"
haul	haul
haunch	haunch
haunched tenon	haunched' ten' on
haunching	haunch' ing
hawk	hawk
haydite	hay' dite
haylon	hay' lon
hazard	haz' ard
hazardous	haz' ard ous
haze	haze
he bolt	he' bolt"
head	head
head casing	head' cas' ing
head jamb	head' jamb"

head joint	head' joint"
head piece	head' piece"
head pressure	head' pres' sure
headboard	head' board"
header	head' er
header-high	head' er high"
heading	head' ing
headlap	head' lap"
headmold	head' mold
headroom	head' room"
headwall	head' wall"
headway	head' way
health care furniture	health' care' fur' ni ture
health hazard	health' haz' ard
hearing	hear' ing
heart	heart
heart check	heart' check"
hearth	hearth
hearthstone	hearth' stone"
heartshake	heart' shake"
heartwood	heart' wood"
heat	heat
heat-absorbing glass	heat' ab sorb' ing glass"
heat-actuated cooling	heat' ac' tu at" ed cool' ing
heat durability	heat' du" ra bil' i ty
heat exchanger	heat' ex chang' er
heat flux	heat' flux"
heat gain	heat' gain"
heat of hydration	heat' of hy dra' tion
heat load	heat' load"
heat loss	heat' loss"
heat pump	heat' pump"
heat-resistant paint	heat' re sist' ant paint"
heat-resisting glass	heat' re sist' ing glass"
heat-set nylon	heat' set" ny' lon
heat sink	heat' sink"
heat-strengthened	heat' strength' ened
heat transmission	heat' trans mis' sion
heat-treatable	heat' treat' a ble
heat-treated	heat' treat' ed
heater	heat' er
heating	heat' ing

heating degree-day	heat' ing de gree' day
heave	heave
heavy-duty	heav' y du' ty
heavy-timber construction	heav' y tim' ber con struc' tion
heavyweight	heav' y weight"
heavyweight aggregate	heav' y weight" ag' gre gate
hectare	hec' tare
heddle	hed' dle
hedge	hedge
hedgerow	hedge' row"
heel	heel
heel bead	heel' bead"
heel bend	heel' bend"
heel radius	heel' ra' di us
heelpost	heel' post"
height	height
Heli-arc process	Hel' i arc pro' cess
helical	hel' i cal
helical reinforcement	hel' i cal re" in force' ment
helical thread	hel' i cal thread"
helically grooved nail	hel' i cal ly grooved' nail
helices	hel' i ces"
helicline	hel' i cline"
heliodon	he' li o don"
heliostat	he' li o stat"
heliotropism	he" li ot' ro pism"
heliport	hel' i port"
helistop	hel' i stop"
helium	he' li um
helix	he' lix
Hellenic	Hel len' ic
Hellenistic	Hel" len is' tic
Hellmuth, George F.	Hel' muth, George' F.
helm roof	helm' roof"
helmet	hel' met
Helmholtz resonator	Helm' holtz res' o na" tor
helve	helve
hem	hem
hem-fir	hem' fir'
hematite	he' ma tite"
hemicycle	hem' i cy" cle
hemihydrate	hem" i hy' drate

hemisphere	hem' i sphere'
hemispherical	hem" i spher' i cal
hemispheroid	hem' i spher' oid
hemitriglyph	hem" i tri' glyph
hemlock	hem' lock"
hempseed oil	hemp' seed oil
henequen	hen' e quen
henry	hen' ry
Hepplewhite	Hep' ple white"
heptachlor	hep' ta chlor"
herm	herm
hermetic	her met' ic
hermetically	her met' i cal ly
herringbone	her' ring bone"
herringbone weave	her' ring bone" weave"
herse	herse
hertz	hertz
heterogeneity	het" er o ge ne' i ty
heterogeneous	het" er o ge' ne ous
heuristic	heu ris' tic
hew	hew
hewed	hewed
hewing	hew' ing
hewn	hewn
hex head	hex' head"
hex tapping screw	hex' tap' ping screw"
hexagon	hex' a gon
hexastyle	hex' a style"
hi-load nail	hi' load" nail
hick joint	hick' joint"
hick-joint pointing	hick' joint" point' ing
hickey	hick' ey
hickory	hick' o ry
H.I.D. lighting	H' I' D' light' ing
hidden lines	hid' den lines"
hiding	hid' ing
hiding power	hid' ing pow' er
high-bay lighting	high' bay' light' ing
high-build coating	high' build' coat' ing
high-calcium lime	high' cal' ci um lime
high-conductivity copper	high' con duc tiv' i ty cop' per
high definition television	high' def" i nit' tion tel' e vi' sion

high density	high' den' si ty
high-density overlay	high' den' si ty ov' er lay
high-early-strength concrete	high' ear' ly strength" con' crete
high hat	high' hat'
high-hazard occupancy	high' haz' ard oc' cu pan cy
high-intensity discharge lamp	high' in ten' si ty dis' charge lamp
high-lift grouting	high' lift grout' ing
high-output fluorescent	high' out' put fluo res' cent
high-piled storage	high' piled' stor' age
high-pressure laminate	high' pres' sure lam' i nate
high-pressure overlay	high' pres' sure ov' er lay
high-rise	high' rise"
high school	high' school"
high-silicon bronze	high' sil' i con bronze"
high-strength bolt	high' strength' bolt"
high-tech	high' tech"
high-tension bolt	high' ten' sion bolt"
high-velocity dual duct	high' ve loc' i ty dual' duct
highboy	high' boy"
highchair	high' chair"
Highland Danby	High' land Dan' by
highlight	high' light"
hinge	hinge
hinge backset	hinge' back' set"
hinge jamb	hinge' jamb"
hinge stile	hinge' stile"
hip	hip
hip-and-valley roof	hip' and val' ley roof"
hip knob	hip' knob"
hip rafter	hip' raf' ter
hip roof	hip' roof"
hipped gable roof	hipped' ga' ble roof
hippodrome	hip' po drome
hiss	hiss
histogram	his' to gram
historic preservation	his tor' ic pres" er va' tion
historical	his tor' i cal
historicism	his tor' i cism"
history	his' to ry
hit-and-miss	hit' and miss'
hitch	hitch
hoarding	hoard' ing

hob	hob
hod	hod
Hoffmann, Josef	Hof' fmann, Jo' sef
hog	hog
hogging	hog' ging
hogsback tile	hogs' back" tile"
hoist	hoist
hoist tower	hoist' tow' er
hoistway	hoist' way"
hold-down clip	hold' down' clip"
hold harmless	hold' harm' less
holdback	hold' back
hole cutter	hole' cut' ter
holiday	hol' i day"
Hollein, Hans	Hol' lein, Hans'
hollow brick	hol' low brick"
hollow-core door	hol' low core' door"
hollow knot	hol' low knot"
hollow masonry unit	hol' low mas' on ry u' nit
hollow metal door	hol' low me' tal door"
hollow-wall anchor	hol' low wall' an' chor
homeostasis	ho" me o sta' sis
homogeneity	ho" mo ge ne' i ty
homogeneous	ho" mo ge' ne ous
homopolymer	hom" o pol' y mer
Honduras mahogany	Hon du' ras ma hog' a ny
hone	hone
honed	honed
honeycomb	hon' ey comb
honeycombing	hon' ey comb" ing
honeysuckle ornament	hon' ey suck" le or' na ment
honing	hon' ing
hood	hood
hood mold	hood' mold"
hook	hook
hook bolt	hook' bolt"
hook strip	hook' strip"
hooked bar	hooked' bar"
hooked rug	hooked' rug"
Hooke's law	Hooke's' law
hoop reinforcement	hoop' re" in force' ment
hopper	hop' per

hopper window	hop' per win' dow
hopsacking	hop' sack" ing
horizon	ho ri' zon
horizontal	hor" i zon' tal
horizontal branch	hor" i zon' tal branch"
horizontal shear	hor" i zon' tal shear"
horizontally pivoted	hor" i zon' tal ly piv' ot ed
horn	horn
horologium	hor" o lo' gi um
horse	horse
horsepower	horse' pow" er
horseshoe arch	horse' shoe" arch"
horticultural building	hor" ti cul' tur al build' ing
hose bibb	hose' bibb"
hose cabinet	hose' cab' i net
hose cock	hose' cock"
hose-stream test	hose' stream" test
hospice	hos' pice
hospital	hos' pi tal
hospital arm pull	hos' pi tal arm" pull
hospital latch	hos' pi tal latch"
hostel	hos' tel
hot-air furnace	hot' air fur' nace
hot-applied sealant	hot' ap plied' seal' ant
hot-cathode tube	hot' cath' ode tube
hot-dip galvanizing	hot' dip' gal' va niz" ing
hot-dipped galvanized	hot' dipped' gal' va nized"
hot glue	hot' glue"
hot-laid	hot' laid"
hot-melt adhesive	hot' melt' ad he' sive
hot plate	hot' plate"
hot press	hot' press"
hot-pressing	hot' pres' sing
hot-rolled finish	hot' rolled" fin' ish
hot tub	hot' tub"
hot-water heating	hot' wa' ter heat' ing
hot-water supply	hot' wa' ter sup' ply
hot working	hot' work' ing
hotel	ho tel'
hothouse	hot' house"
house	house
house drain	house' drain"

house sewer	house' sew' er
housed	housed
housed stair	housed' stair"
housekeeping	house' keep" ing
houselights	house' lights"
housing	hous' ing
hoveling	hov' el ing
Howe truss	Howe' truss"
Howe, George	Howe', George'
howestring truss	howe' string" truss
Hoyer effect	Hoy' er ef fect'
hub	hub
huckaback	huck' a back"
hue	hue
Hughes, Richard	Huges', Ri' chard
humidifier	hu mid' i fi er
humidify	hu mid' i fy
humidistat	hu mid' i stat"
humidity	hu mid' i ty
humiture	hu' mi ture
humus	hu' mus
hurlinge	hur' linge
hurricane	hur' ri cane"
husk	husk
hutch	hutch
hyalography	hy" a log' ra phy
hydrant	hy' drant
hydrate	hy' drate
hydrated lime	hy' drat ed lime"
hydration	hy dra' tion
hydraulic cement	hy drau' lic ce ment'
hydraulic elevator	hy drau' lic el' e va" tor
hydraulic lime	hy drau' lic lime"
hydraulicity	hy" drau lic' i ty
hydraulicking	hy" drau lick' ing
hydraulics	hy drau' lics
hydrex compound	hy' drex com' pound
hydrocal	hy' dro cal
hydrocarbon	hy" dro car' bon
hydrochloric	hy" dro chlo' ric
hydrochlorinator	hy" dro chlo' rin a tor
hydrogen	hy' dro gen

hydrograph	hy' dro graph
hydrolysis	hy drol' y sis
hydronic	hy dron' ic
hydronic heating	hy dron' ic heat' ing
hydrophilic	hy" dro phil' ic
hydrophobic	hy" dro pho' bic
hydroplat	hy' dro plat"
hydropneumatic leveler	hy" dro pneu" ma' tic lev' e ler
hydrostatic head	hy" dro stat' ic head"
hydrostatic pressure	hy" dro stat' ic pres' sure
hydrostone	hy' dro stone"
hydrotherapy	hy" dro ther' a py
hydrous	hy' drous
hygiene	hy' giene
hygienic	hy" gi en' ic
hygrochromic	hy" gro chrom' ic
hygrograph	hy' gro graph"
hygrometer	hy grom' e ter
hygrometric	hy" gro met' ric
hygrometry	hy grom' e try
hygroscopic	hy" gro scop' ic
Hypalon™	Hyp' a lon
hyperbaric room	hy" per bar' ic room"
hyperbolic paraboloid	hy" per bol' ic pa rab' o loid"
hyperboloid	hy per' bo loid"
hypermedia	hy' per me' di a
hypethral	hy pe' thral
hyphen	hy' phen
hypocenter	hy' po cen" ter
hypophyge	hy poph' y ge
hypotenuse	hy pot' e nuse"
hysteresis	hys" ter e' sis

I

I-beam	I beam"
I joist	I' joist"
ibiraro	ib" i ra' ro
ice dam	ice' dam"
ice machine	ice' ma chine'
icehouse	ice' house"
ichnography	ich nog' raph y

icon	i' con
identification	i den" ti fi ca' tion
ideograph	id' e o graph"
igloo	ig' loo
igneous	ig' ne ous
igneous rock	ig' ne ous rock
ignitability	ig nit" a bil' i ty
ignite	ig nite'
ignition	ig ni' tion
ignition pilot	ig ni' tion pi' lot
ikat	i' kat
illuminance	il lu' mi nance
illuminant	il lu' mi nant
illuminate	il lu' mi nate"
illumination	il lu" mi na' tion
illuminator	il lu' mi na" tor
illustrate	il' lus trate"
illustration	il" lus tra' tion
image	im' age
imageability	im" age a bil' i ty
imbibed eraser	im bib' ed e ra' ser
imbow	im' bow
imbrex	im' brex
imbricated	im' bri cat" ed
imbrication	im" bri ca' tion
imbuya	im bu' ya
imitative	im' i ta" tive
immanent space	im' ma nent space"
immersion coating	im mer' sion coat' ing
immersion heater	im mer' sion heat' er
immunity	im mu' ni ty
impact insulation class	im' pact in" su la' tion class"
impact load	im' pact load"
impact noise	im' pact noise"
impact noise rating	im' pact noise" rat' ing
impact resistance	im' pact re sis' tance
impedance	im ped' ance
impeller	im pel' ler
imperfection	im" per fec' tion
Imperial Mahogany	Im pe' ri al Ma hog' a ny
impermeability	im per" me a bil' i ty
impervious	im per' vi ous

implanted core	im plant' ed core"
implied	im plied'
implied contract	im plied' con' tract
implied warranty	im plied' war' ran ty
importer	im port' er
imposed load	im posed' load
impossibility of performance	im pos" si bil' i ty of per for' mance
impossible specification	im pos' si ble spec" i fi ca' tion
impost	im' post
impracticability	im prac" ti ca bil' i ty
impregnated	im preg' nat ed
impregnation	im" preg na' tion
improve	im prove'
improvement	im prove' ment
in-line centrifugal fan	in" line' cen trif' u gal fan
in-line circulator	in" line' cir' cu la" tor
in situ	in si' tu
in-situ concrete	in si' tu con' crete
inaccessible	in" ac ces' si ble
inactive leaf	in ac' tive leaf"
incandesce	in" can desce'
incandescence	in" can des' cence
incandescent	in" can des' cent
incense cedar	in' cense ce' dar
incentive	in cen' tive
incentive clause	in cen' tive clause"
inch	inch
incidental	in" ci den' tal
incinerator	in cin' er a" tor
incipient	in cip' i ent
incipient decay	in cip' i ent de cay'
incipient fusion	in cip' i ent fu' sion
incise	in cise'
incised	in cised'
incising	in cis' ing
inclination	in" cli na' tion
incline	in' cline
inclined conveyor	in' clined con vey' or
income property	in' come prop' er ty
Inconel™	In' co nel"
incorporation	in cor" po ra' tion
increaser	in creas' er

incrustation	in" crus ta' tion
incubator	in' cu ba" tor
indemnification	in dem" ni fi ca' tion
indemnify	in dem' ni fy"
indemnity	in dem' ni ty
indent	in dent'
indented joint	in dent' ed joint"
indeterminate	in" de ter' mi nate
index of refraction	in' dex of re frac' tion
Indian	In' di an
Indiana limestone	In" di an' a lime' stone"
indicator	in' di ca" tor
indicator bolt	in' di ca" tor bolt"
indicator button	in' di ca" tor but' ton
indirect	in" di rect'
indirect expense	in" di rect' ex pense'
indirect gain	in" di rect' gain"
indirect lighting	in" di rect' light' ing
indirect solar radiation	in" di rect' so' lar ra" di a' tion
indoor-outdoor carpeting	in' door" out' door" car' pet ing
induced draft	in duced' draft"
inductance	in duct' ance
induction	in duc' tion
induction brazing	in duc' tion braz' ing
induction system	in duc' tion sys' tem
induction unit	in duc' tion u' nit
inductive reactance	in duc' tive re ac' tance
industrial	in dus' tri al
industrial occupancy	in dus' tri al oc' cu pan cy
industrialized building	in dus' tri al ized" build' ing
inelastic behavior	in" e las' tic be hav' ior
inert	in ert'
inert filler	in ert' fil' ler
inert-gas metal-arc welding	in ert' gas met' al arc weld' ing
inertia	in er' tia
inertia block	in er' tia block"
inertia pad	in er' tia pad"
inerting	in ert' ing
infill	in' fill"
infilling	in' fill" ing
infiltration	in" fil tra' tion
infinite	in' fi nite

infirmary	in fir' ma ry
inflatable	in flat' a ble
inflected arch	in flect' ed arch"
inflection point	in flec' tion point"
influent	in' flu ent
information	in" for ma' tion
infraculture	in" fra cul' ture
infrared	in" fra red'
infrared radiation	in" fra red' ra" di a' tion
infrared spectroscopy	in" fra red' spec tros' co py
infrasonic frequency	in" fra son' ic fre' quen cy
infringement	in fringe' ment
inglenook	in' gle nook"
ingot	in' got
ingress	in' gress
inherent flame-resistance	in her' ent flame' re sist' ance
inhibiting	in hib' it ing
inhibitor	in hib' i tor
initial prestress	in i' tial pre' stress
initial set	in i' tial set"
initiation	in i" ti a' tion
injection	in jec' tion
injection burner	in jec' tion bur' ner
injection molding	in jec' tion mold' ing
ink jet	ink' jet
ink-jet printer	ink' jet print' er
inlaid	in' laid"
inlaid tile	in' laid" tile"
inlay	in' lay"
inlet	in' let
inline fan	in' line" fan"
inn	inn
inner plies	in' ner plies"
inorganic	in" or gan' ic
inorganic silt	in" or gan' ic silt"
input impedance	in' put" im ped' ance
inscription	in scrip' tion
insect screen	in' sect screen"
insecticide	in" sec' ti cide
insert	in' sert
inserted louver	in sert' ed lou' ver
inset sink	in' set" sink"

inside	in" side'
insolation	in" so la' tion
inspection	in spec' tion
inspector	in spec' tor
install	in stall'
installation	in" stal la' tion
instant-start	in' stant start"
instantaneous	in" stan ta' ne ous
institutional occupancy	in" sti tu' tion al oc' cu pan cy
instron	in' stron
instructions to bidders	in struc' tions to bid' ders
instrument	in' stru ment
instrumentation	in" stru men ta' tion
insulate	in' su late"
insulating	in' su lat" ing
insulation	in" su la' tion
insulator	in' su la" tor
insurance	in sur' ance
intaglio	in tagl' io
intake	in' take
intarsia	in tar' si a
intarsist	in tar' sist
integral	in' te gral
integral lock	in' te gral lock"
integral-type lock	in' te gral type" lock
integrant	in' te grant
integrated ceiling	in' te grat" ed ceil' ing
integrating sphere	in' te grat" ing sphere"
integrity	in teg' ri ty
intellectual property	in" tel lec' tu al prop' er ty
intensity	in ten' si ty
intensity-loudness	in ten' si ty loud' ness
intercepting sewer	in" ter cept' ing sew' er
interceptor	in" ter cep' tor
intercolumniation	in" ter co lum" ni a' tion
intercom	in' ter com
intercommunication	in" ter com mu" ni ca' tion
interconnection	in" ter con nec' tion
intercooling	in' ter cool" ing
interdome	in' ter dome"
interest	in' ter est
interface	in' ter face"

interfacing	in' ter fac" ing
interfenestration	in" ter fen" es tra' tion
interference	in" ter fer' ence
interfile	in" ter file'
interflectance	in" ter flec' tance
interior	in te' ri or
interior designer	in te' ri or de sign' er
interior-exterior plywood	in te' ri or ex te' ri or ply' wood
interior glazed	in te' ri or glazed"
interior-type plywood	in te' ri or type" ply' wood
interlace	in" ter lace'
interlaced arch	in" ter laced' arch"
interlacing arcade	in" ter lac' ing ar cade'
interlayer	in' ter lay" er
interlining	in" ter lin' ing
interlock	in" ter lock'
interlocked	in" ter locked'
interlocking	in" ter lock' ing
intermediate	in" ter me' di ate
intermediate density	in" ter me' di ate den' si ty
intermediate metal conduit	in" ter me' di ate me' tal con' duit
intermediate pivot	in" ter me' di ate piv' ot
intermittent pilot	in" ter mit' tent pi' lot
intermittent weld	in" ter mit' tent weld
intermodulation	in" ter mod" u la' tion
intermural	in" ter mu' ral
intern architect	in' tern ar' chi tect"
internal	in ter' nal
internal glazing	in ter' nal glaz' ing
internal-quality brick	in ter' nal qual' i ty brick
international	in" ter na' tion al
International style	In" ter na' tion al style
internship	in' tern ship"
interpenetration	in" ter pen" e tra' tion
interpolate	in ter' po late"
interpretation	in ter" pre ta' tion
interrupted	in" ter rupt' ed
interrupted pilot	in" ter rupt' ed pi' lot
interrupter	in" ter rup' ter
intersect	in" ter sect'
intersecting	in" ter sect' ing
intersection	in" ter sec' tion

interstitial	in" ter sti' tial
intrados	in' tra dos"
intrinsic	in trin' sic
intrusion	in tru' sion
intuitive	in tu' i tive
intumescence	in" tu mes' cence
intumescent	in" tu mes' cent
intumescent paint	in" tu mes' cent paint
inundation batching	in" un da' tion batch' ing
inventory	in' ven to" ry
inverse	in verse'
inverse-square law	in verse' square" law
inversion	in ver' sion
invert	in' vert
invert elevation	in' vert el" e va' tion
inverted	in vert' ed
investment	in vest' ment
invisible	in vis' i ble
invisible hinge	in vis' i ble hinge"
invitation to bid	in" vi ta' tion to bid"
invoice	in' voice
involute	in' vo lute
ion	i' on
ionic	i on' ic
Ionic order	I on' ic or' der
ionization	i" on i za' tion
ionomer	i on' o mer
Iridian	I rid' i an
iridium	i rid' i um
iroko	i ro' ko
iron	i' ron
iron pipe size	i' ron pipe' size"
ironwood	i' ron wood"
ironwork	i' ron work"
ironworker	i' ron work" er
irradiance	ir ra' di ance
irradiation	ir ra" di a' tion
irregular curve	ir reg' u lar curve"
irregularity	ir reg" u lar' i ty
irrigation	ir" ri ga' tion
irritant	ir' ri tant
isacoustic	is" a cous' tic

island-base cabinet	is' land base" cab' i net
isobar	i' so bar
isochrone	i' so chrone"
isocyanate	i" so cy' a nate
isohel	i' so hel
isolated gain	i' so lat" ed gain"
isolation	i" so la' tion
isolation joint	i" so la' tion joint"
isolator	i' so la" tor
isolux diagram	i' so lux di' a gram"
isolux line	i' so lux line"
isometric	i" so met' ric
isophenolic	i" so phe nol' ic
isopleth	i' so pleth"
isoprene	i' so prene"
isosceles triangle	i sos' ce les" tri' an" gle
isotactic	i" so tac' tic
isotherm	i' so therm"
isothermal	i" so ther' mal
isothermal compression	i" so ther' mal com pres' sion
isotron	i' so tron"
isotropic	i" so trop' ic
isotropy	i sot' ro py
issue method	is' sue meth' od
itactic polypropylene	i tac' tic pol" y pro' pyl ene
Italian	I tal' ian
item	i' tem
iterative impedance	i' ter a" tive im ped' ance
izod impact test	i' zod im' pact test

J

jab saw	jab' saw"
jabot	ja bot'
jack	jack
jack arch	jack' arch"
jack plane	jack' plane"
jack post	jack' post"
jack rafter	jack' raf' ter
jack truss	jack' truss"
jacket	jack' et
jacketed	jack' et ed

jackhammer	jack' ham" mer
jacking	jack' ing
jackknife	jack' knife
Jacobean	Ja" co be' an
Jacobsen, Arne	Ja' cob sen, Arne
Jacobsen, Hugh Newell	Ja' cob sen, Hugh' Newell"
jacquard	jac' quard
Jacquard loom	Jac' quard loom"
Jacuzzi™	Ja cuz' zi
Jahn, Helmut	Jahn', Hel' mut
jail	jail
jaket	ja ket'
jal-awning window	jal' awn' ing win' dow
jalousie	ja' lou sie"
jamb	jamb
jamb anchor	jamb' an' chor
jamb extension	jamb' ex ten' sion
jambstone	jamb' stone"
Japan	Ja pan'
japan	ja pan'
Japanese	Jap" a nese'
Japanese lacquer	Jap' a nese" lac' quer
japanning	ja pan' ning
jardiniere	jar" di nere'
jaspé	jas pe'
jaspé carpet	ja spe' car' pet
jawab	ja wab'
Jeanneret, Charles-Edouard	Jean" ner et', Charles' Ed ouard'
jedding ax	jed' ding ax'
jelled	jelled
jerkinhead	jer' kin head"
jesting beam	jest' ing beam"
jet grouting	jet' grout' ing
Jet Mist	Jet' Mist"
jetting	jet' ting
jetty	jet' ty
jewel	jew' el
jeweling	jew' el ing
jib	jib
jiffler mixer	jif' fler mix' er
jiffy mixer	jif' fy mix' er
jig	jig

jig saw	jig' saw"
jimmer	jim' mer
jitterbug	jit' ter bug"
job	job
job captain	job' cap' tain
jobber	job' ber
jobsite	job' site"
jog	jog
jogged	jog' ged
joggle	jog' gle
joggling	jog' gling
Johansen, John M.	Jo han' sen, John' M.
Johnson, Philip	John' son, Phil' ip
joiner	join' er
joinery	join' er y
joining	join' ing
joint	joint
joint compound	joint' com' pound
joint filler	joint' fil' ler
joint movement	joint' move' ment
joint reinforcement	joint' re" in force' ment
joint treatment	joint' treat' ment
joint venture	joint' ven' ture
jointed	joint' ed
jointer	joint' er
jointing	joint' ing
joist	joist
joist hanger	joist' hang' er
joist-purlin hanger	joist' pur' lin han' ger
Jonesboro Red	Jones' bor o Red"
joule	joule
journal	jour' nal
journeyman	jour' ney man
journeywoman	jour' ney wo" man
Juane Rose	Juane' Rose"
jube	ju' be
judas	ju' das
judgment	judg' ment
judicial	ju di' cial
jumbo	jum' bo
jumbo brick	jum' bo brick"
jumper	jump' er

junction	junc' tion
junction box	junc' tion box"
junior beam	jun' ior beam"
junior college	jun' ior col' lege
juniper	ju' ni per
Jura	Ju' ra
jurisdiction	ju" ris dic' tion
jurisdictional dispute	ju" ris dic' tion al dis pute'
jut window	jut' win' dow
jute	jute
jutty	jut' ty
juvenile wood	ju' ve nile" wood"

K

K-slump test	K' slump' test"
k-value	k' val' ue
kabiki	ka bi' ki
Kahn, Louis I.	Kahn', Lou' is I
kalamein door	kal' a mein door"
kaolin	ka' o lin
kapok	ka' pok
Kasota Antique Rose	Ka so' ta An tique' Rose
Kasota Buff	Ka so' ta Buff"
Kassabaum, George	Kass' a baum, George"
katmon	kat' mon
katsura	kat' su ra
keel molding	keel' mold' ing
Keene's cement™	Keen's' ce ment'
keeper	keep' er
kellastone	kel' la stone"
Kelly ball test	Kel' ly ball' test
kelobra	kel ob' ra
kelvin	kel' vin
kennel	ken' nel
Kentish tracery	Kent' ish trac' ery
Kentucky bluestone	Ken tuck' y blue' stone"
keratin	ker' a tin
kerf	kerf
kerfed	kerfed
kerfing	kerf' ing
kern area	kern' ar' e a

kern zone	kern' zone"
kersey	ker' sey
Kershaw	Ker' shaw
ketone	ke' tone
ketonic	ke ton' ic
kevel	kev' el
key	key
key brick	key' brick"
key card	key' card"
key cornered	key' cor' nered
key plan	key' plan
key plate	key' plate"
key switch	key' switch"
keyboard	key' board"
keydrop	key' drop"
keyed	keyed
keyed-alike cylinders	keyed' a like" cyl' in ders
keyed-in-frame	keyed' in frame"
keyed joint	keyed' joint"
keyhole	key' hole"
keyhole saw	key' hole" saw"
keying-in	key' ing in
keylock hardware	key' lock" hard' ware
keynoting	key' not" ing
keypad	key' pad"
keystone	key' stone"
keyway	key' way"
keyword	key' word"
khaya	kha' ya
kick plate	kick' plate"
kick rail	kick' rail"
kicker	kick' er
kicker plate	kick' er plate"
kickout	kick' out"
kickout latch	kick' out" latch
kilim	ki lim'
Killingsworth, Edward A.	Kil' lings worth", Ed' ward A.
kiln	kiln
kiln-dried	kiln' dried"
kiln-dry	kiln' dry"
kiln-run	kiln' run"
kilo	ki' lo

kiloampere	kil' o am' pere
kilobyte	kil' o byte"
kilogram	kil' o gram"
kilojoule	kil' o joule"
kilometer	kil o' meter
kilovolt	kil' o volt"
kilovolt-ampere	kil' o volt" am' pere
kilowatt	kil' o watt"
kilowatt-hour	kil' o watt" hour"
kinetic energy	ki net' ic en' er gy
king closer	king' clos' er
king post	king' post"
king-post truss	king' post" truss
king stud	king' stud"
Kingstone Cherry Pink	King' stone" Cher' ry Pink
kink	kink
kiosk	ki' osk
kip	kip
kit	kit
kitchen	kitch' en
kitchen equipment	kitch' en e quip' ment
kitchenette	kitch" en ette'
kitchenware	kitch' en ware"
kite winder	kite' wind" er
kited	kit' ed
kiva	ki' va
knapped flint	knapped' flint"
knee	knee
knee brace	knee' brace"
knee wall	knee' wall"
kneehole desk	knee' hole" desk
kneeler	kneel' er
knife-blade fuse	knife' blade' fuse"
knife mark	knife' mark"
knife pleats	knife' pleats"
knob	knob
knob rose	knob' rose"
knobbing	knob' bing
knocked down	knocked' down"
knocked-down frame	knocked' down" frame"
knocker	knock' er
knockout	knock' out"

knot	knot
knot cluster	knot' clus' ter
knothole	knot' hole"
knotting	knot' ting
knotty pine	knot' ty pine"
knowledge management	knowl' edge man' age ment
knuckle	knuck' le
knuckling	knuck' ling
knurl	knurl
knurled	knurled
knurling	knurl' ing
koa	ko' a
Koenig, Pierre	Koe' nig, Pierre'
korina	ko rin' a
kraft-faced insulation	kraft' faced' in" su la' tion
kraft paper	kraft' pa' per
kraft-type vapor barrier	kraft' type" va' por bar' ri er
kraftcord	kraft' cord"
Kurokawa, Kisho	Kur" o kaw' a, Kis' ho
kyanise	ky' an ise

L

L brace	L' brace"
label	la' bel
label stop	la' bel stop"
labeled	la' beled
labeled door	la' beled door"
labeled frame	la' beled frame"
labeled opening	la' beled o' pen ing
labor	la' bor
labor and material payment bond	la' bor and ma te' ri al pay' ment bond"
labor rate	la' bor rate"
laboratory	lab' o ra to" ry
laborer	la' bor er
labyrinth	lab' y rinth
lac	lac
lac burgauté	lac' bur gaute'
Lac Du Bonnet	Lac' du Bon net'
lace	lace
laced valley	laced' val' ley

lacewood	lace' wood"
lacework	lace' work"
lacing	lac' ing
lacing course	lac' ing course"
lacquer	lac' quer
lacquerwork	lac' quer work"
lacuna	la cu' na
lacunar	la cu' nar
lacunaria	lac u nar' i a
ladder	lad' der
ladder-back chair	lad' der back" chair
ladder core	lad' der core"
Lady chapel	La' dy chap' el
lag bolt	lag' bolt"
lag screw	lag' screw"
lag shield	lag' shield"
lagging	lag' ging
laid-on molding	laid' on mold' ing
laid to weather	laid' to weath' er
laitance	lai' tance
lake pitch	lake' pitch'
Lake Placid Blue	Lake' Plac' id Blue
lake sand	lake' sand
Lally column™	Lal' ly col' umn
lambert	lam' bert
Lambert's cosine law	Lam' bert's co' sine law
lambrequin	lam' bre quin
lamb's tongue	lamb's' tongue"
lamella	la mel' la
lamina	lam' i na
laminar flow	lam' i nar flow"
laminate	lam' i nate"
laminate-faced door	lam' i nate" faced door
laminated	lam' i nat" ed
laminated glass	lam' i nat" ed glass"
laminated veneer	lam' i nat" ed ve neer'
laminated wood	lam' i nat" ed wood"
laminating	lam' i nat" ing
lamination	lam" i na' tion
laminator	lam' i na" tor
lamp	lamp
lamp bulb	lamp' bulb"

157

lamp lumen depreciation factor	lamp' lu' men de pre" ci a' tion fac' tor
lamp post	lamp' post"
lampblack	lamp' black"
lampshade	lamp' shade"
lamson tube	lam' son tube"
lanai	la na' i
lancet	lan' cet
lancet arch	lan' cet arch"
lanciform	lan' ci form
land	land
land survey	land' sur' vey
land use	land' use"
land-use analysis	land' use" a nal' y sis
land-use planning	land' use" plan' ning
landform	land' form"
landing	land' ing
landing newel	land' ing new' el
landing tread	land' ing tread"
landlord	land' lord"
landmark	land' mark"
landscape	land' scape"
landscaping	land' scap ing
landslide	land' slide"
lane	lane
langley	lang' ley
lantern	lan' tern
lap	lap
lap joint	lap' joint"
lap-joint weld	lap' joint" weld
lap-riveted	lap' riv' et ed
lap siding	lap' sid' ing
lap splice	lap' splice"
lap weld	lap' weld"
Lapidus, Morris	Lap' i dus, Mor' ris
lapis lazuli	lap' is la zu' li
lappet	lap' pet
lapping	lap' ping
larch	larch
larder	lar' der
laser	la' ser
laser plotter	la' ser plot' ter

latch	latch
latch bolt	latch' bolt"
latching	latch' ing
latchkey	latch' key"
latchset	latch' set"
late wood	late' wood"
latent defect	la' tent de fect'
latent heat	la' tent heat"
lateral	lat' er al
lateral brace	lat' er al brace"
lateral file	lat' er al file"
lateral load	lat' er al load"
lateral support	lat' er al sup port'
laterally	lat' er al ly
latex	la' tex
latex paint	la' tex paint"
latex portland cement	la' tex port' land ce ment'
lath	lath
lathe	lathe
lathhouse	lath' house"
lathing	lath' ing
latitude	lat' i tude"
latrine	la trine"
latrobe	la trobe"
lattice	lat' tice
lattice molding	lat' tice mold' ing
latticework	lat' tice work"
lauan	lau' an
laundry chute	laun' dry chute"
laundry room	laun' dry room"
laurel wood	lau' rel wood"
lavabo	la va' bo
lavalier microphone	lav" a lier' mi' cro phone"
lavatory	lav' a to" ry
lawn	lawn
lawyer	law' yer
lay-up	lay' up"
layer	lay' er
laying out	lay' ing out"
laylight	lay' light"
layout	lay' out"
lazaretto	laz" a ret' to

lazy susan	laz' y su' san
Le Corbusier	Le" Cor bu sier'
leach	leach
leachates	leach' ates
leaching	leach' ing
leaching field	leach' ing field"
lead	lead
lead-bearing glass	lead' bear' ing glass
lead glass	lead' glass"
lead-head nail	lead' head" nail
lead-lined door	lead' lined' door"
lead shield	lead' shield"
leaded brass	lead' ed brass"
leaded light	lead' ed light"
leader	lead' er
leading edge	lead' ing edge
leads	leads
leaf	leaf
leaf-and-dart	leaf' and dart'
leafing	leaf' ing
leak test	leak' test"
lean clays	lean' clays"
lean concrete	lean' con' crete
lean-to	lean' to"
lease	lease
leaseback	lease' back"
leasehold	lease' hold"
least squares	least' squares"
leather	leath' er
leaves	leaves
Lebanon cedar	Leb' a non ce' dar
lectern	lec' tern
ledge	ledge
ledgement	ledge' ment"
ledger	ledg' er
ledger board	ledg' er board"
ledger strip	ledg' er strip"
Lee White	Lee' White"
leeward	lee' ward
left-hand door	left' hand" door"
leg	leg
legging	leg' ging

Legorreta, Ricardo	Leg" or ret' a, Ri card' o
lehr	lehr'
lemon spline	lem' on spline"
length	length
leno weave	le' no weave"
lens	lens
Lesbian cyma	Les' bi an cy' ma
Lesbian rule	Les' bi an rule"
lessee	les see'
lessor	les sor'
let in	let' in"
let-in brace	let' in" brace"
letter accessories	let' ter ac ces' sor ies
letter chute	let' ter chute"
letter of agreement	let' ter of a gree' ment
letterbox	let' ter box"
lettering	let' ter ing
level	lev' el
level return	lev' el re turn'
leveling	lev' el ing
leveling compound	lev' el ing com' pound
leveling course	lev' el ing course"
lever	lev' er
lever arm	lev' er arm"
lever handle	lev' er han' dle
leverage	lev' er age
Levittown	Lev' it town"
lewis	lew' is
lewis bolt	lew' is bolt"
liabilities	li" a bil' i ties
liability	li" a bil' i ty
librarianship	li brar' i an ship"
library	li' brar" y
license	li' cense
lich gate	lich' gate"
lichen	li' chen
lien	lien
lien waiver	lien' waiv' er
lierne	li erne'
life-cycle cost	life' cy' cle cost"
lifeline	life' line"
lift	lift

lift latch	lift' latch"
lift slab	lift' slab"
lift-slab construction	lift' slab' con struc' tion
light	light
light court	light' court"
light loss factor	light' loss fac' tor
light resistance	light' re sist' ance
Light Rosso Marblehaus	Light' Ros' so Mar' ble haus
light well	light' well"
lightfastness	light' fast" ness
lightgage	light' gage
lighthouse	light' house"
lighting	light' ing
lightness	light' ness
lightning arrester	light' ning ar rest' er
lightproof	light' proof
lightstripping	light' strip" ping
lightweight	light' weight"
lightweight aggregate	light' weight" ag' gre gate
lignasan	lig' na san
ligneous	lig' ne ous
lignin	lig' nin
lignin resin	lig' nin res' in
lignocellulosic	lig" no cel" lu los' ic
limba	lim' ba
lime	lime
lime-and-cement mortar	lime' and ce ment' mor' tar
limerock	lime' rock"
limestone	lime' stone"
limewash	lime' wash"
liming	lim' ing
limit control	lim' it con trol'
limit switch	lim' it switch"
limitation	lim" i ta' tion
limonite	li' mo nite"
limpness	limp' ness
lincrusta	lin crus' ta
lindane	lin' dane
linden	lin' den
line	line
line drop	line drop"
line-focus collector	line' fo' cus col lec' tor

line of sight	line' of sight
lineal	lin' e al
linear diffuser	lin' e ar dif fus' er
linear induction motor	lin' e ar in duc' tion mo' tor
linen	lin' en
linen chute	lin' en chute"
liner	lin' er
lining	lin' ing
link	link
Linnebach projector	Lin' ne bach pro jec' tor
linoleum	li no' le um
linseed oil	lin' seed oil"
lintel	lin' tel
linters	lint' ers
lip	lip
lip molding	lip' mold' ing
lip strike	lip' strike"
lip union	lip' un' ion
lipping	lip' ping
liquefaction	liq" ue fac' tion
liquefied	liq' ue fied"
liquid	liq' uid
liquid-crystal coating	liq' uid crys' tal coat' ing
liquid-immersed transformer	liq' uid im mersed' trans for' mer
liquid limit	liq' uid lim' it
liquid-membrane curing compound	liq' uid mem' brane cur' ing com' pound
liquid polymer	liq' uid pol' y mer
liquid state	liq' uid state"
liquid-type dispenser	liq' uid type" dis pens' er
liquid-volume measurement	liq' uid vol' ume meas' ure ment
liquidated damages	liq' ui dat" ed dam' ages
liquidation	liq' ui da' tion
liquidity	li quid' i ty
liquidtight	liq' uid tight"
liquidus	liq' ui dus
list	list
listed	list' ed
listel	lis' tel
listing	list' ing
listing agency	list' ing a' gen cy
lite	lite

liter	li' ter
lithocarbon	lith' o car" bon
lithographic	lith" o graph' ic
lithography	li thog' ra phy
Lithonia granite	Lith on' i a gran' ite
litigation	lit" i ga' tion
litmus	lit' mus
live	live
live acoustic	live' a cous' tic
live load	live' load"
live room	live' room"
liveness	live' ness"
livering	liv' er ing
living room	liv' ing room"
living unit	liv' ing u' nit
Llewelyn-Davies, Richard	Llew el' yn Dav' ies, Rich' ard
load	load
load-bearing wall	load' bear' ing wall
load-carrying	load' car' ry ing
load duration factor	load' dur a' tion fac' tor
load factor	load' fac' tor
load-indicating bolt	load' in' di cat" ing bolt
load-resisting	load' re sist' ing
loader	load' er
loading cycles	load' ing cy' cles
loading dock	load' ing dock"
loading door	load' ing door"
loam	loam
loamy	loam' y
lobby	lob' by
lobe	lobe
local area network	lo' cal ar' e a net' work
local buckling	lo' cal buck' ling
local vent	lo' cal vent"
locale	lo cale'
locate	lo' cate
location	lo ca' tion
lock	lock
lock block	lock' block"
lock nut	lock' nut"
lock rail	lock' rail"
lock stile	lock' stile"

lock-strip gasket	lock' strip gas' ket
locker	lock' er
locking stile	lock' ing stile"
lockout	lock' out"
lockset	lock' set"
lockstrip	lock' strip"
lodge	lodge
lodging house	lodg' ing house"
loess	lo' ess
loft	loft
log	log
logarithm	log' a rithm
logarithmic	log" a rith' mic
loge	loge
loggia	log' gia
long-lead item	long' lead' i' tem
long-life lamp	long' life' lamp"
long lip strike	long' lip' strike"
long-nose pliers	long' nose" pli' ers
long oil	long' oil
longitude	lon' gi tude"
longitudinal	lon" gi tu' di nal
longspan	long' span"
lookout	look' out"
loom	loom
loop	loop
loop back	loop' back"
loop pile	loop' pile"
loop vent	loop' vent"
loophole	loop' hole"
Loos, Adolf	Loos', A' dolf
loose-fill insulation	loose' fill in" su la' tion
loose-joint hinge	loose' joint" hinge
loose-laid membrane	loose' laid" mem' brane
loose lintel	loose' lin' tel
loose-pin hinge	loose' pin" hinge
loper	lop' er
Lorant isolator	Lor ant' i' so la" tor
Loredo Rosato	Lo re' do Ro sat' o
loss	loss
loss of prestress	loss' of pre' stress
lost-wax process	lost' wax' pro" cess

lot	lot
lot line	lot' line"
lot-line wall	lot' line" wall
lotus	lo' tus
loudness	loud' ness"
loudspeaker	loud' speak" er
lounge	lounge
louver	lou' ver
louver door	lou' ver door"
louvered ceiling	lou' vered ceil' ing
louvered door	lou' vered door
love seat	love' seat"
low-alkali cement	low' al' ka li ce ment'
low-back chair	low' back chair"
low-emissivity	low' em" is siv' i ty
low-hazard contents	low' haz' ard con' tents
low-modulus sealant	low' mod' u lus seal' ant
low-noise lamp	low' noise" lamp
low-pressure boiler	low' pres' sure boil' er
low-pressure laminate	low' pres' sure lam' i nate
low-temperature	low' tem' per a ture
low-voltage lighting	low' volt' age light' ing
low-voltage protection	low' volt' age pro tec' tion
lowboy	low' boy"
lowest	low' est
lozenge	loz' enge
lubricant	lu' bri cant
lubricate	lu' bri cate"
lucarne	lu carne'
lug	lug
lug end-grain block	lug' end' grain" block
lug sill	lug' sill
lugging	lug' ging
lumber	lum' ber
lumber core	lum' ber core"
lumen	lu' men
lumen method	lu' men meth' od
luminaire	lu" mi naire'
luminaire dirt-depreciation	lu" mi naire' dirt' de pre" ci a' tion
luminaire efficiency	lu" mi naire' ef fi' cien cy
luminance	lu' mi nance
luminescence	lu" mi nes' cence

luminescent	lu" mi nes' cent
luminosity	lu" mi nos' i ty
luminous	lu' mi nous
luminous ceiling	lu' mi nous ceil' ing
luminous efficacy	lu' mi nous ef' fi ca cy
luminous flux	lu' mi nous flux"
luminous intensity	lu' mi nous in ten' si ty
luminous-intensity distribution	lu' mi nous in ten' si ty dis" tri- bu' tion
lump lime	lump' lime"
lump sum	lump' sum'
lump-sum contract	lump' sum' con' tract
lunette	lu nette'
luster	lus' ter
luthern	lu' thern
lux	lux
Lyndon, Donlyn	Lyn' don, Don' lyn

M

macadam	mac ad' am
macaya	ma cay' a
Macciavecchia	Mac" ci a vec' chi a
machinability	ma chin" a bil' i ty
machine bolt	ma chine' bolt"
machine direction	ma chine' di rec' tion
machine-screw anchor	ma chine' screw' an' chor
machine stress rated	ma chine' stress' rat' ed
machined	ma chined'
machinery	ma chin' er y
macro	mac' ro
macro-fractures	mac' ro frac' tures
macrolite	mac' ro lite
macromolecule	mac" ro mol' e cule
macroscopic	mac" ro scop' ic
macroseismic	mac" ro seis' mic
Madison Pink	Mad' i son Pink"
magazine	mag" a zine'
magenta	ma gen' ta
magnesia	mag ne' sia
magnesian	mag ne' sian
magnesian marble	mag ne' sian mar' ble

magnesite	mag' ne site"
magnesite flooring	mag' ne site" floor' ing
magnesium	mag ne' si um
magnesium-oxychloride	mag ne' si um ox" y chlo' ride
magnetic catch	mag net' ic catch"
magnetic switch	mag net' ic switch"
magnitude	mag' ni tude"
magnolia	mag no' lia
mahogany	ma hog' a ny
mail chute	mail' chute"
mailbox	mail' box"
mailroom	mail' room"
main	main
main disconnect	main' dis" con nect'
main runner	main' run' ner
main vent	main' vent"
mainframe	main' frame"
maintainability	main tain" a bil' i ty
maintenance	main' te nance
maintenance factor	main' te nance fac' tor
makeup air	make' up" air"
makeup water	make up" wa' ter
makoré	ma kore'
male plug	male' plug"
male thread	male' thread"
maleic resin	ma le' ic res' in
mall	mall
malleability	ma" le a bil' i ty
malleable	mal' le a ble
mallet	mal' let
malm	malm
malpais	mal" pa is'
malpractice	mal prac' tice
manage	man' age
management	man' age ment
manager	man' ag er
mandatory	man' da to" ry
mandrel	man' drel
manège	ma nege'
manganese	man' ga nese"
manhole	man' hole"
manifold	man' i fold"

manipulation	ma nip" u la' tion
Mankato Golden Buff	Man ka' to Gold' en Buff"
manlift	man' lift"
manometer	ma nom' e ter
mansard roof	man' sard roof"
mansion	man' sion
mansonia	man son' i a
mantel	man' tel
mantelpiece	man' tel piece"
manteltree	man' tel tree"
manual	man' u al
manual fire station	man' u al fire' sta' tion
manufactured	man" u fac' tured
manufacturer's bond	man" u fac' tur er's bond"
maple	ma' ple
mapping	map' ping
maprail	map' rail"
maquette	ma quette'
marble	mar' ble
marble chips	mar' ble chips"
Marblehaus Beige	Mar' ble haus" Beige"
marbleized	mar' ble ized"
marbleizing	mar' ble iz" ing
marblewood	mar' ble wood"
marbling	mar' bling
marbly	mar' bly
marezzo	ma rez' zo
margin	mar' gin
marginal bar	mar' gin al bar
marguerite	mar" gue rite'
marine	ma rine"
marine-grade panel	ma rine" grade" pan' el
Mariposa Danby	Mar' i po' sa Dan' by
mark number	mark' num' ber
marked face	marked' face"
market price	mar' ket price"
marketing	mar' ket ing
marketplace	mar' ket place"
marking	mark' ing
marking guage	mark' ing guage"
marl	marl
Marmor	Mar' mor

marmoraceous	mar" mo rac' e ous
marquee	mar quee'
marquetry	mar' que try
marquise	mar quise'
marquisette	mar" qui sette'
marsh	marsh
martensite	mar' tens ite"
Martindale test	Mar' tin dale test"
mascaron	mas' ca ron"
mash hammer	mash' ham' mer
mask	mask
masking	mask' ing
mason	ma' son
Masonite™	Ma' so nite
masonry	ma' son ry
masonry anchor	ma' son ry an' chor
masonry cement	ma' son ry ce ment'
masonry tie	ma' son ry tie"
mason's putty	ma' son's put' ty
mass concrete	mass' con' crete
mass foundation	mass' foun da' tion
masstone	mas' stone"
mast	mast
mastaba	mas' ta ba
master key	mas' ter key"
master-keyed lock	mas' ter keyed" lock
Masterformat	Mas' ter for" mat
mastic	mas' tic
mastic-set	mas' tic set"
mastication	mas" ti ca' tion
mat	mat
mat-formed	mat' formed'
mat foundation	mat' foun da' tion
mat well	mat' well
match line	match' line"
matchboards	match' boards"
matched lumber	matched' lum' ber
matching	match' ing
matelassé	mat' e las se"
material	ma te' ri al
material hoist	ma te' ri al hoist"
material lift	ma te' ri al lift"

mathematical	math" e mat' i cal
mathematics	math" e mat' ics
matrices	ma' tri ces
matrix	ma' trix
matte	matte
matte-surfaced glass	matte' sur' faced glass"
matted	mat' ted
matting	mat' ting
mattress	mat' tress
maturing	ma tur' ing
maul	maul
mausoleum	mau" so le' um
maximum	max' i mum
Mayan	Mayan
Maybeck, Bernard	May' beck, Ber nard'
maze	maze
McGrath, Raymond	Mc Grath', Ray' mond
McHarg, Ian	Mc Harg', I' an
McKinnell, Noel Michael	Mc Kin' nell, No' el Mi' chael
mean	mean
mean radiant temperature	mean ' ra' di ant tem' per a ture
meander	me an' der
measure	meas' ure
measured drawing	meas' ured draw' ing
measurement	meas' ure ment
mechanic	me chan' ic
mechanical	me chan' i cal
mechanical connection	me chan' i cal con nec' tion
mechanical-draft chimney	me chan' i cal draft" chim' ney
mechanical engineer	me chan' i cal en" gi neer'
mechanical finish	me chan' i cal fin' ish
mechanic's lien	me chan' ic's lien"
medallion	me dal' lion
median	me' di an
mediation	me" di a' tion
medicine cabinet	med' i cine cab' i net
medieval	me" di e' val
medium	me' di um
medium-carbon steel	me' di um car' bon steel"
medium checks	me' di um checks"
medium density fiberboard	me' di um den' si ty fi' ber board"
medium density overlay	me' di um den' si ty o" ver lay'

medium-duty	me' di um du' ty
medium voltage	me' di um volt' age
medullary ray	med' ul lar" y ray"
meeting rail	meet' ing rail"
meeting stile	meet' ing stile"
megabyte	meg' a byte"
megajoule	meg' a joule"
megalith	meg' a lith"
megalithic	meg' a lith' ic
megalopolis	meg' a lop' o lis
Meier, Richard	Mei' er, Rich' ard
melamine-formaldehyde	mel' a mine form al' de hyde"
melamine resin	mel' a mine" res' in
melt	melt
melt-thru	melt' thru"
melting	melt' ing
melton	mel' ton
member	mem' ber
membrane	mem' brane
membrane condition index	mem' brane con di' tion in' dex
membrane curing	mem' brane cur' ing
membrane waterproofing	mem' brane wa' ter proof" ing
memo sample	mem' o sam' ple
memorial	me mo' ri al
memorial plaque	me mo' ri al plaque"
Mendelsohn, Eric	Men' del sohn, Er' ic
mending plate	mend' ing plate"
menhir	men' hir
meniscus	me nis' cus
mensa	men' sa
mensuration	men" su ra' tion
men's room	men's' room"
Mercalli scale	Mer cal' li scale'
mercantile	mer' can tile"
mercerization	mer" cer i za' tion
mercerizing	mer' cer iz" ing
mercury	mer' cu ry
mercury-contact switch	mer' cu ry con' tact switch"
mercury-halide lamp	mer' cu ry ha' lide lamp"
mercury-vapor lamp	mer' cu ry va' por lamp"
meridian line	me rid' i an line"
mesh	mesh

mesh partition	mesh' par ti' tion
mesopic	me sop' ic
Mesopotamian	Mes" o po ta' mi an
metabolic	met" a bol' ic
metal	met' al
metal-arc welding	met' al arc weld' ing
metal casing	met' al cas' ing
metal-cutting blade	met' al cut' ting blade"
metal deck	met' al deck"
metal lath	met' al lath"
metal lock fastener	met' al lock fas' ten er
metal stud	met' al stud"
metal-wood system	met' al wood sys' tem
metalizing	met' al iz" ing
metallic insulation	me tal' lic in" su la' tion
metallurgic	met" al lur' gic
metalwork	met' al work"
metalworking	met' al work" ing
metameric	met" a mer' ic
metamerism	me tam' er ism"
metamers	met' a mers
metamorphic	met" a mor' phic
metamorphic rock	met" a mor' phic rock"
metamorphism	met" a mor' phism
meter	me' ter
metes and bounds	metes' and bounds'
methane	meth' ane
Methenamine pill test	Me the' na mine" pill' test
methodology	meth" od ol' o gy
methyl chloride	meth' yl chlo' ride
methyl ethyl ketone	meth' yl eth' yl ke' tone
methyl methacrylate	meth' yl meth ac' ry late"
methylpentene polymer	meth' yl pen" tene pol' y mer
metope	met' o pe
metric	met' ric
metric system	met' ric sys' tem
metrification	met" ri fi ca' tion
mews	mews
Mexican	Mex' i can
Meyer, Hannes	Mey' er, Hannes'
mezzanine	mez' za nine"
mezzo-relievo	mez' zo re lie' vo

mica	mi' ca
micro-fractures	mi' cro frac' tures
microclimate	mi' cro cli" mate
microclimatology	mi' cro cli" ma tol' o gy
microcomputer	mi' cro com put" er
microcracking	mi' cro crack" ing
microcracks	mi' cro cracks"
microcrystalline limestone	mi' cro crys' tal line lime' stone"
microculture	mi' cro cul" ture
microfiche	mi' cro fiche"
microfilm	mi' cro film"
microform	mi' cro form"
micrographics	mi" cro graph' ics
microimage	mi' cro im" age
microinch	mi' cro inch"
microlambert	mi' cro lam" bert
microlumen	mi' cro lu' men
micrometer	mi crom' e ter
micron	mi' cron
microphone	mi' cro phone"
micropublishing	mi' cro pub" lish ing
microscopic	mi" cro scop' ic
microseism	mi' cro seism"
microseismic	mi' cro seis" mic
microwave	mi' cro wave"
middle rail	mid' dle rail"
midpoint	mid' point"
midspan	mid' span"
Mies van der Rohe, Ludwig	Mies' van der Ro' he, Lud' wig
migration	mi gra' tion
mil	mil
mil-foot	mil' foot'
mild steel	mild' steel'
mildew	mil' dew
mildewstat	mil' dew stat"
Milford Buff	Mil' ford Buff"
Milford Pink	Mil' ford Pink"
milkiness	milk' i ness
mill	mill
mill finish	mill' fin' ish
mill length	mill' length"
mill run	mill' run"

mill-run	mill' run"
mill scale	mill' scale"
milled surface	milled' sur' face
millimeter	mil' li me" ter
milling	mill'ing
milliphot	mill' i phot"
millshop	mill' shop"
millstone	mill' stone"
millwork	mill' work"
millwright	mill' wright"
minaret	min" a ret'
mineral	min' er al
mineral-core door	min' er al core" door
mineral fiber felt	min' er al fi' ber felt"
mineral granules	min' er al gran' ules
mineral naphtha	min' er al naph' tha
mineral spirits	min' er al spir' its
mineral streak	min' er al streak"
mineral-surfaced roofing	min' er al sur' faced roof' ing
mineral wool	min' er al wool"
mineralization	min" er al i za' tion
miniature	min' i a ture
minicomputer	min' i com put' er
minimum	min' i mum
Minnesota Pink	Min" ne so' ta Pink"
Minnesota stone	Min" ne so' ta stone"
minus	mi' nus
minute of arc	min' ute of arc"
mirror	mir' ror
misalignment	mis" a lign' ment
miscellaneous iron	mis" cel la' ne ous i' ron
miserere	mis" e re' re
misfile	mis file'
mismatch	mis' match
mismatched	mis' matched
misrepresentation	mis" rep re sen ta' tion
mission	mis' sion
mission tile	mis' sion tile"
Missouri marble	Mis sour' i mar' ble
mistake	mis take'
miter	mi' ter
miter box	mi' ter box"

miter joint	mi' ter joint"
mitered stringer	mi' tered string' er
mitering	mi' ter ing
mix	mix
mix design	mix' de sign'
mixed grain	mixed' grain
mixed-grained lumber	mixed' grained" lum' ber
mixed occupancy	mixed' oc' cu pan cy
mixer	mix' er
mixing valve	mix' ing valve"
mixture	mix' ture
moat	moat
mobile	mo' bile
mobilization	mo" bi li za' tion
mock rafter	mock" raf' ter
mock-up	mock' up"
modacrylic	mod' a cryl' ic
mode	mode
model	mod' el
modeling	mod' el ing
modem	mo' dem
Modernism	mod' ern ism"
modification	mod" i fi ca' tion
modified	mod' i fied
modified bitumen	mod' i fied bi tu' men
Modified Mercalli Intensity Scale	Mod' i fied Mer cal' li In ten' si- ty Scale
modifier	mod' i fi" er
modillion	mo dil' lion
modular	mod' u lar
modular construction	mod' u lar con struc' tion
modular home	mod' u lar home"
modulate	mod' u late"
modulating	mod' u lat" ing
modulating thermostat	mod' u lat" ing ther' mo stat"
modulation	mod" u la' tion
module	mod' ule
modulus of elasticity	mod' u lus of e las tic' i ty
modulus of rigidity	mod' u lus of ri gid' i ty
modulus of rupture	mod' u lus of rup' ture
mogul base	mo' gul base"
mohair	mo' hair"

Mohs' scale	Mohs' scale'
moiré	moi' re
moist cure	moist' cure"
moist curing	moist' cur' ing
moisture	mois' ture
moisture barrier	mois' ture bar' ri er
moisture content	mois' ture con' tent
moisture-resistant	mois' ture re sis' tant
moisture-resistant adhesive	mois' ture re sis' tant ad hes' ive
moistureproof	mois' ture proof"
mold	mold
molded edge	mold' ed edge"
molding	mold' ing
mole run	mole' run"
molly bolt	mol' ly bolt"
molybdenum	mo lyb' de num
moment	mo' ment
moment diagram	mo' ment di' a gram
moment of inertia	mo' ment of in er' tia
moment-resisting space frame	mo' ment re sist' ing space" frame
moment splice	mo' ment splice"
momentary-contact switch	mo' men tar" y con' tact switch
momentum	mo men' tum
monastery	mon' as ter" y
Monel metal™	Mo nel' me' tal
monitor	mon' i tor
monitoring	mon' i tor ing
Monk bond	Monk' bond"
monochords	mon' o chords"
monochromatic	mon" o chro mat' ic
monochrome	mon' o chrome"
monocottura	mon' o cot tur' a
monofil	mon' o fil
monofilament	mon" o fil' a ment
monolith	mon' o lith
monolithic	mon" o lith' ic
monolithic glass	mon' o lith' ic glass"
monolithic terrazzo	mon' o lith' ic ter raz' zo
monomer	mon' o mer
monopod	mon' o pod"
monorail	mon' o rail"

177

monstrance	mon' strance
montage	mon tage'
Montclair Danby	Mont clair' Dan' by
montmorillonite	mont" mo ril' lon ite"
montmorillonoid	mont" mo ril' lon oid"
monument	mon' u ment
monumental	mon" u men' tal
monumental stair	mon" u men' tal stair"
Moore, Arthur Cotton	Moore', Ar' thur Cot' ton
Moore, Charles W.	Moore', Charles' W.
mop-and-flop	mop' and flop'
mop sink	mop' sink"
mopboard	mop' board"
mopping	mop' ping
mopping coat	mop' ping coat"
moquette	mo quette'
mordant	mor' dant
moresque	mo resque'
morgue	morgue
Morris chair	Mor' ris chair"
mortar	mor' tar
mortar joints	mor' tar joints"
mortarboard	mor' tar board"
mortarless	mor' tar less"
mortgage	mort' gage
mortgagee	mort" ga gee'
mortgagor	mort' ga gor
mortise	mor' tise
mortise bolt	mor' tise bolt"
mortise lock	mor' tise lock"
mortise-and-tenon joint	mor' tise and ten' on joint
mortised astragal	mor' tised as' tra gal
mortising	mor' tis ing
mortuary	mor' tu ar" y
mosaic	mo sa' ic
mosque	mosque
motel	mo tel'
mother-of-pearl	moth' er of pearl"
mothproofing	moth' proof" ing
motif	mo tif'
motion	mo' tion
motor	mo' tor

motor generator set	mo' tor gen' erator set"
mottle	mot' tle
mottler	mot' tler
mottling	mot' tling
mouchette	mou chette'
mould	mould
mount	mount
Mount Airy granite	Mount' Air' y gran' ite
mounting	mount' ing
mouse	mouse
mousseline	mousse line'
movable partition	mov' a ble par ti' tion
movement	move' ment
moving ramp	mov' ing ramp"
moving sidewalk	mov' ing side' walk"
mucilage	mu' ci lage
muck	muck
mucking	muck' ing
mud	mud'
mud cracking	mud" crack' ing
mud-jacking	mud' jack' ing
mud room	mud' room"
mud slab	mud' slab"
mudcapping	mud' cap' ping
mudflow	mud' flow"
mudsill	mud' sill"
muffler	muf' fler
mulch	mulch
mulching	mulch' ing
Muller, Peter	Mul' ler, Pe' ter
mulling	mul' ling
mullion	mul' lion
multi-element member	mul' ti el' e ment mem' ber
multi-ply	mul' ti ply'
multi-unit wall	mul' ti u' nit wall
multicentered arch	mul" ti cen' tered arch"
multicolor	mul' ti col" or
multicomponent	mul" ti com po' nent
multidisciplinary	mul" ti dis' ci pli nar" y
multielement prestressing	mul" ti el' e ment pre' stres sing
multifamily	mul" ti fam' i ly
multifoil	mul' ti foil"

multifolding door	mul' ti fold" ing door
multijet burner	mul' ti jet burn' er
multimedia	mul' ti me' di a
multiplate glass	mul' ti plate" glass"
multiple	mul' ti ple
multiple dwelling	mul' ti ple dwel' ling
multiple-family	mul' ti ple fam' i ly
multiple-layer adhesive	mul' ti ple lay' er ad he' sive
multiplier	mul' ti pli" er
multiply	mul' ti ply"
multipurpose	mul" ti pur' pose
multisensory	mul" ti sen' sor y
multispeed	mul' ti speed"
multistage compressor	mul' ti stage" com pres' sor
multistory	mul" ti sto' ry
multiwythe	mul' ti wythe"
multizone	mul' ti zone"
municipal building	mu nic' i pal build' ing
municipality	mu nic" i pal' i ty
muninga	mu nin' ga
Munsell color system	Mun' sell col' or sys' tem
muntin	mun' tin
Muntz metal	Muntz' met" al
mural	mu' ral
muriatic acid	mu" ri at' ic ac' id
Murphy bed	Mur' phy bed"
museum	mu se' um
mushroom construction	mush' room con struc' tion
muskeg	mus' keg
Muslim architecture	Mus' lim ar' chi tec" ture
muslin	mus' lin
mutes	mutes
Mycenaean architecture	My" ce nae' an ar' chi tec" ture
Mylar™	My' lar
myrtle burl	myr' tle burl"

N

nail	nail
nail pop	nail' pop"
nail schedule	nail' sched' ule
nail set	nail' set"

nailable	nail' able
nailer	nail' er
nailhead	nail' head
nailing	nail' ing
nailing pattern	nail' ing pat' tern
naked wall	na' ked wall
named insured	named' in sured'
nameplate	name' plate"
nanometer	nan' o me" ter
nap	nap
naphtha	naph' tha
naphthalene	napht' ha lene
naphthenate	naph' the nate"
naphthol	naph' thol
nappe	nappe
narra	nar' ra
narrow-light door	nar' row light' door
narrow-ringed	nar' row ringed"
narrowcast	nar' row cast"
narrowscope	nar' row scope"
narthex	nar' thex
natatoria	na" ta to' ri a
natatorium	na" ta to' ri um
nattes	nattes
natural	nat' u ral
natural-cleft	nat' u ral cleft"
natural finish	nat' u ral fin' ish
natural frequency	nat' u ral fre' quen cy
natural gas	nat' u ral gas
Naugahyde™	Nau' ga hyde
Navajo rug	Nav' a jo" rug"
naval	na' val
nave	nave
Naxos	Nax' os
neat	neat
neat cement	neat" ce ment'
neat cut	neat' cut"
nebule	neb' ule
neck	neck
neck down	neck' down"
necking	neck' ing
necropolis	ne crop' o lis

needle	nee' dle
needle beam	nee' dle beam"
needle glazing	nee' dle glaz' ing
needle-nose pliers	nee' dle nose" pli' ers
needle-punching	nee' dle punch' ing
needlework	nee' dle work"
needling	nee' dling
negative	neg' a tive
negative moment	neg' a tive mo' ment
negligence	neg' li gence
negotiable	ne go' ti a ble
negotiation	ne go" ti a' tion
neighborhood	neigh' bor hood
Nelson, George	Nel' son, George'
Neo-Gothic	Ne" o Goth' ic
neoclassic	ne" o clas' sic
neoclassicism	ne" o clas' si cism"
neon	ne' on
neoprene	ne' o prene"
neoprene washer nail	ne' o prene" wash' er nail
Nervi, Pier Luigi	Ner' vi, Pi' er Lu i' gi
nested tables	nest' ed ta' bles
net cross-sectional area	net' cross' sec' tion al ar' e a
net floor area	net' floor' ar' e a
net income	net' in' come
net load	net' load
net section	net' sec' tion
net-to-gross ratio	net' to gross' ra' tio
Netsch, Walter A.	Netsch', Wal' ter A.
network	net' work"
networking	net' work" ing
Neutra, Richard J.	Neu' tra, Rich' ard J.
neutral	neu' tral
neutral axis	neu' tral ax' is
neutral conductor	neu' tral con duc' tor
neutralizing	neu' tral iz" ing
New England Colonial	New" Eng' land Co lo' ni al
new town	new' town'
newel	new' el
newel cap	new' el cap"
newel-post	new' el post"
newton	new' ton

newton-meter	new' ton me' ter
nib	nib
nibbler	nib' bler
niche	niche
nicked-bit finish	nicked' bit' fin' ish
nickel	nick' el
niello	ni el' lo
Niemeyer, Oscar	Nie' mey er, Os' car
nigged ashlar	nigged' ash' lar
night latch	night' latch"
night sky radiation	night' sky' ra" di a' tion
ninon	ni' non
nippers	nip' pers
nipple	nip' ple
nit	nit
nitriding	ni' trid ing
nitrile	ni' trile
nitrile rubber	ni' trile rub' ber
nitrocellulose	ni" tro cel' lu lose
nitrogen	ni' tro gen
nitrous oxide	ni' trous ox' ide
no-hub soil pipe	no' hub' soil" pipe
no-slump grout	no' slump ' grout"
no-wax flooring	no' wax' floor' ing
noble metal	no' ble met' al
nodal points	nod' al points'
node	node
nodular	nod' u lar
nogging	nog' ging
Noguchi, Isamu	No gu' chi, I' sa mu"
noil	noil
Noir Fleuri	Noir' Fleu' ri
noise	noise
noise criterion	noise' cri te' ri on
noise reduction	noise' re duc' tion
nominal	nom' i nal
nominal dimension	nom' i nal di men' sion
nominal span	nom' i nal span"
nomogram	nom' o gram
non-air-entrained concrete	non' air' en trained' con' crete
nonambulatory	non am' bu la to" ry
nonautomatic	non" au to mat' ic

nonbearing	non' bear' ing
noncementitious	non" ce" men ti' tious
noncohesive soil	non" co he' sive soil"
noncollusion	non' col lu' sion
noncombustible	non com bus' ti ble
nonconcentrating	non con' cen trat" ing
nonconcurrency	non" con cur' ren cy
nonconcurrent	non" con cur' rent
nonconcurrent force	non" con cur' rent force"
nonconforming	non" con form' ing
noncontractual	non" con trac' tual
noncoplanar	non" co pla' nar
nondestructive test	non" de struc' tive test"
nondrying	non dry' ing
nonevaporable water	non" e vap' o ra ble wa' ter
nonferrous	non fer' rous
nonflammable	non flam' ma ble
nonilluminated	non" il lu' mi nat" ed
noninsurable risk	non" in sur' a ble risk"
nonliquefied	non" liq' ue fied"
non-load-bearing wall	non' load' bear" ing wall
nonlustrous glaze	non lus' trous glaze"
nonmetallic	non" me tal' lic
nonmetallic sheathed cable	non" me tal' lic sheathed' ca' ble
nonoperational mode	non" op er a' tion al mode"
nonpayment	non pay' ment
nonporous	non por' ous
nonpotable	non po' ta ble
nonprestressed	non pre' stressed
nonrecycling	non" re cy' cling
nonreproducible	non" re pro duc' i ble
nonresonant	non res' o nant
nonrising	non ris' ing
non-sag	non sag'
nonselective surface	non" se lec' tive sur' face
nonshrink	non shrink"
nonsiphon trap	non si' phon trap"
non-skinning	non" skin' ning
nonslip	non slip'
nonstaining	non stain' ing
nonstructural	non struc' tur al
nonsynchronous	non syn' chro nous

nontoxic	non tox' ic
nonvitreous tile	non vit' re ous tile"
nonvolatile	non vol' a tile
nonwarp	non warp'
nonwoven	non wov' en
nook	nook
nook-shaft	nook' shaft'
normal consistency	nor' mal con sis' ten cy
normal-weight concrete	nor' mal weight" con' crete
normalization	nor" mal i za' tion
normalized	nor' mal ized"
Norman architecture	Nor' man arch i tec' ture
Norman brick	Nor' man brick"
north	north
northern white pine	north' ern white pine
northlight roof	north' light roof"
nose-and-miter	nose' and mi' ter
nosing	nos' ing
nosing line	nos' ing line"
notations	no ta' tions
notch	notch
notch joist	notch' joist"
notchboard	notch' board"
notched molding	notched' mold' ing
notched spreader	notched' spread' er
notched trowel	notched' trow' el
notching	notch' ing
note	note
notice to bidders	no' tice to bid' ders
notification to proceed	no" ti fi ca' tion to pro ceed'
nouveau	nou' veau
novelty flooring	nov' el ty floor' ing
novolak	no' vo lak
novolid	no' vo lid
noxtane	nox' tane
Noyes, Eliot	Noyes', El' i ot
noys	noys
nozzle	noz' zle
nub	nub
nuclear	nu' cle ar
nulling	nul' ling
nunnery	nun' ner y

nursery	nurs' er y
nurses call system	nurses' call' sys' tem
nursing home	nurs' ing
nut	nut
nut driver	nut' driv' er
nut eyebolt	nut' eye' bolt"
Nuvolato	Nu" vo la' to
nylon	ny' lon
nytril	ny' tril

O

O-ring	O' ring"
oak	oak
oakum	oa' kum
Obata, Gyo	O ba' ta, Gy' o
obelisk	ob' e lisk
objectives	ob jec' tives
obligee	ob" li gee'
obligor	ob" li gor'
oblique	o blique'
obscuration	ob" scu ra' tion
obscure	ob scure'
obscuring window	ob scur' ing win' dow
observation	ob" ser va' tion
observatory	ob serv' a to" ry
obsidian	ob sid' i an
obsolescence	ob" so les' cence
obstetrical hospital	ob stet' ri cal hos' pi tal
obtuse	ob tuse'
obtuse angle	ob tuse' an' gle
occasional chair	oc ca' sion al chair"
occupancy	oc' cu pan cy
occupancy indicator	oc' cu pan cy in' di ca" tor
occupancy permit	oc' cu pan cy per' mit
occupant load	oc' cu pant load"
occupiable	oc' cu pi" a ble
occurrence	oc cur' rence
ocher	o' cher
Oconee	O co' nee
octagon	oc' ta gon
octastyle	oc' ta style"

octave	oc' tave
octave band	oc' tave band"
octave-band analyzer	oc' tave band" an' a lyz" er
oculus	oc' u lus
Odessa	O des' sa
odeum	o de' um
odometer	o dom' e ter
odor nuisance	o' dor nui' sance
oersted	oer' sted
off-center	off' cen' ter
off-site	off' site
off street parking	off' street" park' ing
off-white	off' white
office	of' fice
offset	off' set"
offset bend	off' set" bend"
offset pivot	off' set" piv' ot
ogee	o' gee
Oglesby Blue granite	O' gles by Blue" gran' ite
ohm	ohm
Ohm's law	Ohm's' law"
oil	oil
oil-base paint	oil' base paint"
oil buffer	oil' buf' fer
oil can	oil' can"
oil-canning	oil' can' ning
oil fired	oil' fired'
oil-modified urethane	oil' mod' i fied u' re thane"
oilite bearing hinge	oil' ite bear' ing hinge
oilslip	oil' slip"
oilstone	oil' stone"
oiticica oil	oi" ti ci' ca oil"
Old English bond	Old' Eng' lish bond
old growth	old' growth"
olefin	o' le fin
oleophilic	o" le o phil' ic
oleoresin	o" le o res' in
oleoresinous	o" le o res' in ous
oligomer	o lig' o mer
oligomeric	o lig" o mer' ic
oligomerization	o lig" o mer i za' tion
olive knuckle hinge	ol' ive knuck' le hinge"

Omalon™	O' ma lon
ombré	om bre'
on-center	on" cen' ter
on grade	on' grade"
on-line	on' line'
on-site	on' site'
one-hour wall	one' hour' wall"
one-part	one' part'
one-point perspective	one' point' per spec' tive
one-sided connection	one' sid' ed con nec' tion
one-way joist	one' way' joist"
one-way slab	one' way' slab"
one-way system	one' way' sys' tem
onion dome	on' ion dome"
onyx	on' yx
oolite	o' o lite"
oolitic	o" o lit' ic
oolitic limestone	o" o lit' ic lime' stone"
opacity	o pac' i ty
opal glass	o' pal glass"
opalescence	o" pal les' cence
opalescent	o" pal es' cent
opalized	o' pal ized
opaque	o paque'
opaque finish	o paque' fin' ish
opaquing	o paqu' ing
open back	o' pen back"
open bidding	o' pen bid' ding
open-cell foam	o' pen cell" foam
open-corner fireplace	o' pen cor' ner fire' place"
open cornice	o' pen cor' nice
open-end block	o' pen end' block"
open-graded aggregate	o' pen grad" ed ag' gre gate
open-grain	o' pen grain
open joint	o' pen joint"
open plan	o' pen plan"
open planning	o' pen plan' ning
open-riser stair	o' pen ris' er stair"
open space	o' pen space"
open stair	o' pen stair"
open valley	o' pen val' ley
open-web steel joist	o' pen web' steel" joist

open-web studs	o' pen web' studs
opening	o' pen ing
openwork	o' pen work"
opera house	op' er a house
operable	op' er a ble
operable partition	op' er a ble par ti' tion
operable window	op' er a ble win' dow
operant behavior	op' er ant be hav' i or
operating cost	op' er at" ing cost"
operating engineer	op' er at" ing en' gi neer
operating room	op' er at" ing room"
opposed-blade damper	op posed' blade" damp' er
optical	op' ti cal
optimization	op" ti mi za' tion
optimizing	op' ti miz" ing
optimum moisture content	op' ti mum mois' ture con' tent
option	op' tion
orange peel	or' ange peel"
orangery	or' ange ry
oratory	or' a to" ry
orb	orb
orbicular	or bic' u lar
orbital sander	or' bit al sand' er
orchestra	or' ches tra
orchestra lift	or' ches tra lift"
order	or' der
ordinance	or' di nance
ordinary construction	or' di nar" y con struc' tion
ordinary-hazard contents	or' di nar" y haz' ard con' tents
ordinate	or' di nate
organic	or gan' ic
Organic architecture	Or gan' ic arc' hi tec" ture
organic coating	or gan' ic coat' ing
organic felt	or gan' ic felt"
organisol	or gan' i sol
organzine	or' gan zine"
oriel	o' ri el
oriel window	o' ri el win' dow
orient	o' ri ent
Oriental	O" ri en' tal
oriental rug	o" ri en' tal rug"
orientation	o" ri en ta' tion

oriented strandboard	o' ri ent" ed strand' board"
orifice	or' i fice
origin	or' i gin
orlo	or' lo
Orlon™	Or' lon
ormolu	or' mo lu"
ornament	or' na ment
ornamental	or" na men' tal
ornamentation	or" na men ta' tion
ornate	or nate'
orphanage	or' phan age
orthochromatic	or" tho chro mat' ic
orthoclase	or' tho clase"
orthogonal	or thog' o nal
orthograph	or' tho graph"
orthographic projection	or" tho graph' ic pro jec' tion
orthography	or thog' ra phy
orthophoto	or' tho pho' to
orthostyle	or' tho style"
orthotropic	or" tho trop' ic
Osage	O' sage
oscillate	os' cil late"
oscillating	os' cil lat" ing
oscillating load	os' cil lat" ing load"
oscillation	os" cil la' tion
oscillator	os' cil la" tor
osmosis	os mo' sis
osmotic	os mot' ic
osmotic pressure	os mot' ic pres' sure
osnaburg	os' na burg"
Ostwald color system	Ost' wald col' or sys' tem
Otto, Frei	Ot' to, Frei'
ottoman	ot' to man
Oud, J. J. P.	Oud', J. J. P.
out-of-plumb	out' of plumb"
out-of-round	out' of round"
out-of-square	out' of square"
out-of-true	out' of true"
outband	out' band"
outbond	out' bond"
outbuilding	out' build' ing
outcrop	out' crop"

outcropping	out' crop" ping
outdoor	out' door"
outdoor design temperature	out' door" de sign' tem' per a ture
outer court	out' er court
outfall	out' fall"
outgassing	out' gas" sing
outlet	out' let
outline	out' line"
outline specification	out' line" spec" i fi ca' tion
outlooker	out' look" er
outrigger	out' rig" ger
outside air	out' side air
outside-air intake	out' side air' in' take
outside corner molding	out' side cor' ner mold' ing
outside diameter	out' side di am' e ter
outside glazing	out' side glaz' ing
ovalness	o' val ness
ovals	o' vals
ovendry	ov' en dry
overall	o' ver all"
overall span	o' ver all" span"
overburden	o" ver bur' den
overcast	o' ver cast'
overcompaction	o' ver com pac' tion
overconsolidated	o' ver con sol' i dat" ed
overcurrent	o' ver cur' rent
overdesign	o' ver de sign"
overdoor	o' ver door"
overdying	o" ver dy' ing
overflow	o" ver flow'
overgraining	o' ver grain" ing
overhand work	o' ver hand" work'
overhang	o' ver hang'
overhaul	o" ver haul'
overhead	o' ver head'
overhead concealed closer	o' ver head' con cealed' clos' er
overhead crane	o' ver head' crane"
overhead door	o' ver head' door"
overhead factor	o' ver head' fac' tor
overhead pot rack	o' ver head' pot' rack
overhead and profit	o' ver head' and prof' it
overlaid	o' ver laid"

overlap	o' ver lap"
overlapping astragal	o' ver lap" ping as' tra gal
overlay	o' ver lay"
overload	o' ver load"
overloading	o' ver load" ing
overmantel	o' ver man" tel
overshoot	o" ver shoot'
oversize brick	o' ver size brick"
overspray	o' ver spray"
overstretching	o" ver stretch' ing
overthrow	o' ver throw"
overtime	o' ver time"
overtone	o' ver tone"
overturning	o' ver turn" ing
overturning moment	o' ver turn" ing mo' ment
overvibration	o' ver vi bra" tion
overvoltage	o' ver volt" age
ovola	o' vo la"
ovolo	o' vo lo"
Owings, Nathaniel	Ow' ings, Na than' iel
owner	own' er
owner-architect agreement	own' er arc' hi tect" a gree' ment
owner-contractor agreement	own' er con' trac tor a gree' ment
owner-supplied	own' er sup plied'
ownership	own' er ship"
oxalic acid	ox al' ic ac' id
oxbow front	ox' bow front"
oxeye	ox' eye
oxidation	ox i da' tion
oxide	ox' ide
oxidized	ox' i dized"
oxidized bronze	ox' i dized" bronze"
oxter piece	ox' ter piece"
oxyacetylene	ox" y a cet' y lene
oxychloride	ox" y chlo' ride
oxychloride cement	ox" y chlo' ride ce ment'
oxychloride terrazzo	ox" y chlo' ride ter raz' zo
oxyfuel welding	ox' y fuel weld' ing
oxygen	ox' y gen
oxyhydrogen welding	ox" y hy' dro gen weld' ing
oxypropane cutting	ox" y pro' pane cut' ting
oyelet	oye' let

oylet	oy' let
oyster veneer	oys' ter ve neer'
ozone	o' zone
ozone resistance	o' zone re sist' ance

P

P-trap	P' trap"
P-waves	P waves"
pace	pace
package trim	pack' age trim'
packaged boiler	pack' aged boil' er
packer	pack' er
packing	pack' ing
pad foot	pad' foot"
padding	pad' ding
paddle mixer	pad' dle mix' er
paddock	pad' dock
padlock	pad' lock
padouk	pa douk'
page	page
pagoda	pa go' da
pai-loo	pai' loo'
pailing	pail' ing
paillon	pail lon'
Paimio chair	Pai' mi o" chair"
paint	paint
paint brush	paint' brush"
paint spraying	paint' spray' ing
paintable	paint' a ble
painter	paint' er
pair	pair
paisley	pais' ley
palace	pal' ace
palatial	pa la' tial
palazzo	pa laz' zo
paldao	pal da' o
pale	pale
palette	pal' ette
palette knife	pal' ette knife"
paling	pal' ing
palisade	pal" i sade'

Palladian	Pal la' di an
Palladian terrazzo	Pal la' di an ter raz' zo
palladium	pal la' di um
pallet	pal' let
pallet nail	pal' let nail"
palletized	pal' let ized"
palm capital	palm' cap' i tal
palmate	pal' mate
palmette	pal mette'
palmwood	palm' wood"
pan	pan
pan construction	pan' con struc' tion
pan form	pan' form"
pan-and-roll roofing	pan' and roll roof' ing
pan-type tread	pan' type' tread"
panache	pa nache'
panchromatic	pan" chro mat' ic
pane	pane
panel	pan' el
panel-back chair	pan' el back chair"
panel building system	pan' el build' ing sys" tem
panel clip	pan' el clip"
panel door	pan' el door"
panel heating	pan' el heat' ing
panel length	pan' el length"
panel point	pan' el point"
panel schedule	pan' el sched' ule
panelboard	pan' el board"
paneling	pan' el ing
panelized	pan' el ized
panic bolt	pan' ic bolt"
panic exit	pan' ic ex' it
panic hardware	pan' ic hard' ware"
panicproof lock	pan' ic proof" lock"
panier	pan' ier
panne	panne
pannier	pan' nier
panopticon	pan op' ti con"
pantile	pan' tile"
pantograph	pan' to graph"
pantry	pan' try
paper	pa' per

paper form	pa' per form"
paperhanger	pa' per hang" er
paperhanging	pa' per hang" ing
paperholder	pa' per hold" er
papering	pa' per ing
PAR lamp	PAR' lamp"
parabola	pa rab' o la
parabolic	par" a bol' ic
parabolic antenna	par" a bol' ic an ten' na
paraboloid	pa rab' o loid"
paracentric	par" a cen' tric
paracyl reflector	par' a cyl" re flec' tor
paradigm	par' a digm"
paradise	par' a dise"
paraffin	par' af fin
paragraph	par' a graph"
parallel	par' al lel"
parallel-blade damper	par' al lel" blade' damp' er
parallel strand lumber	par' al lel" strand' lum' ber
parallelepiped	par" al lel" e pi' ped
parallelogram	par" al lel' o gram"
parameter	pa ram' e ter
parametric	par" a met' ric
parapet	par' a pet
parclose	par' close"
Pardais	Par" da' is
parenchyma	pa ren' chy ma
parent material	par' ent ma ter' i al
parent metal	par' ent met' al
paretta	pa ret' ta
parge	parge'
parge coat	parge' coat"
parget	par' get
pargeting	par' get ing
pargework	parge' work
parging	parg' ing
parish house	par' ish house"
parison	par' i son
park	park
parkerized	par' ker ized
parkerizing	par' ker iz" ing
parking	park' ing

parking lot	park' ing lot"
parliament hinge	par' lia ment hinge"
parlor	par' lor
parquet	par quet'
parquetry	par' quet ry
parrel	par' rel
parsonage	par' son age
Parsons table	Par' sons ta' ble
parterre	par terre'
Parthenon	Par' the non
parti	par ti'
partial occupancy	par' tial oc' cu pan cy
partial payment	par' tial pay' ment
particle board	par' ti cle board
particle-board core	par' ti cle board" core"
particle size	par' ti cle size
particle-size distribution	par' ti cle size' dis' tri bu' tion
particulate matter	par tic' u late mat' ter
parting	part' ing
parting bead	part' ing bead"
parting strip	part' ing strip"
partition	par ti' tion
partnership	part' ner ship"
parts per million	parts' per mil' lion
party wall	par' ty wall"
parvis	par' vis
pascal	pas' cal
pass	pass
pass-through	pass' through'
passage set	pas' sage set"
passageway	pas' sage way"
passementerie	passe men' terie
passenger elevator	pas' sen ger el' e va" tor
passings	pass' ings
passive solar	pas' sive so' lar
passkey	pass' key"
paste	paste
paste filler	paste' fil' ler
patch	patch
patch panel	patch" pan' el
patching	patch' ing
patent	pat' ent

patent defect	pat' ent de' fect
patent hammer	pat' ent ham' mer
patera	pa ter' a
path	path
pathogen	path' o gen
patina	pat i' na
patio	pat' i o
patio lock	pat' i o lock"
patten	pat' ten
pattern	pat' tern
pattern cracking	pat' tern crack' ing
patterned glass	pat' terned glass'
patterning	pat' tern ing
paumelle hinge	pau melle' hinge
pavement	pave' ment
paver	pav' er
pavilion	pa' vil' ion
paving brick	pav' ing brick"
Pavonazzo	Pav" o naz' zo
payback	pay' back"
payback period	pay' back" pe' ri od
payment	pay' ment
payment certificate	pay' ment cer tif' i cate
pea gravel	pea' grav' el
peak	peak
peak-load controller	peak' load con trol' ler
peak shear strength	peak' shear' strength
peaked roof	peaked' roof"
pearl molding	pearl' mold' ing
pearwood	pear' wood"
peat	peat
peat moss	peat' moss"
pebble	peb' ble
pebble dash	peb' ble dash"
pebble dashing	peb' ble dash' ing
pebbled	peb' bled
pecan	pe can'
peck	peck
pecky cypress	peck' y cy' press
pecky timber	peck' y tim' ber
pedestal	ped' es tal
pedestal table	ped' es tal ta' ble

pedestrian	pe des' tri an
pediment	ped' i ment
peel test	peel' test"
peeler log	peel' er log"
peeling	peel' ing
peen	peen
peening	peen' ing
peg	peg
pegboard	peg' board"
Pei, I. M.	Pei', I. M.
pellet	pel' let
Pelli, Cesar	Pel' li, Ce sar'
pellon	pel' lon
pelmet	pel' met
pembroke table	pem' broke ta' ble
penalty clause	pen' al ty clause"
pencil	pen' cil
pencil holder	pen' cil hold' er
pencil rod	pen' cil rod"
penciling	pen' cil ing
pendant	pend' ant
pendant finial	pend' ant fin' i al
pendentive	pen den' tive
pendulum	pen' du lum
penetrability	pen" e tra bil' i ty
penetrating stain	pen' e trat" ing stain"
penetration	pen" e tra' tion
penetrometer	pen" e trom' e ter
peninsula-base cabinet	pen in' su la base" cab' i net
penitentiary	pen" i ten' tia ry
Pennsylvania slate	Penn' syl va' nia slate"
penny	pen' ny
penstock	pen' stock
pent roof	pent' roof"
penta	pen' ta
penta resin	pen' ta res' in
pentachlorophenol	pen" ta chlo' ro phe' nol
pentagon	pen' ta gon"
pentagram	pen' ta gram"
penthouse	pent' house"
pentrometer	pen" trom e ter
people mover system	peo' ple mov' er sys' tem

percale	per cale'
percent	per cent'
percent compaction	per cent' com pac' tion
percentage	per cent' age
perception	per cep' tion
perceptual	per cep' tu al
perch	perch
perched water table	perched' wat' er ta' ble
percolation	per" co la' tion
percussion cone	per cus' sion cone"
percussion drill	per cus' sion drill"
Pereira, William L.	Pe rei' ra, Wil' liam L.
perennial	per en' ni al
perfect	per' fect
perfection	per fec' tion
perforated	per' fo rat" ed
perforated gypsum lath	per' fo rat" ed gyp' sum lath
perforated metal	per' fo rat" ed met' al
perforating	per' fo rat" ing
perform	per form'
performance	per for' mance
performance bond	per for' mance bond"
pergola	per' go la
periclase	per' i clase"
perimeter	pe rim' e ter
perimeter heating	pe rim' e ter heat' ing
period	pe' ri od
periodic	pe" ri od' ic
periodical room	pe" ri od' i cal room
peripheral	pe riph' er al
peristyle	per' i style"
Perkins, Lawrence B.	Per' kins, Law' rence B.
perling	perl' ing
perlite	per' lite
perm	perm
permafrost	per' ma frost"
permanence	per' ma nence
permanent	per' ma nent
permanent set	per' ma nent set"
permeability	per" me a bil' i ty
permeability-compression test	per" me a bil' i ty com pres' sion test"

permeameter	per' me a me" ter
permeance	per' me ance
permeation	per" me a' tion
permissible	per mis' si ble
permit	per' mit
permittivity	per" mit tiv' i ty
perpend stone	per' pend stone"
perpender	per' pen der
perpendicular	per" pen dic' u lar
perpeyn wall	per' pe yn wall"
perron	per' ron
Persian rug	Per' sian rug"
persiennes	per" si ennes'
personal	per' son al
personal injury	per' son al in' ju ry
personal space	per' son al space"
personalization	per" son al i za' tion
personnel	per" son nel'
perspective	per spec' tive
PERT schedule	PERT' sched' ule
pet cock	pet' cock"
Petite Granite	Pe tite' Gran' ite
petroglyph	pet' ro glyph"
petrographic analysis	pet" ro graph' ic a nal' y sis
petrography	pe trog' ra phy
petrolene	pet' ro lene"
petroleum	pe tro' le um
petrolic ether	pe trol' ic e' ther
petty cash	pet' ty cash"
pew	pew
pewter	pew' ter
pH value	p' H' val' ue
pharmacy	phar' ma cy
phase	phase
phase change	phase' change"
phase delay	phase' de lay'
phased development	phased' de vel' op ment
phellem	phel' lem
phenocryst	phe' no cryst
phenol	phe' nol
phenol resorcinol	phe' nol res or' cin ol"
phenol-formaldehyde	phe' nol form al' de hyde

phenolic resin	phe" no' lic res' in
phenylene	phen' yl ene"
phenylpropane	phen" yl pro' pane
phi factor	phi' fac' tor
Philippine cedar	Phil' ip pine" ce' dar
Philippine mahogany	Phil' ip pine" ma hog' a ny
Phillips head	Phi' lips head"
phloem	phlo' em
phlogopite	phlog' o pite"
pholads	pho' lads
phon	phon
phosphate-coated	phos' phate coat' ed
phosphated	phos' phat ed
phosphatized	phos' pha tized"
phosphatizing	phos' pha tiz" ing
phosphor	phos' phor
phosphor-bronze	phos' phor bronze"
phosphorescence	phos" pho res' cence
phosphorescent	phos" pho res' cent
phosphorized copper	phos' pho rized" cop' per
phot	phot
photo drafting	pho' to draft' ing
photo mechanical transfer	pho' to me chan" i cal trans' fer
photocell	pho' to cell"
photochemical	pho' to chem" i cal
photochromic coating	pho" to chro' mic coat' ing
photochromism	pho" to chro' mism
photocopy	pho' to cop" y
photodetector	pho' to de tec" tor
photodiode	pho' to di" ode
photoelasticity	pho' to e las tic' i ty
photoelectric	pho' to e lec' tric
photoelectric cell	pho' to e lec' tric cell'
photoelectric effect	pho' to e lec' tric ef fect'
photoflood	pho' to flood"
photogrammetrist	pho" to gram' me trist
photogrammetry	pho" to gram' me try
photoluminescence	pho" to lu" mi nes' cence
photolysis	pho tol' y sis
photometer	pho tom' e ter
photometric	pho" to met' ric
photometry	pho tom' e try

photomicroscopy	pho" to mi cros' co py
photomural	pho' to mur" al
photopic	pho top' ic
photoplotting	pho' to plot' ting
Photostat™	Pho' to stat"
phototube	pho' to tube"
photovoltaic	pho" to vol ta' ic
phyrheliometric scale	phyr' he" li o met' ric scale
physically disabled	phys' i cal ly dis a' bled
piano hinge	pi an' o hinge"
piazza	pi az' za
pick	pick
picket	pick' et
picketing	pick' et ing
pickled	pick' led
pickling	pick' ling
pickup	pick' up"
pictorial	pic to' ri al
picture molding	pic' ture mold' ing
picture plane	pic' ture plane"
picture window	pic' ture win' dow
picturesque	pic' turesque
piece-dyed	piece' dyed"
piece dyeing	piece' dye' ing
piece mark	piece' mark"
pien	pien'
piend	piend
pier	pier
pierced louver	pierced' lou' ver
piezoelectric effect	pi e" zo e lec' tric ef fect'
piezometer	pi" e zom' e ter
piezometric	pi e" zo met' ric
pigeonhole	pi' geon hole"
pigment	pig' ment
pigtail	pig' tail"
pilaster	pi las' ter
pile	pile
pile cap	pile' cap"
pile driver	pile' driv' er
pile height	pile' height"
piling	pil' ing
pill test	pill' test"

pillar	pil' lar
pillar-stone	pil' lar stone"
pilling	pil' ling
pillow	pil' low
pillowwork	pil' low work"
pilot hole	pi' lot hole"
pilot light	pi' lot light"
piloti	pi lo' ti
pilotis	pi lo' tis
pimples	pim' ples
pin	pin
pin-connected truss	pin' con nec' ted truss"
pin joint	pin' joint
pin knot	pin' knot
pin rail	pin' rail"
pin registered overlay	pin' reg' is tered o' ver lay"
pincers	pin' cers
pinch bar	pinch' bar"
pinch mark	pinch' mark"
pinchers	pinch' ers
pine	pine
pine tar	pine' tar"
pinhole	pin' hole"
pinholing	pin' hol" ing
Pink Aurora	Pink' Au ror' a
Pink Buff Mansota	Pink' Buff' Man sot' a
pink noise	pink' noise"
pinnacle	pin' na cle
pinning	pin' ning
pintle	pin' tle
pipe	pipe
pipe column	pipe' col' umn
pipe fitter	pipe' fit' ter
pipe fitting	pipe' fit' ting
pipe hanger	pipe hang' er
pipe size	pipe' size"
pipe threads	pipe' threads"
pipeline	pipe' line"
piping	pip' ing
piqué	pi que'
piscina	pis ci' na
pise	pi se'

piston	pis' ton
pit	pit
pit-run gravel	pit' run' grav' el
pitch	pitch
pitch board	pitch' board"
pitch-faced	pitch' faced"
pitch pan	pitch' pan"
pitch pocket	pitch' pock' et
pitch streak	pitch' streak"
pitched roof	pitched' roof"
pitched stone	pitched' stone"
pitchhole	pitch' hole"
pith	pith
pith fleck	pith' fleck"
pitting	pit' ting
pivot	piv' ot
pivoted	piv' ot ed
pixel	pix' el
placage	plac' age
place	place
place of assembly	place' of as sem' bly
placement	place' ment
placing	plac' ing
plafond	pla fond'
plain concrete	plain' con' crete
plain-cut joint	plain' cut' joint"
plain-sawn	plain' sawn"
plan	plan
planceer	plan ceer'
plancer	plan' cer
plancier	plan cier'
plane	plane
plane of weakness	plane' of weak' ness
planed-to-caliper hardboard	planed' to cal' i per hard' board"
planed lumber	planed' lum' ber
planer	plan' er
planetarium	plan" e tar' i um
planimeter	pla nim' e ter
planing	plan' ing
planish finish	plan' ish fin' ish
plank	plank
planking	plank' ing

planned unit development	planned' u' nit de vel' op ment
planning	plan' ning
plano-convex	pla' no con vex'
plant	plant
plant-mix base	plant' mix' base"
planted	plant' ed
planter	plant' er
planting	plant' ing
plaque	plaque
plaster	plas' ter
plaster bead	plas' ter bead"
plaster guard	plas' ter guard"
plaster lath	plas' ter lath"
plaster of Paris	plas' ter of Par' is
plaster ring	plas' ter ring"
plasterboard	plas' ter board"
plastering	plas' ter ing
plasterwork	plas' ter work"
plastic	plas' tic
plastic cement	plas' tic ce ment'
plastic clad window	plas' tic clad" win' dow
plastic design	plas' tic de sign'
plastic laminate	plas' tic lam' i nate
plastic limit	plas' tic lim' it
plastic piping	plas' tic pip' ing
plastic screw anchor	plas' tic screw" an' chor
plasticity	plas tic' i ty
plasticity index	plas tic' i ty in' dex
plasticize	plas' ti cize"
plasticizer	plas' ti ciz" er
plastisol	plas' ti sol"
plastomeric	plas" to mer' ic
plat	plat
plate	plate
plate tectonics	plate' tec ton' ics
plate-type	plate' type"
Plateau Danby	Pla teau' Dan' by
plated	plat' ed
platen	plat' en
platform	plat' form
platform frame	plat' form frame"
plating	plat' ing

platinum	plat' i num
Platner, Warren	Plat' ner, War' ren
platted	plat' ted
play	play
playback	play' back"
playfield	play' field"
playground	play' ground"
playhouse	play' house"
plaza	pla' za
pleading	plead' ing
pleating	pleat' ing
pleats	pleats
plenum	ple' num
plenum barrier	ple' num bar' ri er
plenum-rated cable	ple' num rat' ed ca' ble
pliers	pli' ers
plinth	plinth
plinth block	plinth' block"
plissé	plis se'
plot	plot
plot plan	plot' plan"
plotter	plot' ter
plotting	plot' ting
plough	plough
plow	plow
plucked finish	plucked' fin' ish
plug	plug
plug weld	plug' weld"
plugging	plug' ging
plum	plum
plumb	plumb
plumb bob	plumb' bob'
plumb cut	plumb' cut
plumb line	plumb' line"
plumber	plumb' er
plumbing	plumb' ing
plumbing fixture	plumb' ing fix' ture
plumbing system	plumb' ing sys' tem
plumbness	plumb' ness
plume	plume
plunge	plunge
plunger	plung' er

plunging	plung' ing
plush	plush
plush carpet	plush' car' pet
ply	ply
plyclips	ply' clips"
plyform	ply' form"
Plymouth White	Plym' outh White"
plyron	ply' ron
plywood	ply' wood"
pneumatic	pneu mat' ic
pneumatically	pneu mat' i cal ly
poché	po che'
pocher	poch' er
pock marks	pock' marks"
pocket	pock' et
pocket butt	pock' et butt"
pocket door	pock' et door"
pocket rot	pock' et rot"
pockmarking	pock' mark" ing
podium	po' di um
point	point
point-bearing pile	point' bear' ing pile"
point of inflection	point' of in flec' tion
point load	point' load"
point source	point' source"
pointed arch	point' ed arch"
pointing	point' ing
pointing trowel	point' ing trow' el
poise	poise
poisons	poi' sons
Poisson's ratio	Pois son's' ra' tio
polar coordinate	po' lar co or' di nate"
polariscope	po lar' i scope"
polarity	po lar' i ty
polarization	po" lar i za' tion
polarized	po' lar ized"
polarized light	po' lar ized" light"
pole	pole
pole construction	pole' con struc' tion
pole piece	pole' piece"
policyholder	pol' i cy hold" er
polish	pol' ish

polished finish	pol' ished fin' ish
polishing	pol' ish" ing
pollution	pol lu' tion
Polshek, James Stewart	Pol' shek, James' Stew' art
polyacrylate	pol" y ac' ry late
polyallomers	po" ly al' lo mers
polyamide	pol" y a mide'
polyamide-epoxy	pol" y am' ide e pox' y
polyblends	pol' y blends"
polybutene	pol" y bu' tene
polybutylene	pol" y bu' tyl ene
polycarbonate	pol" y car' bo nate
polychloroprene	pol" y chlo' ro prene
polychromatic	pol" y chro mat' ic
polychrome	pol' y chrome"
polychromy	pol' y chro" my
polyester	pol' y es" ter
polyester pneumacel	pol' y es" ter pneu' ma cel
polyether	pol' y e' ther
polyethylene	pol" y eth' yl ene"
polygon	pol' y gon"
polygonal masonry	po lyg' o nal ma' son ry
polyimides	pol" y im' ides
polyisobutylene	pol" y i" so bu' tyl ene
polyisocyanurate	pol" y i" so cy an' u rate
polymer	pol' y mer
polymercaptan	pol" y mer cap' tan
polymeric	pol" y mer' ic
polymerization	po lym' er i za' tion
polymethyl methacrylate	pol" y meth' yl meth ac' ry late"
polyol	pol' y ol"
polyolefin	pol" y o' le fin
polyoxymethylene	pol" y ox" y meth' yl ene"
polypropylene	pol" y pro' pyl ene"
polypropylene-olefin	pol" y pro' ply ene" o' le fin
polystyle	pol' y style"
polystyrene	pol" y sty' rene
polysulfide	pol" y sul' fide
polytrophic	pol" y troph' ic
polyurea	pol" y u re' a
polyurethane	pol" y u' re thane"
polyvinyl	pol" y vi' nyl

polyvinyl acetal	pol" y vi' nyl ac' e tal"
polyvinyl acetate	pol" y vi' nyl ac' e tate"
polyvinyl acetate emulsion	pol" y vi' nyl ac' e tate" e mul' sion
polyvinyl chloride	pol" y vi' nyl chlo' ride
polyvinyl fluoride	pol" y vi' nyl fluor' ide
polyvinylidene chloride	pol" y vi nyl' i dene" chlo' ride
polyvinylidene fluoride	pol" y vi nyl' i dene" fluor' ide
pommel	pom' mel
ponding	pond' ing
pongee	pon gee'
Ponti, Gio	Pon' ti, Gi' o
pool	pool
pool deck	pool' deck
pop-corn concrete	pop' corn" con' crete
pop-out	pop' out"
poplar	pop' lar
poplin	pop' lin
poppyhead	pop' py head"
population	pop" u la' tion
porcelain	por' ce lain
porcelain enamel	por' ce lain e nam' el
porcelain-on-steel chalkboard	por' ce lain on steel' chalk' board"
porch	porch
pore water	pore' wa' ter
porosity	po ros' i ty
porous	po' rous
porous wood	po' rous wood"
porphyry	por' phy ry
port	port
portable	port' a ble
portal	por' tal
porte-cochère	porte co chere'
portico	por' ti co"
portland cement	port' land ce ment'
portland-pozzolan cement	port' land poz' zo lan ce ment'
Portman, John	Port' man, John'
Portoghesi, Paolo	Por" to ghe' si, Paolo
position indicator	po si' tion in' di ca tor
positive moment	pos' i tive mo' ment
post	post
post anchor	post' an' chor
post-and-beam framing	post' and beam' fram' ing

post cap	post' cap"
post-completion	post" com ple' tion
post-construction services	post" con struc' tion ser' vi ces
post-cure	post' cure"
post-occupancy evaluation	post" oc' cu pan cy e val" u a' tion
post office	post' of' fice
postern	pos' tern
postflare	post' flare"
postformed plywood	post' formed" ply' wood"
postheating	post" heat' ing
postiche	pos tiche'
postmodern	post' mod' ern
postmodernism	post' mod' ern ism"
posttensioned	post ten' sioned
posttensioning	post ten' sion ing
pot life	pot' life"
pot sink	pot' sink"
potable	po' ta ble
potential	po ten' tial
potential energy	po ten' tial en' er gy
potentiometer	po ten" ti om' e ter
pottery	pot' ter y
pouch	pouch
Pouillenay	Pouil le nay'
pounce	pounce
pounce powder	pounce' pow' der
pour coat	pour' coat"
powder post beetle	pow' der post' bee' tle
powder room	pow' der room"
powdering	pow' der ing
power	pow' er
power-actuated fastener	pow' er ac' tu at" ed fas' ten er
power amplifier	pow' er am' pli fi" er
power of attorney	pow' er of at tor' ney
power boiler	pow' er boil' er
power-driven fastener	pow' er driv' en fas' ten er
power factor	pow' er fac' tor
power plant	pow' er plant"
power pole	pow' er pole
powered	pow' ered
powerhouse	pow' er house"
pozzolanic	poz" zo lan' ic

pozzolan	poz' zo lan
pozzolana	poz" zo la' na
Pratt truss	Pratt' truss"
pre-excavation	pre ex" ca va' tion
pre-existing duty	pre ex ist' ing du' ty
pre-posttensioned	pre' post ten' sioned
pre-posttensioning	pre' post ten' sion ing
preamplifier	pre am' pli fi" er
preassembled	pre" as sem' bled
prebid	pre' bid
prebid conference	pre' bid con' fer ence
precast concrete	pre cast' con' crete
precedence diagram	prec' e dence di' a gram
precipitation	pre cip' i ta' tion
precipitator	pre cip' i ta" tor
precision	pre ci' sion
precompressed zone	pre" com pressed' zone"
preconsolidation	pre" con sol" i da' tion
preconstruction	pre" con struc' tion
precontract	pre con' tract
precoring	pre cor' ing
precure	pre cure'
precut	pre cut'
predecorated	pre dec' o rat" ed
predella	pre del' la
preengineered structure	pre en" gin neered' struc' ture
prefab	pre' fab"
prefabricate	pre fab' ri cate"
prefabricated	pre fab' ri cat" ed
prefabrication	pre" fab ri ca' tion
prefecture	pre' fec ture
preferred angle	pre ferred' an' gle
prefilter	pre' fil ter
prefinished	pre fin' ished
preformed	pre' formed'
preformed joint seal	pre' formed' joint' seal
preglazed	pre glazed'
preheat	pre heat'
preheat coil	pre heat' coil"
preheating	pre heat' ing
prehung	pre hung'
preliminary	pre lim' i nar" y

preloading	pre load' ing
premature stiffening	pre" ma ture' stif' fen ing
premiated	pre' mi at" ed
premises	prem' ises
premium	pre' mi um
premium grade	pre' mi um grade"
premix	pre mix'
premixed	pre mixed'
premolded	pre mold' ed
premounted tile sheets	pre mount' ed tile' sheets"
preparation	prep" a ra' tion
preplaced-aggregate concrete	pre placed' ag' gre gate con' crete
prepolymer	pre pol' y mer
prequalification	pre" qual i fi ca' tion
prerinse spray	pre rinse' spray"
presbytery	pres' by ter" y
prescriptive specification	pre scrip' tive spec' i fi ca' tion
present value	pres' ent val' ue
preservation	pres" er va' tion
preservative	pre serv' a tive
preshimmed	pre shimmed'
preshrunk	pre shrunk'
pressbrake	press' brake"
pressed	pressed
pressure	pres' sure
pressure drop	pres' sure drop"
pressure-injected footing	pres' sure in jec' ted foot' ing
pressure-locked grating	pres' sure locked" grat' ing
pressure-reducing valve	pres' sure re duc' ing valve"
pressure-relief damper	pres' sure re lief' damp' er
pressure relief valve	pres' sure re lief' valve"
pressure-relieving joint	pres' sure re liev' ing joint"
pressure-sensing device	pres' sure sens' ing de vice'
pressure-sensitive	pres' sure sen' si tive
pressure-treated lumber	pres' sure treat' ed lum' ber
pressurized	pres' sur ized"
prestained	pre stained'
prestress	pre stress'
prestressed concrete	pre' stressed con' crete
prestressing	pre' stress ing
pretensioned concrete	pre ten' sioned con' crete
pretensioning	pre ten' sion ing

pretinning	pre tin' ning
pretrial	pre" tri' al
pretrimmed	pre trimmed'
prevailing wages	pre vail' ing wa' ges
primary air	pri' ma ry air"
primary branch	pri' ma ry branch"
primary colorant	pri' ma ry col' or ant
primary colors	pri' ma ry col' ors
prime	prime
prime contract	prime' con' tract
prime contractor	prime' con' trac tor
primer	prim' er
primer-sealer	prim' er seal' er
priming	prim' ing
princess posts	prin' cess posts"
principal	prin' ci pal
principal-in-charge	prin' ci pal in charge'
principle	prin' ci ple
printer	print' er
printout	print' out
priory	pri' o ry
prism	prism
prismatic	pris mat' ic
prismoidal formula	pris moi' dal for' mu la
prison lock	pris' on lock"
privacy	pri' va cy
privacy fence	pri' va cy fence"
privacy set	pri' va cy set"
private	pri vate
private stairway	pri' vate stair' way
privity	priv' i ty
probability	prob" a bil' i ty
process	proc' ess
Proctor compaction test	Proc' tor com pac' tion test
producer	pro duc' er
product	prod' uct
productivity	pro" duc tiv' i ty
professional	pro fes' sion al
profile	pro' file
profitability	prof" it a bil' i ty
program	pro' gram
programming	pro' gram ming

progress payment	prog' ress pay' ment
progressive	pro gres' sive
progressive failure	pro gres' sive fail' ure
project	proj' ect
project management	proj' ect man' age ment
project manager	proj' ect man a ger
project manual	proj' ect man' u al
project representative	proj' ect rep" re sen' ta tive
projected	pro ject' ed
projected window	pro ject' ed win' dow
projecting	pro ject' ing
projection	pro jec' tion
projector	pro jec' tor
projet	pro' jet"
promenade	prom" e nade'
promisee	prom" is ee'
promisor	prom' i sor'
promissory note	prom' is so" ry note"
proof	proof
propagance	prop' a gance
propane	pro' pane
propeller fan	pro pel' ler fan"
property	prop' er ty
property insurance	prop' er ty in sur' ance
property line	prop' er ty line"
property-line wall	prop' er ty line" wall"
propinquity	pro pin' qui ty
proportion	pro por' tion
proportional	pro por' tion al
proportional limit	pro por' tion al lim' it
proportioning	pro por' tion ing
proposal	pro pos' al
proprietary	pro pri' e tar" y
proprietorship	pro pri' e tor ship"
propylene	pro' pyl ene"
proration	pro ra' tion
proscenium	pro sce' ni um
proscenium arch	pro sce' ni um arch"
prospect	pros' pect
prospectus	pro spec' tus
prostyle	pro' style
protected	pro tect' ed

protected opening	pro tect' ed o' pen ing
protection	pro tec' tion
protective	pro tec' tive
protective covenant	pro tec' tive cov' e nant
prototype	pro' to type"
protractor	pro trac' tor
protrusion	pro tru' sion
proved pilot	proved' pi' lot
proxemics	prox e' mics
proximal storage	prox' i mal stor' age
proximate cause	prox' i mate" cause"
proximity switch	prox im' i ty switch"
proxylin	prox' y lin
pry bar	pry' bar"
psychiatric	psy" chi at' ric
psychosocial	psy" cho so' cial
psychrograph	psy' chro graph"
psychrometer	psy chrom' e ter
psychrometric chart	psy" chro met' ric chart'
psychrometrics	psy" chro met' rics
psychrometry	psy chrom' e try
public-address system	pub' lic ad dress' sys' tem
public corridor	pub' lic cor' ri dor
public housing	pub' lic hous' ing
public way	pub' lic way
puckering	puck' er ing
puddle	pud' dle
puddle weld	pud' dle weld"
puddling	pud' dling
pueblo	pueb' lo
pugging	pug' ging
pull	pull
pull bar	pull' bar"
pull box	pull' box"
pull-chain operator	pull' chain' op' er a" tor
pull-down utility shelf	pull' down" u til' i ty shelf"
pull hardware	pull' hard' ware"
pulley	pul' ley
pulling	pull' ing
pulpit	pul' pit
pulpitum	pul' pi tum
pulsation absorber	pul sa' tion ab sorb' er

pulverize	pul' ver ize"
pulvinated	pul' vi nat" ed
pumice	pum' ice
pumice block	pum' ice block"
pump	pump
pumpability	pump" a bil' i ty
pumpable	pump' a ble
pumped	pumped
pumped concrete	pumped' con' crete
pumping	pump' ing
punch	punch
punch list	punch' list"
puncheon	pun' cheon
punching	punch' ing
punching shear	punch' ing shear"
puncture resistance	punc' ture re sist' ance
punty	punt' y
purchase order	pur' chase or' der
purchaser	pur' chas er
pure coat	pure' coat"
purfled	pur' fled
purge	purge
purger	purg' er
purging	purg' ing
purity	pu' ri ty
purlin	pur' lin
purpleheart	pur' ple heart"
push bar	push' bar"
push button	push' but' ton
push-in-type soap dispenser	push' in' type" soap dis pen' ser
push plate	push' plate"
push-pull cabinet lock	push' pull' cab' i net lock
pusher	push' er
putlog	put' og"
putty	put' ty
pylon	py' lon
pyramid	pyr' a mid
pyramidal	py ram' i dal
pyranometer	pyr" a nom' e ter
pyrgeometer	pyrg" e om' e ter
pyrheliometer	pyr" he li om' e ter
pyrite	py' rite

pyrobitumen	py" ro bi tu' men
pyrolysis	py rol' y sis
pyrolytic action	py" ro lyt' ic ac' tion
pyrometer	py rom' e ter
pyroxylin	py rox' y lin
pyrradiometer	pyr rad' i om' e ter

Q

quad	quad
quadra	quad' ra
quadrangle	quad' ran" gle
quadrant	quad' rant
quadrel	quad' rel
quadrilateral	quad" ri lat' e ral
quadripartite	quad" ri par' tite
quadripartite vault	quad' ri par' tite vault"
quadrominium	quad" ro min' i um
qualification	qual" i fi ca' tion
quality assurance	qual' i ty as sur' ance
quality control	qual' i ty con trol'
quantify	quan' ti fy"
quantity	quan' ti ty
quantity takeoff	quan' ti ty take' off
quarrel	quar' rel
quarried	quar' ried
quarry	quar' ry
quarry-faced	quar' ry faced"
quarry run	quar' ry run"
quarry tile	quar' ry tile"
quarrying	quar' ry ing
quarter bend	quar' ter bend"
quarter-pace	quar' ter pace"
quarter point	quar' ter point"
quarter round	quar' ter round"
quartered	quar' ter ed
quartered grain	quar' ter ed grain"
quartering	quar' ter ing
quartersawing	quar' ter saw" ing
quartersawn	quar' ter sawn"
quartz	quartz
quartz-iodine lamp	quartz' i' o dine" lamp"

quartzite	quartz' ite
quartzitic	quartz it' ic
quatrefoil	quat' re foil"
Queen Anne	Queen' Anne'
Queen Anne arch	Queen' Anne' arch"
queen closer	queen' clos' er
queen-post truss	queen' post" truss
queen truss	queen' truss"
quench	quench
quenched	quenched
quenching	quench' ing
quick-connect coupling	quick' con nect' cou' pling
quick drying	quick' dry' ing
quick-ship	quick' ship"
quick sweep	quick' sweep
quicklime	quick' lime"
quilt insulation	quilt' in su la' tion
quilted fabric	quilt' ed fab' ric
quilting	quilt' ing
quincunx	quin' cunx
quirk	quirk
quirk molding	quirk' mold' ing
quitclaim deed	quit' claim" deed"
quoin	quoin
Quonset™ hut	Quon' set hut"
quota sampling	quo' ta sam' pling
quotation	quo ta' tion

R

R lamp	R' lamp"
R value	R' val' ue
rab	rab
rabbet	rab' bet
raceway	race' way"
rack	rack
racked	racked
racking	rack' ing
radial	ra' di al
radial arch roof	ra' di al arch' roof"
radial-arm saw	ra' di al arm' saw"
radial brick	ra' di al brick"

radial rubber flooring	ra' di al rub' ber floor' ing
radial saw	ra' di al saw"
radially-cut grating	ra' di al ly cut grat' ing
radian	ra' di an
radiance	ra' di ance
radiant energy	ra' di ant en' er gy
radiant flux	ra' di ant flux"
radiant flux density	ra' di ant flux" den' si ty
radiant glass	ra' di ant glass"
radiant heater	ra' di ant heat' er
radiating chapels	ra' di ant chap' els
radiation	ra" di a' tion
radiation-shielding concrete	ra" di a' tion shield' ing con' crete
radiator	ra' di a" tor
radii	ra' di i
radioactive	ra" di o ac' tive
radioactivity	ra" di o ac tiv' i ty
radiographic	ra" di o graph' ic
radiography	ra" di og' ra phy
radioisotopic	ra" di o i" so top' ic
radiology	ra" di ol' o gy
radiometer	ra" di om' e ter
radiometric	ra" di o met' ric
radiometry	ra" di om' e try
radius	ra' di us
radius edge	ra' di us edge"
radius of gyration	ra' di us of gy ra' tion
radius rod	ra' di us rod"
radon	ra' don
raft foundation	raft' foun da' tion
rafter	raf' ter
rafter seat	raf' ter seat"
rag felt	rag' felt"
rag-rolling	rag' rol' ling
raggle	rag' gle
ragwork	rag' work"
rail	rail
railing	rail' ing
railroading	rail' road" ing
rain leader	rain' lead' er
rain screen	rain' screen"
rainbow	rain' bow"

rainfall frequency	rain' fall" fre' quen cy
rainproof	rain' proof"
rainwater piping	rain' wa" ter pip' ing
raise	raise
raised grain	raised' grain"
raised letters	raised' let' ters
raising	rais' ing
rake	rake
rake molding	rake' mold' ing
raked joint	raked' joint"
raker	rak' er
raking bond	rak' ing bond"
raking out	rak' ing out"
ramie	ram' ie
rammed earth	rammed' earth'
rammer	ram' mer
ramming	ram' ming
ramp	ramp
rampant arch	ram' pant arch"
rampant vault	ram' pant vault"
rampart	ram' part
ramped	ramped
rance	rance
ranch house	ranch' house"
random	ran' dom
random ashlar	ran' dom ash' lar
random error	ran' dom er' ror
random match	ran' dom match"
random-sheared carpet	ran' dom sheared" car' pet
random spacing	ran' dom spac' ing
randomization	ran" dom i za' tion
range	range
range hood	range' hood"
range line	range' line"
ranged rubble	ranged' rub' ble
ranger	rang' er
rangework	range' work"
ranging bond	rang' ing bond"
rapid-curing asphalt	rap' id cur' ing as' phalt
rapid-start lamp	rap' id start' lamp
raschel knit	ras' chel knit"
rasp	rasp

raster	ras' ter
rat stop	rat' stop"
rat-tail hinge	rat' tail" hinge"
ratchet	ratch' et
ratchet-lever hoist	ratch' et lev' er hoist"
ratchet nail	ratch' et nail
rate	rate
rate of flow	rate' of flow"
rate of rise	rate' of rise"
rated load	rat' ed load"
rated speed	rat' ed speed"
rating	rat' ing
ratio	ra' tio
rattan	rat tan'
rattrap bond	rat' trap" bond"
ravel	rav' el
raveling	rav' el ing
rawlplug	rawl' plug"
ray	ray
Raymond pile	Ray' mond pile"
rayon	ray' on
Rayonnant style	Ray' on nant" style"
raze	raze
reach-in refrigerator	reach' in" re frig' er a" tor
reactance	re ac' tance
reactant	re ac' tant
reaction	re ac' tion
reactive aggregate	re ac' tive ag' gre gate
reading-room	read' ing room"
readjustment	re" ad just' ment
readvertisement	re" ad ver tise' ment
ready-mixed concrete	read' y mixed' con' crete
real estate	real' es tate'
real property	real' prop' er ty
Realtor™	Re' al tor
ream	ream
reamed	reamed
reamer	ream' er
reaming	ream' ing
rear yard	rear' yard"
reassessed	re as sessed'
rebar	re' bar

rebate	re' bate
rebidding	re bid' ding
rebound	re' bound
receding color	re ced' ing co' lor
receivables	re ceiv' a bles
receiver	re ceiv' er
receptacle	re cep' ta cle
receptor	re cep' tor
recess	re' cess
recessed	re' cessed
recessed cup dispenser	re' cessed cup" dis pens' er
recessed fixture	re' cessed fix' ture
recharge	re charge'
recharging	re charg' ing
reciprocal	re cip' ro cal
reciprocating	re cip' ro cat" ing
reciprocity	rec" i proc' i ty
recirculated	re cir' cu lat" ed
recirculating	re cir' cu lat" ing
recirculation	re" cir cu la' tion
reclining chair	re clin' ing chair"
recommendation	rec" om men da' tion
reconditioned	re" con di' tioned
reconstructed	re" con struc' ted
record drawing	re' cord draw' ing
recording	re cord' ing
recovering	re cov' er ing
recovery	re cov' er y
recrystallized limestone	re crys' tal lized" lime' stone"
rectangle	rec' tan" gle
rectangular	rec tan' gu lar
rectifier	rec' ti fi" er
rectilinear	rec" ti lin' e ar
rectory	rec' to ry
recycle	re cy' cle
red brass	red' brass"
red cedar	red' ce' dar
Red Levanto	Red' Le van' to
redevelopment	re" de vel' op ment
redraw	re draw'
reducer	re duc' er
reducing agent	re duc' ing a" gent

reduction	re duc' tion
redundant	re dun' dant
redwood	red' wood"
reed	reed
reed-and-tie molding	reed' and tie' mold' ing
reeding	reed' ing
reedmark	reed' mark
reek	reek
reel-and-bead molding	reel' and bead' mold' ing
reentrant corner	re en' trant cor' ner
refectory	re fec' to ry
reference	ref' er ence
refined	re fined'
refinishing	re fin' ish ing
reflectance	re flect' ance
reflected	re flect' ed
reflected ceiling plan	re flect' ed ceil' ing plan"
reflected glare	re flect' ed glare"
reflection	re flec' tion
reflective	re flec' tive
reflective insulation	re flec' tive in" su la' tion
reflectivity	re" flec tiv' i ty
reflectometer	re" flec tom' e ter
reflectometry	re" flec tom' et ry
reflector	re flec' tor
refracted	re fract' ed
refraction	re frac' tion
refractory	re frac' to ry
refrigerant	re frig' er ant
refrigerated	re frig' er at" ed
refrigerating	re frig' er at" ing
refrigeration	re frig" er a' tion
refrigerator	re frig' er a" tor
refuge area	ref' uge ar' e a
refusal	re fus' al
refuse	ref' use
Regal Gray	Re' gal Gray"
Regal Midnight	Re' gal Mid' night
Regal Red	Re' gal Red"
Regal Rose	Re' gal Rose"
Regal Russet	Re' gal Rus' set
Regency	Re' gen cy

register	reg' is ter
registered architect	reg' is tered arc' hi tect
registration equipment	reg" is tra tion e quip' ment
reglet	reg' let
regrading	re grad' ing
regrate	re grate'
regression	re gres' sion
regula	reg' u la
regulator	reg' u la" tor
rehabilitation	re" ha bil" i ta' tion
reheat	re heat'
reheat system	re' heat" sys' tem
reheating	re heat' ing
reimbursable	re" im burs' a ble
reimbursable expense	re" im burs' a ble ex' pense
reinforced	re" in forced'
reinforced concrete	re" in forced' con' crete
reinforced-grouted brick masonry	re" in forced' grout' ed brick mas' on ry
reinforcement	re" in force' ment
reinforcing bar	re" in forc' ing bar
reinforcing mesh	re" in forc' ing mesh"
rejection	re jec' tion
rejection of work	re jec' tion of work"
relamped	re lamped'
relamping	re lamp' ing
related trades	re lat' ed trades"
relative compaction	rel' a tive com pac' tion
relative humidity	rel' a tive hu mid' i ty
relaxation	re" lax a' tion
relay	re' lay
release agent	re lease' a' gent
release of lien	re lease' of lien"
release paper	re lease' pa' per
reliability	re li" a bil' i ty
reliction	re lic' tion
relief	re lief'
relief damper	re lief' damp' er
relief map	re lief' map"
relief valve	re lief' valve"
relieve	re lieve'
relieved work	re lieved' work"

relieving arch	re liev' ing arch"
relievo	re lie' vo
relocatable	re" lo cat' a ble
relocatable partition	re" lo cat' a ble par ti' tion
relocate	re lo' cate
remainder	re main' der
Remington Gray	Rem' ing ton Gray"
remnant	rem' nant
remodeled	re mod' eled
remodeling	re mod' el ing
remoldability	re mold" a bil' i ty
remolded soil	re mold' ed soil"
remote	re mote'
remote-control wiring	re mote' con trol' wir' ing
removable mullion	re mov' a ble mul' lion
Renaissance	Ren" ais sance'
render	ren' der
rendering	ren' der ing
rendition	ren di' tion
rendu	ren' du
renewable	re new' a ble
renovation	ren" o va' tion
rentable	rent' a ble
rental	rent' al
repair	re pair'
repeat	re peat'
repeatability	re peat' a bil' i ty
replacement	re place' ment
replica	rep' li ca
replication	rep" li ca' tion
repointing	re point' ing
repose	re pose'
repoussé	re pous se'
repp	repp
repro drafting	re' pro draft' ing
reprocessed	re proc' essed
reproducible	re" pro duc' i ble
reproduction	re" pro duc' tion
reprographic	rep" ro graph' ic
reprography	re prog' ra phy
reradiation	re ra" di a' tion
reredos	rere' dos

rerolled steel	re' rolled steel"
reroofing	re roof' ing
resaw	re saw'
resawed face	re sawed' face"
rescind	re scind'
reseau	re seau'
reserve	re serve'
reservoir	res' er voir"
resetting	re set' ting
reshoring	re shor' ing
residence	res' i dence
residential	res" i den' tial
residual	re sid' u al
residual deflection	re sid' u al de flec' tion
residual stress	re sid' u al stress"
resilience	re sil' ience
resiliency	re sil' ien cy
resilient channel	re sil' ient chan' nel
resilient-floor layer	re sil' ient floor" lay' er
resilient flooring	re sil' ient floor' ing
resilient tile	re sil' ient tile"
resiliently	re sil' ient ly
resin	res' in
resin-bonded	res' in bond' ed
resin-coated	res' in coat' ed
resin-emulsion paint	res' in e mul' sion paint
resin-impregnated wood	res' in im preg' nat ed wood
resinoid	res' in oid"
resinous	res' in ous
resist	re sist'
resistance	re sist' ance
resistance brazing	re sist' ance braz' ing
resistance welding	re sist' ance weld' ing
resistivity	re" sis tiv' i ty
resistor	re sis' tor
resite	res' ite
resitol	res' i tol
resol	re sol'
resolution	res" o lu' tion
resonance	res' o nance
resonant	res' o nant
resonant frequency	res' o nant fre' quen cy

resonant load	res' o nant load"
resonate	res' o nate
resonator	res' o na tor
resorcinol	res or' cin ol"
resorcinol adhesive	res or' cin ol" ad he' sive
resources	re' sources
respirator	res' pi ra" tor
respond	re spond'
response	re sponse'
responsibility	re spon" si bil' i ty
restaurant	res' tau rant
restitution	res" ti tu' tion
restoration	res' to ra' tion
restretch	re stretch'
restriction	re stric' tion
restrictive covenant	re stric' tive cov' e nant
resubmission	re" sub mis' sion
resubmitted	re" sub mit' ted
resultant of forces	re sult' ant of forces'
resurfacing	re sur' fac ing
retable	re ta' ble
retainage	re tain' age
retained earnings	re tained' earn' ings
retainer	re tain' er
retaining wall	re tain' ing wall"
retard	re tard'
retardant	re tard' ant
retardation	re" tar da' tion
retarded hemihydrate	re tard' ed hem" i hy' drate
retarder	re tard' er
retempering	re tem' per ing
retention	re ten' tion
reticulate	re tic' u late"
reticulated	re tic' u lat" ed
reticulation	re tic" u la' tion
retractable	re tract' a ble
retrochoir	ret' ro choir"
retrofit	ret' ro fit"
retrogradation	ret" ro gra da' tion
retroreflection	ret" ro re flec' tion
retroreflector	ret" ro re flec' tor
retting	ret' ting

return	re turn'
return air	re turn' air"
return-air intake	re turn' air" in' take
reveal	re veal'
reverberant	re ver' ber ant
reverberation	re ver" ber a' tion
reverse	re verse'
reverse bevel	re verse' bev' el
reverse box match	re verse' box" match"
reverse diamond match	re verse' dia' mond match
reverse-engraved	re verse' en graved'
reversible lock	re vers' i ble lock"
reversion	re ver' sion
revertment	re vert' ment
revet	re vet'
revetment	re vet' ment
revibration	re" vi bra' tion
revision	re vi' sion
Revival style	Re viv' al style
revocation	rev" o ca' tion
revolution	rev" o lu' tion
revolving	re volv' ing
revolving door	re volv' ing door"
rezoning	re zon' ing
rheology	rhe ol' o gy
rheostat	rhe' o stat
rheostatic control	rhe" o stat' ic con trol'
rhodium	rho' di um
rhomboid	rhom' boid
rhombus	rhom' bus
rib	rib
rib lath	rib' lath"
rib weave	rib' weave"
riband	rib' and
ribband-back	rib' band" back"
ribbed arch	ribbed' arch"
ribbing	rib' bing
ribbon	rib' bon
ribbon process	rib' bon proc' ess
ribbon strip	rib' bon strip"
ribbon-stripe veneer	rib' bon stripe" ve neer'
rice brush	rice brush"

rich mix	rich' mix"
Richter scale	Rich' ter scale"
ride	ride
ridge	ridge
ridge beam	ridge' beam"
ridge course	ridge' course"
ridge roll	ridge' roll"
ridge roof	ridge' roof"
ridgeboard	ridge' board"
ridgecap	ridge' cap"
ridgepiece	ridge' piece"
ridging	ridg' ing
Rietveld, Gerrit	Riet' veld, Ger' rit
rift	rift
rift cut	rift' cut"
rift plane	rift' plane"
rift sawn	rift' sawn"
rift-sliced	rift' sliced"
rig	rig
rigger	rig' ger
rigging	rig' ging
right-hand door	right' hand' door"
right-hand stairway	right' hand' stair' way
right triangle	right' tri' an" gle
right-of-way	right' of way"
rigid	rig' id
rigid conduit	rig' id con' duit
rigid connection	rig' id con nec' tion
rigid frame	rig' id frame"
rigid insulation	rig' id in" su la' tion
rigid urethane foam	rig' id u' re thane" foam
rigidity	ri gid' i ty
rim	rim
rim joist	rim' joist"
rim lock	rim' lock"
rime	rime
rinceau	rin ceau'
ring pull	ring' pull"
ring shake	ring' shake"
ring-shank nail	ring shank" nail
ringhole	ring' hole"
rink	rink

rip	rip
riparian	ri par' i an
ripper	rip' per
ripping size	rip' ping size"
ripple finish	rip' ple fin' ish
riprap	rip' rap
ripsaw	rip' saw"
rise	rise
rise and run	rise' and run'
riser	ris' er
rising damp	ris' ing damp"
rising hinge	ris' ing hinge"
rising pin	ris' ing pin
rive	rive
rivet	riv' et
riveted	riv' et ed
riveting	riv' et ing
road	road
roadbed	road' bed"
roadside	road' side"
roadway	road' way"
rock	rock
rock asphalt	rock' as' phalt
rock core drilling	rock' core" dril' ling
rock crystal	rock' crys' tal
rock-cut	rock' cut"
rock dash	rock' dash"
rock socket	rock' soc' ket
rock wool	rock' wool"
rockbed	rock' bed"
rocking	rock' ing
rockpocket	rock' pock' et
Rockville White	Rock' ville White"
Rockwell hardness	Rock' well hard' ness
rococo	ro co' co
Rococo architecture	Ro co' co ar' chi tec" ture
rod	rod
rod bender	rod' bend' er
rod level	rod' lev' el
rod test	rod' test"
rodability	rod" a bil' i ty
rodding	rod' ding

rodent control	ro' dent con trol'
Rogers, Archibald C.	Rog' ers, Ar' chi bald" C.
Rojo Alicante	Ro' jo Al" i can' te
roll	roll
roll-and-fillet molding	roll' and fil' let mold' ing
roll-grooved	roll' grooved"
roll impression	roll' im pres' sion
roll mark	roll' mark"
roll-over arms	roll' o' ver arms"
roll roofing	roll' roof' ing
roll-top desk	roll' top" desk"
roll-up door	roll' up" door
roll warmer	roll' warm' er
rollback	roll' back"
rolled	rolled
rolled-in scratch	rolled' in scratch"
roller	roll' er
roller blinds	roll' er blinds"
roller catch	roll' er catch"
roller check	roll' er check"
roller guide	roll' er guide"
roller shades	roll' er shades"
roller strike	roll' er strike"
rolling	roll' ing
rollwork	roll' work"
Roman arch	Ro' man arch"
Roman brick	Ro' man brick"
Roman shade	Ro' man shade"
Romanesque	Ro" man esque'
Romex™	Rom' ex
rondelle	ron delle'
rood beam	rood' beam"
roof	roof
roof assembly	roof' as sem' bly
roof condition index	roof' con di' tion in' dex
roof covering	roof' cov' er ing
roof-deck	roof' deck"
roof decking	roof' deck' ing
roof framing	roof' fram' ing
roof jacket	roof' jac' ket
roof rise	roof' rise"
roof run	roof' run"

roofer	roof' er
roofer's knife	roof' er's knife"
roofing	roof' ing
roofline	roof' line"
rooftop	roof' top"
rooftree	roof' tree"
room	room
room ratio	room' ra' tio
root	root
rope	rope
rope calk	rope' calk"
rope molding	rope' mold' ing
ropiness	rop' i ness
ropy	rop' y
Rosa Aurora	Ros' a Au ro' ra
Rosa Vergado	Ros' a Ver ga' do
rosace	ro sace'
rose	rose
rose window	rose' win' dow
rosette	ro sette'
rosewood	rose' wood"
rosin	ros' in
rosin-sized sheathing	ros' in sized" sheath' ing
Rossi, Aldo	Ros' si, Al' do
Rosso Alberato	Ros' so Al ber a to
rostrum	ros' trum
rot	rot
rotary-cut veneer	ro' ta ry cut ve neer'
rotary cutting	ro' ta ry cut' ting
rotary float	ro' ta ry float"
rotary head	ro' ta ry head"
rotary-screen printing	ro' ta ry screen print' ing
rotary slicing	ro' ta ry slic' ing
rotation	ro ta' tion
rotation capacity	ro ta' tion ca pac' i ty
Roth, Alfred	Roth', Al' fred
rotisserie	ro tis' ser ie
roto operator	ro' to op' er a" tor
rotovinyl	ro' to vin" yl
rottenstone	rot' ten stone"
rotunda	ro tun' da
Rouge Fleuri	Rouge' Fleu ri'

rough buck	rough' buck
rough carpentry	rough' car' pen try
rough carriage	rough' car' raige
rough-cut	rough' cut
rough flooring	rough' floor' ing
rough grading	rough' grad' ing
rough-hewn	rough' hewn"
rough lumber	rough' lum' ber
rough opening	rough' o' pen ing
rough sawed	rough' sawed"
rough-sawn	rough' sawn"
roughback	rough' back"
roughcast	rough' cast"
roughened	rough' ened
roughing-in	rough' ing in'
roughometer	rough" om' e ter
roughstring	rough' string"
round	round
roundabout	round' a bout
roundel	roun' del
rout	rout
router	rout' er
router plane	rout' er plane"
routing	rout' ing
rover	rov' er
roving	rov' ing
row house	row' house"
rowlock	row' lock"
royal	roy' al
Royal Pearl	Roy' al Pearl
rubbed finish	rubbed' fin' ish
rubber	rub' ber
rubber insulation	rub' ber in" su la' tion
rubber silencer	rub' ber si' lenc er
rubber tile	rub' ber tile"
rubbing stone	rub' bing stone"
rubble	rub' ble
rubble ashlar	rub' ble ash' lar
rubble stone	rub' ble stone"
rubblework	rub' ble work"
rubrication	ru" bri ca' tion
rudenture	ru den' ture

Rudolph, Paul	Ru' dolph, Paul'
rule	rule
ruling pen	rul' ing pen"
run	run
rung	rung
runner	run' ner
running bond	run' ning bond"
running match	run' ning match"
running trim	run' ning trim"
runoff	run' off"
runout	run' out"
runway	run' way"
rupture	rup' ture
rush seat	rush' seat"
Russian	Rus' sian
rust	rust
rust joint	rust' joint"
rustic	rus' tic
rustic terrazzo	rus' tic ter raz' zo
rusticated	rus' ti cat" ed
rusticating	rus' ti cat" ing
rustication	rus" ti ca' tion
ruthenium	ru the' ni um
ruts	ruts
rya rug	ry' a rug'

S

S beam	S' beam"
S-trap	S' trap"
S-waves	S waves"
Saarinen, Eero	Saa' ri nen, Ee' ro
Saarinen, Eliel	Saa' ri nen, E' li el
saber saw	sa' ber saw"
sabin	sa' bin
Sabine's formula	Sa' bine's for' mu la
sabot	sab' ot
sack	sack
sack rub	sack' rub"
sacking	sack' ing
sacraria	sa crar' i a
sacrarium	sa crar' i um

sacrificial protection	sac" ri fi' cial pro tec' tion
sacristy	sac' ris ty
saddle	sad' dle
saddle-backed coping	sad' dle backed" cop' ing
saddle bar	sad' dle bar"
saddle board	sad' dle board"
saddle tie	sad' dle tie"
saddle valve	sad' dle valve"
saddleback	sad' dle back"
Safdie, Moshe	Saf' die, Mos' he
safe	safe
safe-deposit vault	safe' de pos' it vault"
safety	safe' ty
safety factor	safe' ty fac' tor
safety glass	safe' ty glass"
safety relief valve	safe' ty re lief' valve
safety tread	safe' ty tread"
safing	saf' ing
sag	sag
sagging	sag' ging
sailcloth	sail' cloth"
Saint Corneille	Saint' Cor neille'
salamander	sal' a man" der
salient corner	sa' li ent cor' ner
saline	sa' line
sally port	sal' ly port
salmon brick	salm' on brick"
salon	sa lon'
salt	salt
salt-box	salt' box"
salt-glazed brick	salt' glazed" brick
salt-glazed finish	salt' glazed" fin' ish
salvage	sal' vage
samp	samp
sample	sam' ple
sampling	sam' pling
san	san
sanatorium	san" a to' ri um
sanctuary	sanc' tu ar y
sand	sand
sand-casting	sand' cast' ing
sand-dry	sand' dry"

sand finish	sand' fin' ish
sand-float finish	sand' float" fin' ish
sand grout	sand' grout"
sand interceptor	sand' in ter cep' tor
sand-rubbed finish	sand' rubbed' fin' ish
sand trap	sand' trap"
sandarac	san' da rac"
sandblast	sand' blast"
sandblaster	sand' blast" er
sandblasting	sand' blast" ing
sanded	sand' ed
sanded plaster	sand' ed plas' ter
sander	sand' er
sanding	sand' ing
sanding sealer	sand' ing seal' er
sandpaper	sand' pa" per
sandstone	sand' stone"
sandwich construction	sand' wich con struc' tion
sandy clay	sand' clay"
sandy clay loam	sand' clay" loam
sanitarium	san" i tar' i um
sanitary	san' i tar" y
sanitary base	san' i tar" y base"
sanitary cove	san' i tar" y cove"
sanitary sewer	san' i tar" y sew' er
sanitary tee	san' i tar" y tee
sanitize	san' i tize
sap	sap
sapele	sa pe' le
saponification	sa pon" i fi ca' tion
saponified rayon	sa pon' i fied ray' on
saponify	sa pon' i fy"
sapwood	sap' wood"
sarking	sark' ing
Sasaki, Hideo	Sa sak' i, Hid' e o
sash	sash
sash lift	sash' lift"
sash opening	sash' o' pen ing
sash stop	sash' stop"
sashless window	sash' less win' dow
sateen	sa teen'
satellite	sat' el lite"

satin	sat' in
satin finish	sat' in fin' ish
satinwood	sat' in wood"
satisfaction	sat" is fac' tion
saturant	sat' u rant
saturated	sat' u rat" ed
saturated air	sat' u rat" ed air"
saturated felt	sat' u rat" ed felt"
saturation	sat" u ra' tion
Sauer, Louis	Sau' er, Lou' is
sauna	sau' na
saw	saw
saw kerf	saw' kerf"
sawbuck	saw' buck"
sawcut	saw' cut"
sawdust	saw' dust"
sawed joint	sawed' joint"
sawhorse	saw' horse"
sawtooth roof	saw' tooth" roof"
sawyer	saw' yer
saxony	sax' o ny
scab	scab
scabbing	scab' bing
scabble	scab' ble
scabbled	scab' bled
scabbling	scab' bling
scaffold	scaf' fold
scaffolding	scaf' fold ing
scagliola	scagl io' la
scagliolist	scagl io' list
scale	scale
scale drawing	scale' drawing
scalene triangle	sca' lene tri' an gle
scaling	scal' ing
scallop	scal' lop
scalloped	scal' loped
scalloping	scal' lop ing
scalp	scalp
scalping	scalp' ing
scanner	scan' ner
scantling	scant' ling
scarcement	scarce' ment

scarf	scarf
scarf joint	scarf' joint"
scarfed	scarfed
scarfing	scarf' ing
scarification	scar" i fi ca' tion
scarifier	scar' i fi" er
scarify	scar' i fy
scarifying	scar' i fy" ing
Scarpa, Carlo	Scarp' a, Car' lo
scatter rug	scat' ter rug"
scattering	scat' ter ing
scattering loss	scat' ter ing loss"
scena	sce' na
scene	scene
scenery	scen' er y
scenic	sce' nic
schedule	sched' ule
schedule of values	sched' ule of val' ues
scheduling	sched' ul ing
schematic	sche mat' ic
schematic design	sche mat' ic de sign'
scheme	scheme
schiffli embroidery	schiff' li em broi' der y
Schindler, Rudolph	Schind' ler, Ru' dolph
schist	schist
school	school
schoolroom	school' room"
Schwedler dome	Schwed' ler dome"
scissoring	scis' sor ing
scissors truss	scis' sors truss"
Scivek	Sciv' ek
sclerometer	scle rom' e ter
sconce	sconce
sconcheon	scon' cheon
scoop conveyor	scoop' con vey' or
score	score
scoreboard	score' board"
scoria	sco' ri a
scotch	scotch
Scotchgard™	Scotch' gard"
scotia	sco' tia
scotopic	sco top' ic

Scott Brown, Denise	Scott' Brown', De nise'
scour	scour
scouring	scour' ing
SCR brick	S' C' R' brick"
scrabbled rubble	scrab' bled rub' ble
scraffeto	scraf fet' o
scrap	scrap
scraped finish	scraped' fin' ish
scraper	scrap' er
scratch	scratch
scratch coat	scratch' coat"
scratch hardness test	scratch' hard' ness test
scratcher	scratch' er
scratches	scratch' es
scratching	scratch' ing
screed	screed
screeding	screed' ing
screen	screen
screen-back hardboard	screen' back" hard' board"
screen door catch	screen' door" catch
screenings	screen' ings
screw	screw
screw anchor	screw' an' chor
screw-on-bead	screw' on bead"
screw eye	screw' eye"
screw hook	screw' hook"
screw nail	screw' nail"
screwdriver	screw' driv" er
screwed joint	screwed' joint"
screwless knob	screw' less" knob"
scribe	scribe
scribed joint	scribed' joint"
scriber	scrib' er
scribing	scrib' ing
scrim	scrim
scroll	scroll
scroll arm	scroll' arm"
scroll-back chair	scroll' back" chair
scroll foot	scroll' foot"
scrollwork	scroll' work"
scrub sink	scrub' sink"
scrubber	scrub' ber

scuff	scuff
scullery	scul' ler y
scullery sink	scul' ler y sink"
sculpting	sculp' ting
sculptor	sculp' tor
sculptural	sculp' tur al
sculpture	sculp' ture
sculptured	sculp' tured
scum	scum
scumble	scum' ble
scumbling	scum' bling
scumming	scum' ming
scupper	scup' per
scutch	scutch
scuttle	scut' tle
seal	seal
seal coat	seal' coat"
sealant	seal' ant
sealed insulating glass	sealed' in' su lat" ing glass
sealer	seal' er
sealing	seal' ing
seam	seam
seamer	seam' er
seaming	seam' ing
seamless	seam' less
season crack	sea' son crack"
seasoned	sea' soned
seasoning	sea' son ing
seasoning check	sea' son ing check"
seat	seat
seat cut	seat' cut"
seating	seat' ing
second	sec' ond
second growth	sec' ond growth"
secondary air	sec' ond ar" y air"
secondary backing	sec' ond ar" y back' ing
secondary colors	sec' ond ar" y co' lors
seconds	sec' onds
secret nailing	se' cret nail' ing
secrétaire	sec" re taire'
secretary	sec' re tar" y
sectilia	sec til' i a

section	sec' tion
section modulus	sec' tion mod' u lus
sectional	sec' tion al
security	se cu' ri ty
sediment	sed' i ment
sedimentary	sed" i men' ta ry
sedimentary rock	sed" i men' ta ry rock"
sedimentation	sed" i men ta' tion
seediness	seed' i ness
seeds	seeds
seedy	seed' y
seep	seep
seepage	seep' age
seepage bed	seep' age bed"
Segal, Walter	Se' gal, Wal' ter
segment	seg' ment
segmental arch	seg men' tal arch"
segregation	seg" re ga' tion
seismic	seis' mic
seismic coefficient	seis' mic co" ef fi' cient
seismogram	seis' mo gram"
seismograph	seis' mo graph"
seismographic	seis" mo graph' ic
seismology	seis mol' ogy
seismometer	seis mom' e ter
seizing	seiz' ing
seizure	sei' zure
select	se lect'
selected bidder	se lect' ed bid' der
selenium	se le' ni um
self-adhesive	self' ad he' sive
self-ballasted	self' bal' last ed
self-clinching	self" clinch' ing
self-closing	self" clos' ing
self-contained	self' con tained"
self-desiccation	self' des" ic ca' tion
self-edged	self' edged"
self-energized	self" en' er gized"
self-extinguishing	self' ex tin' guish ing
self-furring	self' fur' ring
self-ignition	self' i g ni tion
self-leveling	self" lev' el ing

self-spacing	self" spac' ing
self-supporting	self" sup port' ing
self-tapping	self' tap' ping
self-vulcanizing	self" vul' can iz" ing
selvage	sel' vage
selvage edges	sel' vage edges"
semi-ambulatory	sem" i am' bu la to" ry
semiautomated	sem" i au' to mat" ed
semiautomatic	sem" i au" to mat' ic
semichord	sem" i chord"
semicircle	sem" i cir" cle
semicircular	sem" i cir' cu lar
semiconcealed closer	sem" i con cealed' clos' er
semidetached dwelling	sem" i de tached' dwel' ling
semidirect lighting	sem" i di rect' light' ing
semiflexible joint	sem" i flex' i ble joint"
semigloss	sem" i gloss"
semihollow	sem" i hol' low
semi-indirect lighting	sem" i in" di rect' light' ing
semiintermediate section	sem" i in" ter med' i ate sec' tion
semimatte tile	sem" i matte' tile"
semi-metric camera	sem" i met' ric cam' er a
seminar	sem' i nar"
seminary	sem' i nar" y
semipermanent	sem" i per' ma nent
semirigid	sem" i rig' id
semirigid plastic	sem" i rig' id plas' tic
semi-rubbed	sem" i rubbed'
semisolid asphalt	sem" i sol' id as' phalt
sensible cooling effect	sen' si ble cool' ing ef fect'
sensible heat	sen' si ble heat"
sensitivity	sen" si tiv' i ty
sensitizer	sen' si tiz" er
sensor	sen' sor
sensory	sen' so ry
separate	sep' a rate
separate contract	sep' a rate con' tract
separation	sep" a ra' tion
sepia	se' pi a
septfoil	sept' foil
septic tank	sep' tic tank"
sepulcher	sep' ul cher

sequence	se' quence
sequence match	se' quence match"
serging	serg' ing
series circuit	se' ries cir' cuit
Serpeggiante	Ser peg" gi an' te
serpentine	ser' pen tine"
serpentining	ser' pen tin" ing
serrated	ser' rat ed
serration	ser ra' tion
Sert, José Luis	Sert', Jo se' Lu is'
service counter door	serv' ice count' er door"
service disconnect	serv' ice dis' con nect
service drop	serv' ice drop"
service-entrance cable	serv' ice en' trance ca' ble
service panel	serv' ice pan' el
serviceability	serv" ice a bil' i ty
set	set
set-retardant coating	set' re tard' ant coat' ing
setback	set' back"
setscrew	set' screw"
settee	set tee'
setter	set' ter
setting bed	set' ting bed"
setting block	set' ting block"
setting shrinkage	set' ting shrink' age
settle	set' tle
settle-table	set' tle ta' ble
settlement	set' tle ment
settling	set' tling
severy	sev' er y
sewage	sew' age
sewage ejector	sew' age e jec' tor
sewer	sew' er
sewerage	sew' er age
sgraffito	sgraf fi' to
shack	shack
shade	shade
shade line	shade' line"
shadow	shad' ow
shadowgraph	shad' ow graph"
shaft	shaft
shafting	shaft' ing

shaftwall	shaft' wall"
shag carpet	shag' car' pet
shake	shake
Shaker furniture	Shak' er fur' ni ture
shakes	shakes
shaking test	shak' ing test"
shale	shale
shank	shank
Shantung	Shan' tung'
shanty	shan' ty
shape	shape
shaper	shap' er
shaping	shap' ing
shark fin	shark' fin"
sharks teeth	sharks' teeth"
sharp	sharp
sharpening	sharp' en ing
shatterproof	shat' ter proof"
shaving	shav' ing
she bolt	she' bolt'
sheaf-back chair	sheaf' back' chair"
shear	shear
shear connector	shear' con nec' tor
shear plane	shear' plane"
shear plate	shear' plate"
shear-plate connector	shear' plate" con nec' tor
shear splice	shear' splice"
shear strength	shear' strength"
shearhead	shear' head"
sheariness	shear' i ness
shearing	shear' ing
shearing strength	shear' ing strength"
shearwall	shear' wall"
sheathe	sheathe
sheathed cable	sheathed' ca' ble
sheathing	sheath' ing
sheave	sheave
shed	shed
shed roof	shed' roof"
shedding	shed' ding
sheen	sheen
sheepsfoot roller	sheeps' foot" rol' ler

sheer	sheer
sheet	sheet
sheet metal screw	sheet' met' al screw
sheet metal work	sheet' met' al work
sheet molding compound	sheet' mold' ing com' pound
sheet pile	sheet' pile"
sheet piling	sheet' pil' ing
sheeting	sheet' ing
Sheetrock™	Sheet' rock"
shelf	shelf
shelf angle	shelf' an' gle
shelf life	shelf' life"
shell	shell
shellac	shel lac'
shelter	shel' ter
shelving	shelv' ing
sherardizing	sher' ard iz" ing
Sheraton chair	Sher' a ton chair"
sheveret	shev e ret'
shield-back chair	shield' back" chair"
shielded	shield' ed
shielding	shield' ing
shim	shim
shingle	shin' gle
shingle style	shin' gle style"
shingling	shin' gling
shiplap	ship' lap"
shiplapped siding	ship' lapped" sid' ing
shirred	shirred
shirring	shirr' ing
shivered edge	shiv' ered edge"
shockproof	shock' proof"
shoe	shoe
shoe molding	shoe' mold' ing
shoji screen	sho' ji screen"
shoot	shoot
shooting board	shoot' ing board"
shop	shop
shop drawing	shop' draw' ing
shop painting	shop' paint' ing
shop primer	shop prim' er
shop weld	shop' weld"

shopping center	shop' ping cen' ter
shopwork	shop' work"
shore	shore
Shore "A" hardness	Shore' "A" hard' ness
Shore hardness number	Shore' hard' ness num' ber
shoring	shor' ing
short	short
short circuit	short' cir' cuit
short column	short' col' umn
short-term load	short' term" load
shortness	short' ness
shot	shot
shot-ground finish	shot' ground" fin' ish
shot-sawn	shot' sawn"
shotblasting	shot' blast" ing
shotcrete	shot' crete"
shotcreting	shot' cret" ing
shoulder	shoul' der
shouldered arch	shoul' dered arch"
shouldering	shoul' der ing
shoved joint	shoved' joint"
shoving	shov' ing
show rafter	show' raft' er
shower	show' er
shower-bath drain	show' er bath' drain"
shower head	show' er head"
shower pan	show' er pan"
showroom	show' room"
shrine	shrine
shrink	shrink
shrinkage	shrink' age
shrinkage cracking	shrink' age crack' ing
shrinkage limit	shrink' age lim' it
shrub	shrub
shutter	shut' ter
shutter bar	shut' ter bar"
shuttering	shut' ter ing
siamese	si" a mese'
siamese connection	si" a mese' con nec' tion
siamoise	sia moise'
sick building syndrome	sick' build' ing syn' drome
side chair	side' chair"

side stake	side' stake"
sideboard	side' board"
sideflash	side' flash"
sidelight	side' light"
sidesway	side' sway"
sidewalk	side' walk"
sidewall	side' wall"
sidewall sprinkler	side' wall" sprin' kler
sideyard	side' yard"
siding	sid' ing
Siegel, Robert	Sie' gel, Rob' ert
sienna	si en' na
Sierra Madre	Si er' ra Mad' re
Sierra White	Si er' ra White"
sieve analysis	sieve' a nal' y sis
sight glass	sight' glass"
sightline	sight' line"
sign	sign
signage	sign' age
signal	sig' nal
signal operation	sig' nal op" er a' tion
silane	sil' ane
silanol polymer	sil' a nol pol' y mer
silencer	si' lenc er
silhouette	sil" hou ette'
silica	sil' i ca
silica fume	sil' i ca fume
silica gel	sil' i ca gel"
silicate	sil' i cate
siliceous	si li' ceous
silicon	sil' i con
silicon bronze	sil' i con bronze"
silicon carbide	sil' i con car' bide
silicone	sil' i cone
silicone sealant	sil' i cone seal' ant
siliconized	sil' i con ized"
siliconized polyester	sil' i con ized" pol' y es" ter
siliconized polymer	sil i con ized" pol' y mer
silk	silk
silk-screened	silk' screened"
silking	silk' ing
sill	sill

sill anchor	sill' an' chor
sill plate	sill' plate"
sillcock	sill' cock"
silo	si' lo
siloxane	si lox' ane
silt	silt
silting	silt' ing
siltstone	silt' stone"
silty clay	silt' y clay"
silty loam	silt' y loam"
silty sand	silt' y sand"
silver	sil' ver
silver brazing	sil' ver braz' ing
silver grain	sil' ver grain"
silver halide	sil' ver ha' lide
silvered-bowl lamp	sil' vered bowl" lamp
silverwood	sil' ver wood"
sima	si' ma
simple beam	sim' ple beam"
simply-supported beam	sim' ply sup port' ed beam
simulated	sim' u lat" ed
simulated stone	sim' u lat" ed stone"
simulation	sim" u la' tion
simulator	sim' u la" tor
sine	sine
sine wave	sine' wave"
singeing	singe' ing
single-acting door	sin' gle act' ing door"
single compartment sink	sin' gle com part' ment sink
single-duct system	sin' gle duct' sys' tem
single-family dwelling	sin' gle fam' i ly dwel' ling
single-hung window	sin' gle hung" win' dow
single phase	sin' gle phase"
single-pole switch	sin' gle pole" switch"
single proprietorship	sin' gle pro pri' e tor ship"
single-rabbet frame	sin' gle rab' bet frame"
single-weld joint	sin' gle weld " joint"
sink	sink
sinkage	sink' age
sinking	sink' ing
sintering	sin' ter ing
sintering grade	sin' ter ing grade"

sinusoidal	si" nus oi' dal
siphon	si' phon
siphoning	si' phon ing
Sirocco Green	Si roc' co Green"
sisal	si' sal
site	site
site drainage	site' drain' age
site furnishings	site' fur' nish ings
site plan	site' plan"
sitework	site' work"
siting	sit' ing
Sitka spruce	Sit' ka spruce'
sitz bath	sitz' bath"
six-cut finish	six' cut" fin' ish
size	size
sizing	siz' ing
skater's cracks	skat' er's cracks"
skein	skein
skein-dyed yarn	skein' dyed' yarn"
skeleton	skel' e ton
skeleton construction	skel' e ton con struc' tion
skene arch	ske' ne arch"
sketch	sketch
skew	skew
skew arch	skew' arch"
skewback	skew' back"
skewed	skewed
skewed beam	skewed' beam"
skid	skid'
Skidmore, Louis	Skid' more, Lou' is
skim	skim
skim coat	skim' coat"
skimmer	skim' mer
skimming	skim' ming
skimming tank	skim' ming tank"
skin	skin
skinning	skin' ning
skintled brickwork	skin' tled brick' work"
skip	skip
skirt	skirt
skirting	skirt' ing
skiving	skiv' ing

skotch fasteners	skotch' fas' ten ers
skydome	sky' dome"
skylight	sky' light"
skyscraper	sky' scrap" er
skyshaft	sky' shaft"
slab	slab
slab-on-grade	slab' on grade'
slab schedule	slab' sched' ule
slabbing	slab' bing
slabjacking	slab' jack" ing
slack	slack
slag	slag
slake	slake
slaking	slak' ing
slamming strip	slam' ming strip"
slant	slant
slant-top desk	slant' top' desk"
slat	slat
slat-back	slat' back"
slate	slate
slater's nails	slat' er's nails"
slating	slat' ing
sled runner	sled' run' ner
sledge	sledge
sleek	sleek
sleeper	sleep' er
sleepiness	sleep' i ness
sleeve	sleeve'
slenderness	slen' der ness
slenderness ratio	slen' der ness ra' tio
slicing cut	slic' ing cut
slick line	slick' line
slicker	slick' er
slide	slide
slider	slid' er
sliding door	slid' ing door"
sliding-door lock	slid' ing door lock"
sliding sash	slid' ing sash"
sliding window	slid' ing win' dow
slime	slime
slimline lamp	slim' line" lamp"
sling	sling

sling psychrometer	sling' psy chrom' e ter
slip	slip
slip form	slip' form"
slip forming	slip' form' ing
slip joint	slip' joint"
slip match	slip' match"
slip-resistant	slip' re sist' ant
slip sheet	slip' sheet"
slipcover	slip' cov er
slippage	slip' page
slitting	slit' ting
slop sink	slop' sink"
slope	slope
sloped footing	sloped' foot' ing
slot diffuser	slot' dif fus' er
slot weld	slot' weld
slotted angle	slot' ted an' gle
slotted-head	slot' ted head
sloughing	slough' ing
slow drying	slow dry' ing
slubbed fabric	slubbed' fab' ric
slubs	slubs
sludge	sludge
slug	slug
slum	slum
slump	slump
slump test	slump' test"
slurry	slur' ry
slurry wall	slur' ry wall"
slushed joint	slushed' joint"
small knot	small' knot"
smartwindows	smart' win" dows
smoke	smoke
smoke alarm	smoke' a larm'
smoke chamber	smoke' cham' ber
smoke detector	smoke' de tec' tor
smoke-developed rating	smoke' de vel' oped rat' ing
smoke screen	smoke' screen"
smoke shelf	smoke' shelf"
smoke vent	smoke' vent"
smoked	smoked
smokemeter	smoke' me" ter

smokeproof	smoke' proof"
smokeproof tower	smoke' proof" tow' er
smokestack	smoke' stack"
smokestop	smoke' stop"
smoking	smok' ing
smoldering	smol' der ing
smooth	smooth
smooth finish	smooth' fin' ish
smooth-surfaced	smooth' sur' faced
smudge	smudge
snack bar	snack' bar"
snagging	snag' ging
snake	snake
snaking	snak' ing
snap	snap
snap-off anchor	snap' off an' chor
snap tie	snap' tie"
sneck	sneck
snecked rubble	snecked' rub' ble
snips	snips
snow guard	snow' guard"
snow load	snow' load"
snow-melting	snow' melt' ing
soap	soap
soap bubble test	soap' bub' ble test
soaping	soap' ing
soapstone	soap' stone"
sociofugal	so" ci o fug' al
sociopetal	so" ci o pet' al
socket	sock' et
socketing	sock' et ing
socle	so' cle
sod	sod
soda-acid fire extinguisher	so' da ac' id fire" ex tin' guish er
soda ash	so' da ash"
soda fountain	so' da foun' tain
sodding	sod' ding
sodium bisulfate	so' di um bi sul' fate
sodium hydroxide	so' di um hy drox' ide
sodium hypochlorite	so' di um hy" po chlo' rite
sodium light	so' di um light"
sodium montmorillonite	so' di um mont" mo ril' lon ite"

sodium-vapor lamp	so' di um va' por lamp
sofa	so' fa
sofa-bed	so' fa bed'
soffit	sof' fit
soft clay	soft' clay"
soft mud process	soft' mud" pro' cess
soft rot	soft' rot"
soft solder	soft' sol' der
soft water	soft' wa' ter
softening point	soft' en ing point"
softness	soft' ness"
software	soft' ware"
softwood	soft' wood
soil	soil
soil-cement	soil" ce' ment
soil pipe	soil' pipe"
soil profile	soil' pro' file
soil stack	soil' stack
soil test	soil' test"
soil vent	soil' vent"
sol-air effect	sol' air' ef fect'
sol-air temperature	sol' air' tem' per a ture
solar altitude	so' lar al' ti tude
solar azimuth	so' lar az' i muth
solar collector	so' lar col lec' tor
solar constant	so' lar con' stant
solar heat	so' lar heat"
solar orientation	so' lar o" ri en ta' tion
solar screen	so' lar screen"
solar time	so' lar time"
solarium	so lar' i um
solarization	so" lar i za' tion
solder	sol' der
solder joint	sol' der joint"
solderability	sol" der a bil' i ty
soldering	sol' der ing
solderless connector	sol' der less con nec' tor
soldier	sol' dier
soldier arch	sol' dier arch"
soldier course	sol' dier course'
sole	sole
sole proprietorship	sole' pro pri' e tor ship"

solenoid	so' le noid"
solenoid valve	so' le noid" valve"
soleplate	sole' plate"
Soleri, Paolo	So le' ri, Pao' lo
solid	sol' id
solid bridging	sol' id bridg' ing
solid-core door	sol' id core' door"
solid modeling	sol' id mod' el ing
solid-mopping	sol' id mop' ping
solid struck	sol' id struck"
solid vinyl tile	sol' id vi' nyl tile
solidification	so lid" i fi ca' tion
solids	solids
solidus	sol' i dus
solifluction	so" li fluc' tion
solstice	sol' stice
solubility	sol" u bil' i ty
soluble	sol' u ble
solution	so lu' tion
solution-dyed yarn	so lu' tion dyed' yarn"
solvency	sol' ven cy
solvent	sol' vent
solvent welding	sol' vent weld' ing
solvent wiping	sol' vent wip' ing
sommer	som' mer
sone	sone
Soriano, Raphael	Sor" i an' o, Raph' a el
sound	sound
sound absorption	sound' ab sorp' tion
sound absorption coefficient	sound' ab sorp' tion co" ef fi' cient
sound-amplification system	sound' am" pli fi ca' tion sys' tem
sound attenuation	sound' at ten" u a' tion
sound-control booth	sound' con trol' booth"
sound-insulating glass	sound' in' su lat" ing glass
sound knot	sound' knot"
sound level	sound' lev' el
sound-level meter	sound' lev' el me' ter
sound power	sound' pow' er
sound power level	sound' pow' er lev' el
sound pressure	sound' pres' sure
sound pressure level	sound' pres' sure lev' el
sound-rated door	sound' rat' ed door"

sound transmission class	sound' trans mis' sion class"
sounding board	sound' ing board"
sounding well	sound' ing well"
soundness	sound' ness
soundproofing	sound' proof" ing
soutache	sou tache'
south-light roof	south' light' roof"
southern pine	south' ern pine"
spa	spa
space	space
space frame	space' frame
spaced column	spaced' col' umn
spacer	spac' er
spacing	spac' ing
spacing-to-mounting height ratio	spac' ing to mount' ing height ra' tio
Spackle™	Spack' le
spackling compound	spack' ling com' pound
spade bit	space' bit"
spade foot	spade' foot"
spading	spad' ing
spall	spall
spaller	spall' er
spalling	spal' ling
span	span
Span-deck™	Span' deck
spandrel	span' drel
spandrel beam	span' drel beam"
spandrel glass	span' drel glass"
Spanish architecture	Span' ish ar' chi tec" ture
spanpiece	span' piece"
spar	spar
spar varnish	spar' var' nish
sparge pipe	sparge' pipe"
spark arrester	spark' ar rest' er
sparpiece	spar' piece"
sparver	spar' ver
spatial	spa' tial
spatter	spat' ter
spatterdash	spat' ter dash"
spattering	spat' ter ing
special conditions	spe' cial con di' tions

special district	spe' cial dis' trict
special-purpose tile	spe' cial pur' pose tile
specialties	spe' cial ties
specific gravity	spe cif' ic grav' i ty
specific heat	spe cif' ic heat"
specification	spec" i fi ca' tion
specifier	spec' i fi" er
specimen	spec' i men
specks	specks
spectral	spec' tral
spectral emissivity	spec' tral em" is siv' i ty
spectrocolorimeter	spec" tro col" o rim' e ter
spectrometer	spec trom' e ter
spectrophotometer	spec" tro pho tom' e ter
spectrophotometry	spec" tro pho tom' e try
spectroradiometer	spec" tro ra" di om' e ter
spectroscopy	spec tros' co py
spectrum	spec' trum
spectrum locus	spec' trum lo' cus
specular	spec' u lar
specular angle	spec' u lar an' gle
speculative	spec' u la" tive
speech interference level	speech' in" ter fer' ence lev" el
speech privacy	speech" pri' va cy
speed	speed
spelter	spel' ter
spherical	spher' i cal
spier	spi' er
spigot	spig' ot
spike	spike
spike grid	spike' grid"
spike knot	spike' knot"
spike-plate connector	spike' plate con nec' tor
spile	spile
spill	spill
spindle	spin' dle
spindle-back chair	spin' dle back" chair
spine wall	spine' wall"
spinnerette	spin' ner ette"
spinning	spin' ning
spiral	spi' ral
spiral reinforcement	spi' ral re" in force' ment

spiral stair	spi' ral stair"
spiralled column	spi' ralled col' umn
spirally reinforced	spi' ral ly re" in forced'
spire	spire
spirit level	spir' it le' vel
spit	spit'
splashblock	splash' block"
splashboard	splash' board"
splat	splat
splatter finish	splat' ter fin' ish
splay	splay
splayed	splayed
splayed edge	splayed' edge"
splice	splice
splice plate	splice' plate"
splice point	splice' point"
spline	spline
spline miter	spline' mi' ter
splined flooring	splined' floor' ing
splint seat	splint' seat"
split	split
split astragal	split' as' tra gal
split-face block	split' face' block"
split frame	split' frame"
split-level	split' lev' el
split-ring connector	split' ring' con nec' tor
split truss	split' truss
splitter	split' ter
splitting	split' ting
splush carpet	splush' car' pet
spoil	spoil
spokeshave	spoke' shave"
sponge rubber	sponge' rub' ber
sponging	spong' ing
spontaneous combustion	spon ta' ne ous com bus' tion
spot	spot
spot elevation	spot' el" e va' tion
spot ground	spot' ground"
spot-mopping	spot' mop' ping
spot weld	spot' weld"
spot welding	spot' weld' ing
spotlight	spot' light"

spotting	spot' ting
spout	spout
spray booth	spray' booth"
spray-on insulation	spray' on" in" su la' tion
spray paint	spray' paint"
spray-painting	spray' paint' ing
spray-pond roof	spray' pond" roof
sprayed	sprayed
sprayed fireproofing	sprayed' fire' proof" ing
spraying	spray' ing
spread	spread
spread footing	spread' foot' ing
spread spectrum technology	spread' spec' trum tech nol' o gy
spreader	spread' er
spreader bar	spread' er bar"
spreading	spread' ing
spreading rate	spread' ing rate
spreadsheet	spread' sheet"
sprig	sprig
sprigging	sprig' ging
sprigging lawn	sprig' ging lawn"
spring	spring
spring back	spring' back"
spring buffer	spring' buf' fer
spring hinge	spring' hinge"
spring line	spring' line"
spring-supported flooring	spring' sup port' ed floor' ing
spring-wing toggle bolt	spring' wing' tog' gle bolt
springer	spring' er
springing	spring' ing
springpiece	spring' piece"
springwood	spring' wood"
sprinkle	sprin' kle
sprinkle-mopping	sprin' kle mop' ping
sprinkler	sprin' kler
sprinkler alarm	sprin' kler a larm'
sprinkler head	sprin' kler head"
sprinklered	sprink' lered
sprinkling	sprin' kling
sprocket	sprock' et
sprouting	sprout' ing
spruce	spruce

sprung molding	sprung' mold" ing
spud	spud'
spudding	spud' ding
spun-bonded	spun' bon' ded
spun-fiber yarn	spun' fib' er yarn
spunware	spun' ware"
spur	spur'
square	square
square cut	square' cut"
square-edge	square' edge"
square mil	square' mil"
square-plate washer	square' plate' wash' er
squared	squared
squareness	square' ness
squaring	squar' ing
squash court	squash' court"
squeeze time	squeeze' time"
squeezed joint	squeezed' joint"
squeezeout	squeeze' out"
squinch	squinch
squint	squint
squint quoin	squint' quoin"
squirrel cage motor	squir' rel cage" mo' tor
stab saw	stab' saw"
stability	sta bil' i ty
stabilization	sta" bi li za' tion
stabilize	sta' bi lize"
stabilizer	sta' bi liz" er
stable	sta' ble
stack	stack
stack bond	stack' bond"
stack effect	stack' ef fect'
stack vent	stack' vent"
stacked bond	stacked' bond"
stacking	stack' ing
stadia	sta' di a
stadium	sta' di um
staff	staff
stage	stage
stage door	stage' door"
stagehouse	stage' house"
stagger	stag' ger

staggered	stag' gered
staggered-stud partition	stag' gered stud' par ti' tion
staging	stag' ing
stagnation	stag na' tion
stain	stain
stained glass	stained' glass"
stained-glass window	stained' glass" win' dow
staining	stain' ing
stainless steel	stain' less steel"
stair	stair
stair rise	stair' rise"
stair tread	stair' tread"
staircase	stair' case"
stairstep	stair' step"
stairway	stair' way"
stairwell	stair' well"
stake	stake
stall	stall
stamba	stam' ba
stamping	stamp' ing
stamptin	stamp' tin
stanchion	stan' chion
stand	stand
stand-alone	stand' a lone"
standard	stand' ard
standard of conduct	stand' ard of con' duct
standard deviation	stand' ard de" vi a' tion
standard penetration test	stand' ard pen" e tra' tion test
standard proctor test	stand' ard proc' tor test
standard time/temperature curve	stand' ard time' tem' per a ture curve"
standardization	stand" ard i za' tion
standby lighting	stand' by" light' ing
standee	stand ee'
standing seam	stand' ing seam"
standing wave	stand' ing wave"
standpipe	stand' pipe"
Stanstead	Stan' stead
staple	sta' ple
stapler	sta' pler
star drill	star' drill"
star expansion bolt	star' ex pan' sion bolt"

starshake	star' shake"
start	start
starter	start' er
starter strip	start' er strip"
starting course	start' ing course"
starved joint	starved joint"
stateroom	state' room"
static control	stat' ic con trol'
static head	stat' ic head"
static load	stat' ic load"
static pressure	stat' ic pres' sure
statically	stat' i cal ly
statically determinate	stat' i cal ly de ter' mi nate
statically indeterminate	stat' i cal ly in' de ter" mi nate
statics	stat' ics
station	sta' tion
station point	sta' tion point"
stationary	sta' tion ar' y
statuary bronze	stat' u ar" y bronze"
Statuary Vein	Stat' u ar" y Vein
statue	stat' ue
statuette	stat" u ette'
status	sta' tus
statute	stat' ute
statute of limitations	stat' ute of lim i ta' tions
statutory	stat' u to" ry
statutory bond	stat' u to" ry bond"
stave	stave
stave-core wood door	stave' core" wood door
stay bar	stay' bar"
stay log	stay' log"
steady state	stead' y state"
steady-state vibration	stead' y state" vi bra' tion
steam	steam
steam-curing cycle	steam' cur' ing cy' cle
steam heating	steam' heat' ing
steam pipe	steam' pipe"
steam table	steam' ta' ble
stearate	ste' a rate"
steatite	ste' a tite"
steel	steel
steel casement	steel' case' ment

steel-frame construction	steel' frame" con struc' tion
steel-sectional door	steel' sec' tion al door
steel stud anchor	steel' stud' an' chor
steel troweling	steel' trow' el ing
steel-viscoelastomer	steel' vis" co e las' to mer
steelworker	steel' work' er
steening	steen' ing
steep asphalt	steep' as' phalt
steeple	stee' ple
Steiner tunnel test	Stei' ner tun' nel test
stele	ste' le
stem	stem
stencil	sten' cil
stenciling	sten' cil ing
step	step
step-down ceiling diffuser	step' down" ceil' ing dif fus' er
step flashing	step' flash' ing
step-plank	step' plank"
stepladder	step' lad" der
stepped flashing	stepped' flash' ing
stepped footing	steeped' foot' ing
stepping	step' ping
steppingstone	step' ping stone"
steradian	ste ra' di an
stereobate	ster' e o bate"
stereophonic	ster" e o phon' ic
stereoscopic	ster" e o scop' ic
stereotomy	ster' e ot' o my
sterilization	ster" i li za' tion
Stern, Robert A. M.	Stern', Rob' ert A. M.
stick	stick
stick-back	stick' back"
stickbuilt construction	stick' built" con struc' tion
sticker	stick' er
sticking	stick' ing
stiff mud process	stiff' mud' pro' cess
stiffener	stif' fen er
stiffness	stiff' ness
stilb	stilb
stile	stile
stilt	stilt
stilted arch	stilt' ed arch"

262

stinger	sting' er
stipple	stip' ple
stippled finish	stip' pled fin' ish
stippler	stip' pler
stippling	stip' pling
stipulated	stip' u lat" ed
stipulated damages	stip' u lat" ed dam' ages
stipulation	stip" u la' tion
Stirling, James	Stir' ling, James'
stirrup	stir' rup
stoa	sto' a
stock	stock
stock-dyed yarn	stock' dyed ' yarn"
stock size	stock' size"
stockpile	stock' pile"
stoker	stok' er
stolon	sto' lon
stolonizing lawn	sto' lon iz" ing lawn
stone	stone
stone mason	stone' mas' on
Stone Mountain granite	Stone' Moun' tain gran' ite
Stone, Edward Durell	Stone', Ed' ward Du rell'
stonecutter	stone' cut" ter
stonework	stone' work"
Stoney Creek	Ston' ey Creek'
stool	stool
stoop	stoop
stop	stop
stop chamfer	stop' cham' fer
stop work order	stop' work' or' der
stopcock	stop' cock"
stope	stope
stopped dado	stopped' da' do
stopwork	stop' work'
storage	stor' age
store	store
storefront	store' front"
storeroom	store' room"
storm clip	storm' clip
storm drain	storm' drain"
storm sewer	storm' sew' er
storm-sewer system	storm' sew' er sys' tem

storm water	storm' wa' ter
story	sto' ry
story height	sto' ry height"
story pole	sto' ry pole
stoup	stoup
stove bolt	stove' bolt"
stovepipe	stove' pipe"
straight-grained	straight' grained"
straight-run stair	straight' run" stair
straight-shank	straight' shank"
straight-split shakes	straight' split" shakes"
straightedge	straight' edge"
strain	strain
strain hardening	strain' hard' en ing
strainer	strain' er
straining piece	strain' ing piece"
strake	strake
strand	strand
stranded wire	strand' ed wire"
strap	strap
strap hinge	strap' hinge"
strapping	strap' ping
strapwork	strap' work"
strata	stra' ta
stratification	strat" i fi ca' tion
stratum	stra' tum
strawberry	straw' ber" ry
strawboard	straw' board"
streak	streak
streaking	streak' ing
streamline	stream' line
street	street
street elbow	street' el' bow
street floor	street' floor"
street furniture	street' fur' ni ture
street gas main	street" gas' main"
street line	street' line"
strength	strength
strength ratio	strength' ra' tio
strength-reducing defect	strength' re duc' ing de' fect
stress	stress
stress crack	stress' crack"

stress diagram	stress' di' a gram
stress-graded lumber	stress' grad' ed lum' ber
stressed-skin panel	stressed' skin" pan' el
stresses	stress' es
stretch-forming	stretch' form' ing
stretcher	stretch' er
stretcher bar	stretch' er bar"
stretcher bond	stretch' er bond"
stretcher leveling	stretch' er lev' el ing
stretchout	stretch' out"
stria carpet	stri' a car' pet
striae	stri' ae
striated	stri' at ed
striation	stri" a' tion
strié	stri e'
strike	strike
strike edge	strike' edge"
strike jamb	strike' jamb"
strike off	strike' off
strike plate	strike' plate"
strike stile	strike' stile"
striker	strik' er
striking	strik' ing
striking off	strik' ing off"
string	string
stringcourse	string' course"
stringer	string' er
stringerless	string' er less
stringiness	string' i ness
stringing	string' ing
strip	strip
strip flooring	strip' floor' ing
strip-mopping	strip' mop' ping
striplight	strip' light"
strippable	strip' pa ble
stripping	strip' ping
strongback	strong' back"
struck joint	struck' joint"
structural	struc' tur al
structural drawings	struc' tur al draw' ings
structural facing unit	struc' tur al fac' ing u' nit
structural glass	struc' tur al glass"

structural particleboard	struc' tur al par' ti cle board"
structural steel	struc' tur al steel"
structural tee	struc' tur al tee"
structure	struc' ture
structureborne sound	struc' ture borne" sound"
strut	strut
strutting	strut' ting
stub	stub
stub tenon	stub' ten' on
Stubbins Jr., Hugh A.	Stub' bins Jr., Hugh' A.
stuc	stuc
stucco	stuc' co
stuck	stuck
stud	stud
stud driver	stud' driv' er
studding	stud' ding
studio	stu' di o
studio apartment	stu' di o a part' ment
studwork	stud' work"
study	stud' y
stuffers	stuff' ers
stump	stump
stumper	stump' er
stunning	stun' ning
style	style
stylobate	sty' lo bate
stylolite	sty' lo lite
styrene	sty' rene
styrene butadiene	sty' rene bu" ta di' ene
styrene butadiene copolymer	sty' rene bu" ta di' ene co pol' y-mer
styrene resin	sty' rene res' in
styrene-rubber	sty' rene rub' ber
Styrofoam™	Sty' ro foam
sub-subcontractor	sub' sub con' trac tor
subarch	sub" arch'
subassemblage	sub" as sem' blage
subbase	sub' base"
subbasement	sub' base" ment
subbid	sub' bid"
subbidder	sub" bid' der
subcasing	sub cas' ing

subcategory	sub" cat' e go" ry
subchannel	sub" chan' nel
subcontract	sub con' tract
subcontractor	sub con' trac tor
subcooling	sub cool' ing
subdivision	sub' di vi" sion
subdrainage	sub" drain' age
subduction	sub duc' tion
subfeeder	sub" feed' er
subfloor	sub' floor"
subflooring	sub" floor' ing
subframe	sub' frame"
subgrade	sub' grade"
subharmonic	sub" har mon' ic
subheading	sub' head" ing
sublease	sub' lease"
sublet	sub let'
sublimation	sub" li ma' tion
submaster key	sub mas' ter key"
submerged	sub merged'
submersible	sub mers' i ble
submittal	sub mit' tal
subparagraph	sub par' a graph"
subplatform	sub plat' form
subpoena	sub poe' na
subpurlin	sub pur' lin
subrogation	sub" ro ga' tion
subscribe	sub scribe'
subscription	sub scrip' tion
subsidence	sub' si dence"
subsidiary	sub sid' i ar y
subsidized housing	sub' si dized" hous' ing
subsoil	sub' soil"
substantial completion	sub stan' tial com ple' tion
substation	sub' sta" tion
substitution	sub" sti tu' tion
substrate	sub' strate
substructure	sub struc' ture
subsurface	sub sur' face
subsurface investigation	sub sur' face in ves" ti ga' tion
subtractive	sub tract' tive
suburb	sub' urb

suburban	sub ur' ban
subway	sub' way"
suction	suc' tion
suction diffuser	suc' tion dif fus' er
suction head	suc' tion head"
sugar pine	sug' ar pine"
suite	suite
sulfamic acid	sul fam' ic ac' id
sulfate	sul' fate
sulfate-resistant cement	sul' fate re sis' tant ce ment'
sulfation	sul fa' tion
sulfur	sul' fur
summary of work	sum' ma ry of work"
summer	sum' mer
summerhouse	sum' mer house"
summerwood	sum' mer wood"
summons	sum' mons
sump	sump
sump pump	sump' pump'
sun deck	sun' deck"
sun factor	sun' fac' tor
sun time	sun' time"
sunburst	sun' burst"
sunfast	sun' fast"
sunken	sunk' en
sunroom	sun' room"
sunscreen	sun' screen"
Sunset Beige	Sun' set" Beige"
Sunset Red	Sun' set" Red"
sunshade	sun' shade"
supa	sup' a
super	sup' er
superblock	sup' er block"
supercolumniation	sup" er co lum" ni a' tion
superconductor	sup" er con duc' tor
supergraphics	sup" er graph' ics
superheat	sup" er heat'
superheated	sup" er heat' ed
superimposed	sup" er im posed'
superintendent	sup" er in tend' ent
supermarket	sup' er mar" ket
superplasticizer	sup" er plas' ti ciz" er

superposition	su" per po si' tion
superstructure	sup" er struc' ture
supervised	sup' er vised"
supervision	sup" er vi' sion
supervisory	sup" er vi' so ry
superwindows	sup" er win' dows
supplemental services	sup" ple men' tal serv' ices
supplementary conditions	sup" ple men' ta ry con di' tions
supplementary lighting	sup" ple men' ta ry light' ing
supplier	sup pli' er
supply air	sup' ply air"
supply grille	sup' ply grille"
support	sup port'
surbase	sur' base"
surcharge	sur' charge"
surcharged earth	sur' charged" earth"
surcharges	sur' charges"
surcharging	sur' charg ing
surety	sur' e ty
surety bond	sur' e ty bond"
surface bolt	sur' face bolt"
surface coefficient	sur' face co" ef fi' cient
surface drainage	sur' face drain' age
surface film conductance	sur' face film con duct' ance
surface hinge	sur' face hinge"
surface-mounted	sur' face mount' ed
surface shake	sur' face shake"
surface water	sur' face wa' ter
surface-water drain	sur' face wa' ter drain"
surface waves	sur' face waves"
surfaced lumber	sur' faced lum' ber
surfacing	sur' fac ing
surfactant	sur fac' tant
surge protection	surge' pro tec' tion
surgical lighting	sur' gi cal light' ing
surround	sur round'
surveillance	sur veil' lance
survey	sur' vey
surveying	sur vey' ing
surveyor	sur vey' or
suspended	sus pend' ed
suspended ceiling	sus pend' ed ceil' ing

suspension roof	sus pen' sion roof"
swab	swab
swag	swag
swag light	swag' light"
swage	swage
swaging	swag' ing
swale	swale
swamp	swamp
swan-neck	swan' neck"
swatch	swatch
swaybrace	sway' brace"
sweat joint	sweat' joint"
sweat-out	sweat' out"
sweating	sweat' ing
swedge bolt	swedge' bolt"
sweep	sweep
sweepstrip	sweep' strip"
SweetSearch™	Sweet' Search"
SweetSpec™	Sweet' Spec"
swell	swell
swelling	swell' ing
Swenson Gray	Swen' son Gray"
Swenson Light Woodbury	Swen' son Light" Wood' bury
swift	swift
swimming pool	swim' ming pool"
swing	swing
swing clear hinge	swing' clear" hinge
swing joint	swing' joint"
swing loader	swing' load' er
swinging door	swing' ing door"
swinging panel chalkboard	swing' ing pan' el chalk' board"
swirl	swirl
switch	switch
switch box	switch' box"
switchboard	switch' board"
switchgear	switch' gear"
switching device	switch' ing de vice"
switchplate	switch' plate"
swivel chair	swiv' el chair"
swivel joint	swiv' el joint"
sycamore	syc' a more
syenite	sy' e nite"

symbol	sym' bol
symbolic	sym bol' ic
symbolism	sym' bol ism
symmetric	sym met' ric
symmetrical	sym met' ri cal
synagogue	syn' a gogue
synchronous	syn chro' nous
synchronous motor	syn chro' nous mo' tor
synclastic	syn clas' tic
syneresis	syn er' e sis
synergism	syn' er gism"
synodal hall	syn' od al hall
syntactic cellular plastic	syn tac' tic cel' lu lar plas' tic
synthesis	syn' the sis
synthetic	syn thet' ic
system	sys' tem
systems engineering	sys' tems en" gi neer' ing
systyle	sys' tyle

T

T-bar	T' bar"
T-beam	T' beam"
T bevel	T' bev' el
T-head	T' head"
T-hinge	T' hinge"
T joint	T' joint"
T-plate	T' plate"
T-rated switch	T' rat' ed switch
T square	T' square"
T-waves	T' waves"
tab	tab
tabaret	tab' a ret
tabby	tab' by
Taber test	Ta' ber test"
tabernacle	tab' er nac" le
table	ta' ble
table saw	ta' ble saw"
tablet	tab' let
tablet-arm chair	tab' let arm" chair
tablet chair	tab' let chair"
tabling	ta' bling

tachuelilla	tach" ue lil' la
tachymeter	ta chym' e ter
tack	tack
tack dry	tack' dry"
tack-free dry	tack' free' dry
tack weld	tack' weld"
tackboard	tack' board"
tacker	tack' er
tackiness	tack' i ness
tacking	tack' ing
tackle	tack' le
tackless strip	tack' less" strip"
tacky	tack' y
tactile	tac' tile
tag	tag
tag line	tag' line"
tail	tail
tail joist	tail' joist"
tailing	tail' ing
tailpiece	tail' piece"
takeoff	take' off"
talc	talc
tally stick	tal' ly stick"
talon	tal' on
talus	ta' lus
tamarack	tam' a rack
tambour	tam' bour
tamp	tamp
tamper	tam' per
tamping anchor	tamp' ing an' chor
tandem	tan' dem
tandem welding	tan' dem weld' ing
tang	tang
Tange, Kenzo	Tan' ge, Ken' zo
tangent	tan' gent
tangential	tan gen' tial
tangential shrinkage	tan gen' tial shrink' age
tanguile	tan guile'
tank	tank
tap	tap
tape	tape
taper	ta' per

tapered	ta' pered
tapered edge	ta' per ed edge
tapered fluted pile	ta' pered flut' ed pile"
tapestry	tap' es try
tapia	tap' i a
taping	tap' ing
taping knife	tap' ing knife"
tapping	tap' ping
taproot	tap' root"
tar	tar
target	tar' get
target rod	tar' get rod"
Tarmac™	Tar' mac
tarmacadam	tar' mac ad" am
tarnish	tar' nish
tarpaulin	tar pau' lin
tarred felt	tarred' felt"
task lighting	task' light' ing
tassel	tas' sel
tatami	ta ta' mi
Taut, Bruno	Taut', Bru' no
tavern	tav' ern
tavern-grade flooring	tav' ern grade" floor' ing
tea garden	tea' gar' den
teahouse	tea' house"
teak	teak
teakwood	teak' wood"
tear strength	tear' strength"
tearing strength	tear' ing strength"
teaser	teas' er
technical pen	tech' ni cal pen"
technological	tech" no log' i cal
technology	tech nol' o gy
tectonic	tec ton' ic
tee	tee
tee joint	tee' joint"
Teflon™	Tef' lon
tegular	teg' u lar
teks	teks
telecommunications	tel" e com mu" ni ca' tions
teleconference	tel' e con" fer ence
teleconferencing	tel' e con" fer enc ing

telegraphing	tel' e graph" ing
telephone	tel' e phone"
telescopic	tel" e scop' ic
telescoping jack	tel' e scop" ing jack"
television	tel' e vi" sion
telltale	tell' tale"
telomer	tel' o mer
temper	tem' per
temperature	tem' per a ture
temperature reinforcement	tem' per a ture re" in force' ment
tempered	tem' pered
tempered glass	tem' pered glass"
tempering	tem' per ing
template	tem' plate
template hardware	tem' plate hard' ware
temple	tem' ple
temporary	tem' po rar" y
tenancy	ten' an cy
tenant	ten' ant
tenant's improvement	ten' ant's im prove' ment
tender	ten' der
tendon	ten' don
tenement	ten' e ment
Tennessee marble	Ten" nes see' mar' ble
tenon	ten' on
tenoned	ten' oned
tensile	ten' sile
tensile fatigue resistance	ten' sile fa tigue' re sis' tance
tensile strength	ten' sile strength"
tension	ten' sion
tension bars	ten' sion bars
tension-supported roof	ten' sion sup port' ed roof"
tensioned	ten' sioned
tenter	ten' ter
tentering	ten' ter ing
term	term
terminal	ter' mi nal
terminal reheat system	ter' mi nal re' heat sys' tem
terminated stop	ter' mi nat" ed stop"
terminating	ter' mi nat" ing
termite	ter' mite
terne metal	terne' met' al

terneplate	terne' plate"
terpolymer	ter pol' y mer
terra-cotta	ter' ra cot' ta
terrace	ter' race
terrain	ter rain'
terrain analysis	ter rain' a nal' y sis
terras	ter ras'
terrazzo	ter raz' zo
terrestrial radiation	ter res' tri al rad" i a' tion
territorial	ter" ri to' ri al
territoriality	ter" ri to" ri al' i ty
tertiary	ter' ti ar" y
tessellated	tes' sel lat" ed
tessera	tes' ser a
tesserae	tes' ser ae"
test cut	test' cut"
test cylinder	test" cy' lin der
test pit	test' pit"
tester	test' er
tetrahydrofuran	tet" ra hy" dro fu' ran
tetrastyle	tet' ra style"
tewel	tew' el
Texas Pearl	Tex' as Pearl"
textile	tex' tile
texture	tex' ture
textured finish	tex' tured fin' ish
texturizing	tex' tur iz" ing
thatch	thatch
theater	the' a ter
theater-in-the-round	the' a ter in the round"
theodolite	the od' o lite"
therm	therm
thermal	ther' mal
thermal capacity	ther' mal ca pac' i ty
thermal conductance	ther' mal con duct' ance
thermal conduction	ther' mal con duc' tion
thermal conductivity	ther' mal con" duc tiv' i ty
thermal cycling	ther' mal cy' cling
thermal discharge capacity	ther' mal dis' charge ca pac' i ty
thermal drift	ther' mal drift"
thermal endurance	ther' mal en dur' ance
thermal lag	ther' mal lag

thermal mass	ther' mal mass"
thermal shock	ther' mal shock"
thermal stress	ther' mal stress"
thermal welding	ther' mal weld' ing
thermalized	ther' ma lized
thermistor	therm is' tor
thermochromic coating	ther" mo chrom' ic coat' ing
thermochromism	ther" mo chrom' ism
thermocouple	ther' mo cou" ple
thermodynamic	ther" mo dy nam' ic
thermograph	ther' mo graph"
thermometer	ther mom' e ter
thermo-osmosis	ther" mo os mo' sis
Thermopane™	Ther' mo pane"
thermoplastic	ther" mo plas' tic
thermoset	ther' mo set"
thermosetting	ther' mo set" ting
thermosiphon	ther" mo si' phon
thermosiphoning	ther" mo si' phon ing
thermostat	ther' mo stat"
thermostatic	ther" mo stat' ic
thickness	thick' ness"
thimble	thim' ble
thin-shell	thin' shell"
thin-shell precast	thin' shell pre' cast
thin-wall conduit	thin' wall" con' duit
thinner	thin' ner
thinset	thin' set
thinset terrazzo	thin' set ter raz' zo
third point	third' point"
thixotropic	thix" o trop' ic
thixotropy	thix ot' ro py
tholobate	thol' o bate
thoroughfare	thor' ough fare"
thread	thread
threaded	thread' ed
three-centered arch	three' cen' tered arch"
three-dimensional sign	three' di men' sion al sign
three-phase	three' phase"
three-ply	three' ply'
three-point perspective	three' point" per spec' tive
three-prong plug	three' prong' plug"

three-way switch	three' way" switch"
three-wire circuit	three' wire' cir' cuit
threshold	thresh' old
throat	throat
throat depth	throat' depth"
throat opening	throat' o' pen ing
throating	throat' ing
throttling-type boiler control	throt' tling type" boil' er con' trol
through bolt	through' bolt"
through-wall flashing	through' wall' flash' ing
through-wall joint	through' wall' joint"
throw	throw
throwaway filter	throw' a way" fil' ter
thrust	thrust
thumb latch	thumb' latch"
thumbpiece	thumb' piece"
thumbscrew	thumb' screw"
thurm	thurm
ticking	tick' ing
tie	tie
tie bar	tie' bar
tie beam	tie' beam"
tie rod	tie' rod"
tie wire	tie' wire"
tieback	tie' back"
tier	tier
tiffany	tif' fa ny
Tiffany glass	Tif' fa ny glass"
tig welding	tig' weld' ing
tiger grain	ti' ger grain"
Tigerman, Stanley	Tig' er man, Stan' ley
tigerwood	ti' ger wood"
tight knot	tight' knot"
tile	tile
till	till
tillage	till' age
tilt-top table	tilt' top' ta' ble
tilt-up	tilt' up"
tilth	tilth
tilting fillet	tilt' ing fil' let
timber	tim' ber
timber connector	tim' ber con nec' tor

timber-framed	tim' ber framed"
timbering	tim' ber ing
timbre	tim' bre
time	time
time of completion	time' of com ple' tion
time-lag	time' lag"
tin	tin'
tin plate	tin' plate"
tin-plated	tin' plat' ed
tin snips	tin' snips"
tinning	tin' ning
tint	tint
tinting	tint' ing
tit	tit
titanium	ti ta' ni um
title	ti' tle
title block	ti' tle block"
title sheet	ti' tle sheet"
toaster	toast' er
toe	toe
toe bead	toe' bead"
toe guard	toe' guard"
toeboard	toe' board"
toeing	toe' ing
toenailing	toe' nail" ing
toggle bolt	tog' gle bolt"
toile	toile
toilet	toi' let
toilet paper holder	toi' let pa' per hold' er
tolerance	tol' er ance
tollhouse	toll' house"
toluol	tol' u ol"
tomb	tomb
ton	ton
tone	tone
toner	ton' er
tong mark	tong' mark"
tongs	tongs"
tongue	tongue
tongue-and-groove	tongue' and groove'
tongue joint	tongue' joint"
tonne	tonne

tool	tool
toolbox	tool' box"
tooled	tooled
tooled joint	tooled' joint"
tooling	tool' ing
tooling time	tool' ing time"
tooth	tooth
toothed ring	toothed' ring"
toothing	tooth' ing
top chord	top' chord"
top lap	top' lap"
top plate	top' plate"
top rail	top' rail"
topcoat	top' coat"
tope	tope
topiary	to' pi ar" y
toplighting	top' light" ing
topographic	top" o graph' ic
topographical	top" o graph' i cal
topography	to pog' ra phy
topping	top' ping
topsoil	top' soil"
torch	torch
torchère	tor chere'
torching	torch' ing
torii	to' ri i"
tormentor	tor men' tor
torn grain	torn' grain"
torpedo gravel	tor pe' do grav' el
torque	torque
torque wrench	torque' wrench"
torsade	tor sade'
torsion	tor' sion
torsional	tor' sion al
tort	tort
tortoise shell	tor' toise shell"
tortoise shelling	tor' toise shel" ling
torus	to' rus
tot lot	tot' lot'
total heat load	to' tal heat" load
total rise	to' tal rise"
total run	to' tal run"

totara	to ta' ra
touch latch	touch' latch"
touch sanding	touch' sand' ing
toughness	tough' ness
towel ring	tow' el ring"
tower	tow' er
tower crane	tow' er crane"
town	town
town planning	town' plan" ning
townhouse	town' house"
townscape	town' scape"
township	town' ship
toxic	tox' ic
toxic-treated board	tox' ic treat' ed board
toxicity	tox ic' i ty
toxicology	tox" i col' o gy
trabeated	tra' be at" ed
trace	trace
tracer gas	trac' er gas"
tracery	trac' er y
tracing	trac' ing
track	track
track lighting	track' light' ing
tracking	track' ing
tracking error	track' ing er' ror
trackwork	track' work"
tract	tract
traction machine	trac' tion ma chine'
tractor	trac' tor
trade	trade
trade union	trade' un' ion
trademark	trade' mark"
traditional	tra di' tion al
traffic	traf' fic
traffic cone	traf' fic cone"
traffic paint	traf' fic paint"
trail batch	trail' batch"
trailer	trail' er
trammel	tram' mel
transceiver	trans ceiv' er
transcript	tran' script
transducer	trans duc' er

transept	tran' sept
transfer	trans' fer
transfer bond	trans' fer bond"
transfer grille	trans' fer grille"
transference	trans fer' ence
transformed section	trans formed' sec' tion
transformer	trans form' er
transformer vault	trans form' er vault"
transistor	tran sis' tor
transit	tran' sit
transit mix	tran' sit mix"
transit-mixed concrete	tran' sit mixed" con' crete
transition	tran si' tion
transitional	tran si' tion al
translation	trans la' tion
translucency	trans lu' cen cy
translucent	trans lu' cent
transmissibility	trans mis" si bil' i ty
transmission	trans mis' sion
transmissivity	trans" mis siv' i ty
transmittal	trans mit' tal
transmittance	trans mit' tance
transom	tran' som
transparency	trans par' en cy
transparent	trans par' ent
transparent finish	trans par' ent fin' ish
transparentizing	trans par' ent iz" ing
transported	trans port' ed
transverse	trans verse'
trap	trap
trap seal	trap' seal"
trapdoor	trap' door'
trapeze hanger	tra peze' hang' er
trapezoid	trap' e zoid"
trapunto	tra pun' to
trash chute	trash' chute"
travel	trav' el
travel distance	trav' el dis' tance
traveler	trav' el er
traverse	tra verse'
traverse rod	trav' erse rod"
travertine	trav' er tine"

tray	tray
tread	tread
treadle	trea' dle
treadway	tread' way"
treated	treat' ed
treatment	treat' ment
tree	tree
tree grate	tree' grate"
treenail	tree' nail"
trefoil	tre' foil
treillage	treil' lage
trellis	trel' lis
trelliswork	trel' lis work"
tremie	trem' ie
trench	trench
trench shield	trench' shield"
trencher	trench' er
trenching	trench' ing
trestle	tres' tle
trestle table	tres' tle ta' ble
triacetate	tri ac' e tate"
trial batch	tri' al batch"
triangle	tri' an" gle
triangular	tri an' gu lar
triangulation	tri an" gu la' tion
triapsidal	tri ap' si dal
triaxial	tri ax' i al
triaxial compression test	tri ax' i al com pres' sion test
trichromatic system	tri" chro mat' ic sys' tem
trickling filter	trick' ling fil' ter
triforium	tri fo' ri um
triglyph	tri' glyph"
trigonometry	trig" o nom' e try
trim	trim
trimmed	trimmed
trimmer	trim' mer
trimmer arch	trim' mer arch"
triple glazing	tri' ple glaz' ing
triple-hung window	tri' ple hung" win' dow
triple-wythe	tri' ple wythe"
tripod	tri' pod
triptych	trip' tych

triquetra	tri que' tra
trisect	tri sect'
tristimulus values	tri stim' u lus val' ues
triumphal arch	tri um' phal arch'
troffer	trof' fer
trolley	trol' ley
trolley duct	trol' ley duct"
Trombe wall	Trombe' wall"
trompe	trompe
trompe l'oeil	trompe' l'oeil'
trough	trough
trowel	trow' el
trowel finish	trow' el fin' ish
troweled	trow' eled
troweled finish	trow' eled fin' ish
troweler	trow' el er
troweling	trow' el ing
truck crane	truck' crane"
truckable sill	truck' a ble sill"
true north	true' north'
trundle bed	trun' dle bed"
trunk	trunk
truss	truss
truss plate	truss' plate"
trussed	trussed
trussed-rafter roof	trussed' raf' ter roof
trust deed	trust' deed'
trustee	trust ee'
try square	try' square"
tube	tube
tube steel	tube' steel"
tube stock	tube' stock"
tubeaxial fan	tube" ax' i al fan"
tubing	tub' ing
tubular	tu' bu lar
tubular lock	tu' bu lar lock"
tuck	tuck
tuck-point	tuck' point"
tuck pointing	tuck' point' ing
Tudor architecture	Tu' dor ar' chi tec" ture
tuff	tuff
tuft	tuft

tufted	tuft' ed
tufted carpet	tuft' ed car' pet
tufting	tuft' ing
tulip chair	tu' lip chair"
tulipwood	tu' lip wood"
tumbled	tum' bled
tumbler	tum' bler
tung oil	tung' oil"
tungsten	tung' sten
tungsten carbide	tung' sten car' bide
tungsten halogen	tung' sten hal' o gen
tunnel	tun' nel
tunnel kiln	tun' nel kiln"
tunnel test	tun' nel test"
tunneling	tun' nel ing
tupelo	tu' pe lo"
turbid	tur' bid
turbidimeter	tur" bi dim' e ter
turbidity	tur bid' i ty
turbulence	tur' bu lence
turbulent flow	tur' bu lent flow"
Turkish rug	Turk ish rug"
turn button	turn' but' ton
turn-key job	turn' key" job"
turn-of-the-nut method	turn' of the nut' meth' od
turnbuckle	turn' buck' le
Turnbull Jr., William	Turn' bull Jr., Wil' liam
turned work	turned' work"
turning	turn' ing
turnout	turn' out"
turnover	turn' o" ver
turnstile	turn' stile"
turntable	turn' ta" ble
turpentine	tur' pen tine"
turret	tur' ret
Tuscan order	Tus' can or' der
tusk	tusk
tusking	tusk' ing
tuyère	tu yere'
tweed carpet	tweed' car' pet
twill	twill
twill weave	twill' weave"

twining stem molding	twin' ing stem" mold' ing
twist	twist
twisted	twist' ed
twisted pair	twist' ed pair"
twisting	twist' ing
two-by-four	two' by four'
two-coat system	two' coat' sys' tem
two-hinged arch	two' hinged' arch"
two-part sealant	two' part' seal' ant
two-point perspective	two' point' per spec' tive
two-way joist construction	two' way" joist con struc' tion
two-way slab	two' way" slab
tympanum	tym' pa num
type X wallboard	type" X' wall' board

U

U bolt	U' bolt"
U-factor	U' fac" tor
U-trap	U' trap"
U-value	U' val" ue
UL label	U' L' la' bel
ultimate strength	ul' ti mate strength"
ultrasonic	ul" tra son' ic
ultrasonic testing	ul" tra son' ic test' ing
ultraviolet	ul" tra vi' o let
ultraviolet radiation	ul" tra vi' o let ra" di a' tion
unbacked	un backed'
unbalanced	un bal' anced
unbonded	un bond' ed
unbraced	un braced'
unconfined	un" con fined'
unconsolidated	un" con sol' i dat" ed
uncoursed	un coursed'
uncured	un cured'
undamped	un damped'
underbed	un' der bed"
undercarpet cable	un" der car' pet ca' ble
undercoat	un' der coat"
undercoating	un' der coat' ing
underconsolidation	un' der con sol" i da' tion
undercroft	un' der croft"

undercut	un" der cut'
underdrain	un' der drain"
underfloor	un' der floor"
underframe	un' der frame"
underground	un' der ground'
underlayment	un" der lay' ment
underpass	un' der pass"
underpinning	un' der pin" ning
underslab	un' der slab"
underslung	un' der slung'
underslung car frame	un' der slung' car" frame
undertone	un' der tone"
underwater	un' der wa' ter
Underwriters Laboratories	Un' der writ" ers Lab' o ra to" ries
undeveloped land	un" de vel' oped land"
undisturbed	un" dis turbed'
undisturbed sample	un" dis turbed' sam' ple
undressed	un dressed'
uneven	un e' ven
unexposed	un" ex posed'
unfading	un fad' ing
unglazed	un glazed'
ungroup	un group
uniaxial	u" ni ax' i al
unicellular	u" ni cel' lu lar
Unified Soil Classification System	U' ni fied" Soil" Clas" si fi ca' tion Sys' tem
Unified Thread series	U' ni fied" Thread' ser' ies
uniform	u' ni form"
Uniform Building Code	U' ni form" Build' ing Code
uniform load	u' ni form" load"
uniformity	u" ni form' i ty
unincorporated	un" in cor' po rat" ed
uninterruptible	un" in ter rupt' i ble
union	un' ion
union shop	un' ion shop"
uniplanar	u" ni pla' nar
unit absorber	u' nit ab sorb' er
unit cooler	u' nit cool' er
unit heater	u' nit heat' er
unit lock	u' nit lock"
unit masonry	u' nit mas' on ry

unit price	u' nit price"
unit pricing	u' nit pric' ing
unitary air conditioner	u' ni tar" y air" con di' tion er
united inches	u nit' ed inch' es
unitized	u' nit ized"
universal	u" ni ver' sal
unprotected	un" pro tect' ed
unreinforced	un" re in forced'
unrestrained	un" re strained'
unsound knot	un sound' knot"
unstable	un sta' ble
unvented appliance	un vent' ed ap pli' ance
upflow furnace	up' flow fur' nace
upholster	up hol' ster
upholstered wall	up hol' stered wall"
upholstering	up hol' ster ing
upholstery	up hol' ster y
uplift	up' lift
uppercroft	up' per croft"
upright	up' right
upset	up set'
upsetting	up set' ting
upstairs	up' stairs'
upturned beam	up' turned" beam"
urban	ur' ban
urban renewal	ur' ban re new' al
urbanization	ur" ban i za' tion
urea-formaldehyde	u re' a form al' de hyde"
urea-melamine resin	u re' a mel' a mine res' in
urea resin	u re' a res' in
urethane coating	u' re thane" coat' ing
urethane elastomer	u' re thane e las' to mer
urinal	u' ri nal
urn	urn
usable floor area	us' a ble floor' ar' e a
useful life	use' ful life"
utilities	u til' i ties
utility	u til' i ty
utility grade	u til' i ty grade"
utilization factor	u" ti li za' tion fac' tor
Utzon, Jørn	Ut' zon, Jorn'

V

V-cut	V' cut"
V-groove	V groove"
V joint	V' joint"
V-match	V' match
vacant	va' cant
vacuum	vac' u um
vacuum breaker	vac' u um break' er
vacuum pump	vac' u um pump"
valance	val' ance
valance lighting	val' ance light' ing
valet towel holder	val et' tow' el hold' er
validity	va lid' i ty
valley	val' ley
valley flashing	val' ley flash' ing
valley rafter	val' ley raft' er
valuation	val" u a' tion
value	val' ue
value engineering	val' ue en" gi neer' ing
valve	valve
vamure	va mure'
van Eyck, Aldo	van Eyck', Al' do
vanadium	va na' di um
vandalism	van' dal ism
vane	vane
vaneaxial fan	vane" ax' i al fan"
vanishing point	van' ish ing point"
vanity	van' i ty
vapor barrier	va' por bar' rier
vapor migration	va' por mi gra' tion
vapor pressure	va' por pres' sure
vapor-pressure gradient	va' por pres' sure gra' di ent
vaporization	va" por i za' tion
vaportight	va' por tight"
variability	var" i a bil' i ty
variable air volume	var' i a ble air" vol' ume
variable-volume air system	var' i a ble vol' ume air" sys' tem
variance	var' i ance
variegated	var' i e gat" ed
varnish	var' nish
vase	vase

vat dyed	vat' dyed'
vat dyeing	vat' dye' ing
vault	vault
vaulted	vault' ed
vaulting	vault' ing
vaulting course	vault' ing course'
vector	vec' tor
vee	vee
vegetable preparation sink	veg' e ta ble prep" a ra' tion sink"
vehicle	ve' hi cle
veiling reflection	veil' ing re flec' tion
vein	vein
Veined Black	Veined' Black"
Velcro™	Vel' cro
vellum	vel' lum
velocity	ve loc' i ty
velodrome	ve' lo drome"
velour	ve lour'
velvet	vel' vet
velvet carpet	vel' vet car' pet
vendor	ven' dor
veneer	ve neer'
veneer plaster	ve neer' plas' ter
veneer wall	ve neer' wall"
veneered	ve neered'
veneering	ve neer' ing
Venetian	Ve ne' tian
venetian blind	ve ne' tian blind"
Venetian terrazzo	Ve ne' tian ter raz' zo
Venezuelan Pink	Ven" e zue' lan Pink"
vent	vent
vent pipe	vent' pipe"
vent stack	vent' stack"
vented appliance	vent' ed ap pli' ance
ventilate	ven' ti late"
ventilating	ven' ti lat" ing
ventilation	ven" ti la' tion
ventilator	ven' ti la" tor
venting	vent' ing
Venturi effect	Ven tu' ri ef fect'
Venturi, Robert	Ven tu' ri, Rob' ert
veranda	ve ran' da

verd antique	verd' an tique'
verdigris	ver' di gris"
verge	verge
verge board	verge' board"
vermicular	ver mic' u lar
vermiculated	ver mic' u lat" ed
vermiculation	ver mic" u la' tion
vermiculite	ver mic' u lite"
vermin	ver' min
vernacular architecture	ver nac' u lar ar' chi tec" ture
vernier	ver' ni er
Vert Jade	Vert' Jade"
vertex	ver' tex
vertical	ver' ti cal
vertical blind	ver' ti cal blind"
vertical file	ver' ti cal file"
vertical grain	ver' ti cal grain"
vertical openings	ver' ti cal o' pen ings
vertical slip form	ver' ti cal slip" form"
very fine sandy loam	ver' y fine sand' y loam"
very-high-output fluorescent	ver' y high" out' put fluo res' cent
vesica piscis	ve si' ca pis' cis
vessel	ves' sel
vestibule	ves' ti bule"
vestry	ves' try
viaduct	vi' a duct"
vibrated	vi' brat ed
vibrating	vi' brat ing
vibrating screen	vi' brat ing screen"
vibration	vi bra' tion
vibration isolation	vi' bra' tion i" so la' tion
vibration isolator	vi' bra' tion i' so la" tor
vibrator	vi' bra tor
vibro-flotation	vi' bro flo ta' tion
Victorian	Vic to' ri an
video display terminal	vid' e o" dis play' term' i nal
Vierendeel truss	Vier" en deel' truss"
view	view
vignette	vi gnette'
vignetting	vi gnet' ting
villa	vil' la
vinal	vi' nal

vine	vine
vinette	vin ette'
vinyl	vi' nyl
vinyl acetate	vi' nyl ac' e tate"
vinyl-asbestos tile	vi' nyl as bes' tos tile
vinyl chloride	vi' nyl chlo' ride
vinyl-coated	vi' nyl coat' ed
vinyl-cork tackboard	vi' nyl cork' tack' board"
vinyl-covered gypsum wallboard	vi' nyl cov' ered gyp' sum wall'-board"
vinyl glazing	vi' nyl glaz' ing
vinyl resin	vi' nyl res' in
vinyl tile	vi' nyl tile"
vinylidene chloride	vi nyl' i dene chlo' ride
vinylidene dinitrile	vi nyl' i dene" di ni' trile
virola	vi ro' la
viscoelastic	vis" co e las' tic
viscoelasticity	vis" co e las ti' ci ty
viscoelastomeric	vis" co e las" to mer' ic
viscometer	vis com' e ter
viscose rayon	vis' cose ray' on
viscosity	vis cos' i ty
viscous damper	vis' cous damp' er
viscous damping	vis' cous damp' ing
vise	vise
vise-grip pliers	vise' grip' pli' ers
visibility	vis" i bil' i ty
visible	vis' i ble
vision light	vi' sion light"
vision-light door	vi' sion light" door
vista	vis' ta
visual	vis' u al
visual acuity	vis' u al a cu' i ty
visual angle	vis' u al an' gle
visual comfort probability	vis' u al com' fort prob" a bil' i ty
visual task	vis' u al task"
visualization	vis" u al i za' tion
vitreous	vit' re ous
vitrification	vit" ri fi ca' tion
vitrified	vit' ri fied
vitrified-clay pipe	vit' ri fied clay pipe"
vocational	vo ca' tion al

void ratio	void' ra' tio
void-solid ratio	void' sol' id ra' tio
voids	voids
voile	voile
volatile	vol' a tile
volatile organic compound	vol' a tile or gan' ic com' pound
volatility	vol" a til' i ty
volt	volt
volt-ampere	volt' am' pere
voltage	volt' age
voltage drop	volt' age drop"
voltmeter	volt' me" ter
volume	vol' ume
volume solids	vol' ume sol' ids
volumetric	vol" u met' ric
volute	vo lute'
vomitorium	vom" i to' ri um
vomitory	vom' i to ry
vortex	vor' tex
voussoir	vous soir'
vug	vug
vulcanization	vul" can i za' tion
vulcanize	vul' can ize"

W

wadding	wad' ding
wafer	wa' fer
wafer teks	wa' fer teks"
waferboard	wa' fer board"
waffle slab	waf' fle slab"
wagon	wag' on
wagon stage	wag' on stage"
wainscot	wain' scot
wainscoting	wain' scot ing
waist	waist
waiver	waiv' er
wale	wale
waler	wal' er
walk	walk
walk-in box	walk' in" box"
walk-in cooler	walk' in" cool' er

walk-up	walk' up"
walkway	walk' way"
wall	wall
wall brace	wall' brace
wall-hung toilet	wall' hung" toi' let
wall line	wall' line"
wall opening	wall' o' pen ing
wall outlet	wall' out' let
wall panel	wall' pan' el
wall plate	wall' plate"
wall system	wall' sys' tem
wall-to-wall	wall' to wall'
wall-wash luminaire	wall' wash' lu" mi naire'
wall-washer	wall' wash' er
wall-washing	wall' wash' ing
wallboard	wall' board"
wallcovering	wall' cov' er ing
walling	wal' ling
wallner line	wall' ner line"
wallpaper	wall' pa" per
wallpiece	wall' piece"
walnut	wal' nut
wane	wane
wardrobe	ward' robe
wardrobe hook	ward' robe hook"
warehouse	ware' house"
warm-air furnace	warm' air' fur' nace
warm-setting adhesive	warm' set' ting ad he' sive
Warnecke, John Carl	War' nec ke, John' Carl'
warp	warp
warpage	warp' age
warped	warped
warping	warp' ing
warranty	war' ran ty
Warren truss	War' ren truss"
wash	wash
wash boring	wash' bor' ing
wash coat	wash' coat"
wash-off product	wash' off" prod' uct
wash-out	wash' out"
washable	wash' a ble
washbasin	wash' ba" sin

washboard	wash' board"
washer	wash' er
washing	wash' ing
washroom	wash' room"
Wassily chair	Was' si ly chair"
waste	waste
waste-disposal unit	waste' dis pos' al u' nit
waste stack	waste' stack"
watchman	watch' man
water	wa' ter
water absorption	wa' ter ab sorp' tion
water-base paint	wa' ter base" paint"
water-cement ratio	wa' ter ce ment' ra' tio
water closet	wa' ter clos' et
water-cooled	wa' ter cooled"
water-cooling tower	wa' ter cool' ing tow' er
water curtain	wa' ter cur' tain
water fountain	wa' ter foun' tain
water hammer	wa' ter ham' mer
water-hammer arrester	wa' ter ham' mer ar rest' er
water heater	wa' ter heat' er
water line	wa' ter line"
water main	wa' ter main"
water meter	wa' ter me' ter
water-reducing admixture	wa' ter re duc' ing ad' mix' ture
water-reducing agent	wa' ter re duc' ing a' gent
water-repellant	wa' ter re pel' lant
water repellent	wa' ter re pel' lent
water-resistant glue	wa' ter re sist' ant glue"
water softener	wa' ter soft' en er
water-supply system	wa' ter sup ply' sys' tem
water table	wa' ter ta' ble
water vapor	wa' ter va' por
watercourse	wa' ter course"
waterline	wa' ter line"
waterproof	wa' ter proof"
waterproofing	wa' ter proof" ing
watershed	wa' ter shed"
waterstop	wa' ter stop"
watertight	wa' ter tight"
waterway	wa' ter way"
watt	watt

watt-hour	watt' hour"
watt-hour meter	watt' hour" me' ter
wattle and daub	wat' tle and daub'
wave front	wave' front"
waveform	wave' form"
wavelength	wave' length"
waves	waves
wavy grain	wav' y grain"
wax	wax
waxing	wax' ing
wayfinding	way' find" ing
wear	wear
wear layer	wear' lay' er
wearing surface	wear' ing sur' face
weather	weath' er
weather-exposed surface	weath' er ex posed' sur' face
weather protection	weath' er pro tec' tion
weather resistance	weath' er re sist' ance
weather strip	weath' er strip"
weather stripping	weath' er strip' ping
weather-struck joint	weath' er struck" joint
weatherability	weath er a bil' i ty
weathered	weath' ered
weathered joint	weath' ered joint"
weathering	weath' er ing
weatherize	weath' er ize"
weatherometer	weath' er om' e ter
weatherproof	weath' er proof"
weathertight	weath' er tight"
weave	weave
weaving	weav' ing
web	web
web connection	web' con nec' tion
web crippling	web' crip' pling
web member	web' mem' ber
webbed	webbed
webbing	web' bing
wedge	wedge
wedging	wedg' ing
weep hole	weep' hole"
Weese, Harry	Weese', Har' ry
weft	weft

weft knit	weft' knit"
weight	weight
weir	weir
weld	weld
weld-line	weld' line"
weld penetration	weld' pen" e tra' tion
weld size	weld' size"
weldability	weld" a bil' i ty
welded tube	weld' ed tube"
welded-wire fabric	weld' ed wire' fab' ric
welder	weld' er
welding	weld' ing
welding rod	weld' ing rod"
weldment	weld' ment"
well	well
wellhead	well' head"
wellhole	well' hole"
welt	welt
welting	welt' ing
western	west' ern
western framing	west' ern fram' ing
western hemlock	west' ern hem' lock
western red cedar	west' ern red" ce' dar
wet-bulb temperature	wet' bulb tem' per a ture
wet felting	wet' felt' ing
wet-film thickness	wet' film" thick' ness
wet glazing	wet' glaz' ing
wet-pipe sprinkler system	wet' pipe' sprink' ler sys' tem
wet seal	wet' seal
wet standpipe	wet' stand' pipe"
wet-use adhesive	wet' use" ad he' sive
wetland	wet' land"
wetting	wet' ting
wetting agent	wet' ting a" gent
whaler	whal' er
wheel load	wheel' load"
wheelbarrow	wheel' bar" row
wheelbase	wheel' base"
whetstone	whet' stone"
whiplash curve	whip' lash" curve"
whispering gallery	whis' per ing gal' ler y
White Alabama	White' Al" a bam' a

white latex adhesive	white' la' tex ad he' sive
white noise	white' noise"
white oak	white' oak'
white pine	white' pine'
whitening	whit' en ing
whiteware	white' ware"
whitewood	white' wood"
whiting	whit' ing
wholesale	whole' sale"
wholesaler	whole' sal" er
whorl	whorl
wick	wick
wickability	wick" a bil' i ty
wicker	wick' er
wicket screen	wick' et screen"
wide-flange beam	wide' flange' beam"
wide-throw hinge	wide' throw' hinge"
widow's walk	wid' ow's walk"
Wilton carpet	Wil' ton car' pet
winch	winch
wind	wind
wind brace	wind' brace"
wind energy	wind' en' er gy
wind load	wind' load"
wind pressure	wind' pres' sure
wind rock	wind' rock"
wind shake	wind' shake"
wind tunnel	wind' tun' nel
windbreak	wind' break"
winder	wind' er
winding stair	wind' ing stair"
windlass	wind' lass
window	win' dow
window box	win' dow box"
window sill	win' dow sill"
window unit	win' dow u' nit
window wall	win' dow wall"
windowpane	win' dow pane"
windproof	wind' proof"
windrow	wind' row"
Windsor chair	Wind' sor chair"
wine cellar	wine' cel' lar

wing	wing
wing chair	wing' chair"
wing wall	wing' wall"
winning	win' ning
winterize	win' ter ize"
winterized	win' ter ized"
winterizing	win' ter iz" ing
wiped joint	wiped joint
wire	wire
wire brad	wire' brad"
wire cloth	wire' cloth'
wire-cut brick	wire' cut' brick"
wire cutter	wire' cut' ter
wire glass	wire' glass'
wire-mesh ties	wire' mesh" ties
wire nail	wire' nail"
wire nut	wire' nut"
wire saw	wire' saw"
wire shelving	wire' shelv' ing
wireframe	wire' frame"
wireless	wire' less
Wiremold™	Wire' mold"
wireway	wire' way"
wiring	wir' ing
withdrawal	with draw' al
witness line	wit' ness line"
wobble friction	wob' ble fric' tion
Wolman salts™	Wol' man salts
Wolmanized	Wol man ized
wood	wood
wood flush door	wood' flush" door"
wood-frame construction	wood' frame' con struc' tion
wood preservative	wood' pre serv' a tive
wood screw	wood' screw"
Woodbury	Wood' bur" y
woodcraft	wood' craft
wooden	wood' en
woodgrain	wood' grain"
woodgraining	wood' grain" ing
woodwork	wood' work"
woodworking	wood' work" ing
wool	wool

work	work
work hardening	work' hard' en ing
work triangle	work' tri' an" gle
workability	work" a bil' i ty
workable	work' a ble
worked lumber	worked' lum' ber
worker	work' er
worker's compensation	work' er's com" pen sa' tion
working	work' ing
working drawings	work' ing draw' ings
working life	work' ing life"
working point	work' ing point"
working stress	work' ing stress"
workmanship	work' man ship"
workman's compensation	work' man's com" pen sa' tion
workroom	work' room"
workshop	work' shop"
workspace	work' space"
workstation	work' sta' tion
wormhole	worm' hole
worsted yarn	wor' sted yarn
woven	wo' ven
woven valley	wo' ven val' ley
woven wire	wo' ven wire"
wrap-around frame	wrap' a round" frame
wreath	wreath
wrecking	wreck' ing
wrecking ball	wreck' ing ball"
wrench	wrench
Wright, Frank Lloyd	Wright', Frank' Lloyd'
wrinkle	wrin' kle
wrinkling	wrin' kling
write once, read many	write' once", read' man' y
wrought iron	wrought' i' ron
Wurster, William Wilson	Wurs' ter, Wil' liam Wil' son
wye	wye
wye branch	wye' branch"
wye strainer	wye' strain' er
wythe	wythe
Wyzenbeek test	Wy' zen beek" test

X

X-brace	X' brace"
X-frame	X' frame"
x-ray shielding	x' ray" shield' ing
xenon-arc	xe' non arc"
xerographic	xe" ro graph' ic
xerography	xe rog' ra phy
xylem	xy' lem
xylol	xy' lol

Y

Y-fitting	Y' fit' ting
Yamasaki, Minoru	Ya" ma sa' ki, Mi no' ru
yard	yard
yard lumber	yard' lum' ber
yardage	yard' age
yarn	yarn
yarn-dyed	yarn' dyed"
yarn-dyed fabric	yarn' dyed" fab' ric
yellow	yel' low
yellow birch	yel' low birch"
yellow cypress	yel' low cy' press
yellow pine	yel' low pine"
yellowing	yel' low ing
yield	yield
yield point	yield' point"
yield strength	yield' strength"
yoke	yoke
yoke-back chair	yoke' back" chair
Young's modulus	Young's' mod' u lus

Z

Z-bar	Z' bar"
Z flashing	Z' flash' ing
zebrawood	ze' bra wood"
zee	zee
zeolite equipment	ze' o lite e quip' ment
zero-clearance fireplace	ze' ro clear' ance fire' place
zero-lot-line siting	ze' ro lot ' line" sit' ing

zero-slump concrete	ze' ro slump" con' crete
zeta	ze' ta
ziggurat	zig' gu rat"
zigzag	zig' zag"
zinc	zinc
zinc chromate	zinc' chro' mate
zinc naphthenate	zinc' naph' the nate"
zinc-rich primer	zinc' rich" prim' er
zinc silicate	zinc' sil' i cate"
zinc sulfide	zinc' sul' fide
zipper glazing	zip' per glaz' ing
zone	zone
zoning	zon' ing
zoological	zo" o log' i cal
zoom	zoom

Text abbreviations listed by term

abbreviation	abbr.
abrasive hardness	Ha
acoustical	acous.
acrylonitrile butadiene styrene	ABS
active mass damper system	AMDS
added damping and stiffness system	ADAS
air conditioning	air cond.
air dried	a.d.
alternating current	ac
American	Am.
American Institute of Architects	AIA
American Institute of Steel Construction	AISC
American Institute of Timber Construction	AITC
American National Standards Institute	ANSI
American Society for Testing and Materials	ASTM
American Society of Civil Engineers	ASCE
American Society of Heating, Refrigerating and Air-Conditioning Engineers	ASHRAE
American Society of Mechanical Engineers	ASME
American standard code for information exchange	ASCII
American standard wire gage	ASWG
American wire gage	AWG
ampere	amp
anodized	anod.
apartment	apt.
architectural	arch.
artificial intelligence	AI
assistant	asst.
Associated General Contractors of America	AGC
autoclaved cellular concrete	ACC
automatic	auto.
avenue	ave.
average	avg.
beam	bm
bearing	brg.
bedroom	br.
bell and spigot	B & S
block	blk.
board	bd.

board foot	bd. ft.
board measure	bm
Brinell hardness	Bh
Brinell hardness number	Bhn
British Standard	BS
British Standards Institution	BSI
British thermal unit	Btu
British thermal units per hour	Btuh
Brown and Sharpe gage	B & S
built	blt.
built-up roofing	BUR
cabinet	cab.
calorie	cal.
camber	cam.
Canadian Standards Association	CSA
candela	cd
candlepower	cp
cast iron	CI
catalog	cat.
ceiling	clg.
center to center	c to c
centimeter	cm
central processing unit	CPU
change order	CO
clear	clr.
chlorinated polyethylene	CPE
chlorinated polyvinyl chloride	CPVC
chlorosulfonated polyethylene	CSPE
closed-circuit television	CCTV
coefficient	coef.
coefficient of heat transfer	U
coefficient of thermal conductivity	k
column	col.
combination	comb.
Commission Internationale de l'Eclairage	CIE
common	com.
compact disk—read only memory	CD-ROM
computer-aided design and drafting	CADD
computer-aided drafting	CAD
concrete	conc.
conductance	C
Construction Specifications Institute	CSI

construction manager	CM
continuous	cont.
coordinate	coord.
corporation	corp.
critical path method	CPM
cubic	cu
cubic centimeter	cc
cubic feet per minute	cfm
cubic foot	cu. ft.
cubic inch	cu. in.
cubic meter	cu. m
cubic yard	cu. yd.
cycles per second	cps
decibel	dB
decibel A scale	dBA
degree	deg.
degree Celsius	°C
degree Fahrenheit	°F
department	dept.
dew point	dp.
diagonal	diag.
diameter	diam.
dimension	dim.
direct current	dc
division	div.
dozen	doz.
drain waste and vent	DWV
drainage fixture unit	d.f.u.
drawing	dwg.
each	ea.
electrical	elec.
electrical metallic tubing	EMT
environmental impact statement	EIS
Environmental Protection Agency	EPA
equipment	equip.
equivalent direct radiation	EDR
equivalent temperature differential	ETD
equiviscous temperature range	EVT
errors and omissions	E & O
estimate	est.
existing	exist.
exterior	ext.

Factory Mutual	FM
Fahrenheit (see also degree Fahrenheit)	F
Federal Housing Administration	FHA
Federal Specification	Fed Spec
Fellow of the American Institute of Architects	FAIA
fiber saturation point	fsp
finish	fin.
flashing condition index	FCI
floor	fl.
fluid	fl.
foot	ft.
foot board measure	fbm
foot-pound	ft lb
footcandle	fc
footlambert	fl
for example (Latin: exempli gratia)	e.g.
freight	frt.
gage	ga.
gallon	gal.
gallons per day	gpd
gallons per hour	gph
gallons per minute	gpm
government	govt.
grade B and better	B & Btr.
grade C and better	C & Btr.
grains	gr.
ground	grnd.
gypsum	gyp.
Heating, ventilating, and air conditioning	HVAC
hectare	ha
height	hgt.
hertz	Hz
hexagonal	hex
high definition television	HDTV
high intensity discharge	H.I.D.
high pressure steam	hps
hollow metal	hm
horizontal	horz.
horsepower	hp
hour	hr.
hours	hrs.
hundred weight	cwt

impact insulation class	IIC
impact noise rating	INR
inch	in.
inches per second	ips
incorporated	Inc.
initial graphics exchange specification	IGES
inside diameter	i.d.
Institute of Electrical and Electronics Engineers	IEEE
institute	inst.
insulation	insul.
insulation condition index	ICI
intercommunication system	intercom
International Standards Organization	ISO
inverted roof membrane assembly	IRMA
iron pipe size	ips
joule	J
kelvin	K
kilocalorie	kcal
kilogram	kg
kilogram-meter	kg-m
kilograms per cubic meter	kg/m3
kilohertz	kHz
kilometer	km
kilopascal	kPa
kilovolt	kV
kilovolt-ampere	kVA
kilowatt	kW
kilowatt-hour	kWh
kip	K
kips per square foot	ksf
kips per square inch	ksi
lambert	L
laminated veneer lumber	LVL
lamination	lam.
large document copier	KDC
latent heat	LH
latitude	lat.
left hand	LH
license	lic.
linear foot (feet)	lin. ft.
linear inche(s)	lin. in.
local area network	LAN

logarithm (common)	log
logarithm (natural)	ln
longitude	long.
lumen	lm.
lumens per watt	lm/W
lux	lx
material	mat.
maximum	max.
mean radiant temperature	MRT
medium density fiberboard	MDF
medium density overlay	MDO
membrane condition index	MCI
memorandum	memo
meter	m
methyl ethyl ketone	MKE
millimeter	mm
minimum	min.
minute	min.
miscellaneous	misc.
month	mo.
National Building Code	NBC
National Electric Code	NEC
National Fire Protection Association	NFPA
National Institute of Standards and Technology	NIST
national	nat.
noise reduction coefficient	NRC
north	N
number	no.
Occupational Safety and Health Administration	OSHA
oriented strand board	OSB
ounce	oz.
outside diameter	o.d.
page	p
parts per million	ppm
pascal	Pa
penny	d
phase	PH
photo mechanical transfer	PMT
planned unit development	PUD
polyvinyl acetate	PVA
polyvinyl chloride	PVC
pound	lb.

pounds per cubic foot	pcf
pounds per square foot	psf
pounds per square inch	psi
professional engineer	P.E.
project evaluation and review technique	PERT
public address system	PA
purchase order	P.O.
radian	rad
radius	r or R
reference	ref.
relative humidity	RH
request for proposal	RFP
required	reqd.
return on investment	ROI
right-of-way	ROW
Rockwell hardness	Rh
roof condition index	RCI
Royal Institute of British Architects	R.I.B.A.
second	sec.
shear plate	Sh. Pl.
sheet-metal screw	SMC
single phase	1PH
society	soc.
sound transmission class	STC
specification	spec.
square	sq.
Standard Building Code	SBC
standard wire gage	S.W.G.
standards	stds.
structural	struc.
surfaced four sides	S4S
that is (Latin: id est)	i.e.
thousand	M
thousand board feet	MFBM
thousand foot-pounds	kip-ft
threaded rod	thrd.
three phase	3PH
tongue-and-groove	T & G
turnbuckle	tbkl.
ultrahigh frequency	UHF
ultraviolet	uv
Underwriters Laboratories	UL

Uniform Building Code	UBC
United States Gage	USG
versus	vs.
very high frequency	VHF
video display terminal	VDT
visual comfort probability	VCP
volatile organic compound	VOC
volt	V
volts alternating current	VAC
watt	W or w
week	wk.
weight	wt.
wide flange	WF
wood	wd.
write once read many	WORM
yard	yd.

Text abbreviations listed by abbreviation

1PH	single phase
3PH	three phase
a.d.	air dried
abbr.	abbreviation
ABS	acrylonitrile butadiene styrene
ac	alternating current
ACC	autoclaved cellular concrete
acous.	acoustical
ADAS	added damping and stiffness system
AGC	Associated General Contractors of America
AI	artificial intelligence
AIA	American Institute of Architects
air cond.	air conditioning
AISC	American Institute of Steel Construction
AITC	American Institute of Timber Construction
Am.	American
AMDS	active mass damper system
amp	ampere
anod.	anodized
ANSI	American National Standards Institute
apt.	apartment
arch.	architectural
ASCE	American Society of Civil Engineers
ASCII	American standard code for information exchange
ASHRAE and	American Society of Heating, Refrigerating Air-Conditioning Engineers
ASME	American Society of Mechanical Engineers
asst.	assistant
ASTM	American Society for Testing and Materials
ASWG	American standard wire gage
auto.	automatic
ave.	avenue
avg.	average
AWG	American wire gage
B & Btr.	grade B and better
B & S	bell and spigot
B & S	Brown and Sharpe gage
bd.	board
bd. ft.	board foot

Bh	Brinell hardness
Bhn	Brinell hardness number
blk.	block
blt.	built
bm	beam
bm	board measure
br.	bedroom
brg.	bearing
BS	British Standard
BSI	British Standards Institution
Btu	British thermal unit
Btuh	British thermal units per hour
BUR	built-up roofing
C	conductance
°C	degree Celsius
C & Btr.	grade C and better
c to c	center to center
cab.	cabinet
CAD	computer-aided drafting
CADD	computer-aided design and drafting
cal.	calorie
cam.	camber
cat.	catalog
cc	cubic centimeter
CCTV	closed-circuit television
cd	candela
CD-ROM	compact disk—read only memory
cfm	cubic feet per minute
CI	cast iron
CIE	Commission Internationale de l'Eclairage
clg.	ceiling
clr.	clear
CM	construction manager
cm	centimeter
CO	change order
coef.	coefficient
col.	column
com.	common
comb.	combination
conc.	concrete
cont.	continuous
coord.	coordinate

corp.	corporation
cp	candlepower
CPE	chlorinated polyethylene
CPM	critical path method
cps	cycles per second
CPU	central processing unit
CPVC	chlorinated polyvinyl chloride
CSA	Canadian Standards Association
CSI	Construction Specifications Institute
CSPE	chlorosulfonated polyethylene
cu	cubic
cu. ft.	cubic foot
cu. in.	cubic inch
cu. m	cubic meter
cu. yd.	cubic yard
cwt	hundred weight
d	penny
d.f.u.	drainage fixture unit
dB	decibel
dBA	decibel A scale
dc	direct current
deg.	degree
dept.	department
diag.	diagonal
diam.	diameter
dim.	dimension
div.	division
doz.	dozen
dp.	dew point
dwg.	drawing
DWV	drain waste and vent
E & O	errors and omissions
e.g.	for example (Latin: exempli gratia)
ea.	each
EDR	equivalent direct radiation
EIS	environmental impact statement
elec.	electrical
EMT	electrical metallic tubing
EPA	Environmental Protection Agency
equip.	equipment
est.	estimate
ETD	equivalent temperature differential

EVT	equiviscous temperature range
exist.	existing
ext.	exterior
F	Fahrenheit
°F	degree Fahrenheit
FAIA	Fellow of the American Institute of Architects
fbm	foot board measure
fc	footcandle
FCI	flashing condition index
Fed Spec	Federal Specification
FHA	Federal Housing Administration
fin.	finish
fl	footlambert
fl.	floor
fl.	fluid
FM	Factory Mutual
frt.	freight
fsp	fiber saturation point
ft lb	foot-pound
ft.	foot
ga.	gage
gal.	gallon
govt.	government
gpd	gallons per day
gph	gallons per hour
gpm	gallons per minute
gr.	grains
grnd.	ground
gyp.	gypsum
H.I.D.	high intensity discharge
Ha	abrasive hardness
ha	hectare
HDTV	high definition television
hex	hexagonal
hgt.	height
hm	hollow metal
horz.	horizontal
hp	horsepower
hps	high pressure steam
hr.	hour
hrs.	hours
HVAC	Heating, ventilating, and air conditioning

Hz	hertz
i.d.	inside diameter
i.e.	that is (Latin: id est)
ICI	insulation condition index
IEEE	Institute of Electrical and Electronics Engineers
IGES	initial graphics exchange specification
IIC	impact insulation class
in.	inch
Inc.	incorporated
INR	impact noise rating
inst.	institute
insul.	insulation
intercom	intercommunication system
ips	inches per second
ips	iron pipe size
IRMA	inverted roof membrane assembly
ISO	International Standards Organization
J	joule
K	kelvin
K	kip
k	coefficient of thermal conductivity
kcal	kilocalorie
KDC	large document copier
kg	kilogram
kg-m	kilogram-meter
kg/m3	kilograms per cubic meter
kHz	kilohertz
kip-ft	thousand foot-pounds
km	kilometer
kPa	kilopascal
ksf	kips per square foot
ksi	kips per square inch
kV	kilovolt
kVA	kilovolt-ampere
kW	kilowatt
kWh	kilowatt-hour
L	lambert
lam.	lamination
LAN	local area network
lat.	latitude
lb.	pound
LH	latent heat

LH	left hand
lic.	license
lin. ft.	linear foot (feet)
lin. in.	linear inche(s)
lm.	lumen
lm/W	lumens per watt
ln	logarithm (natural)
log	logarithm (common)
long.	longitude
LVL	laminated veneer lumber
lx	lux
M	thousand
m	meter
mat.	material
max.	maximum
MCI	membrane condition index
MDF	medium density fiberboard
MDO	medium density overlay
memo	memorandum
MFBM	thousand board feet
min.	minimum
min.	minute
misc.	miscellaneous
MKE	methyl ethyl ketone
mm	millimeter
mo.	month
MRT	mean radiant temperature
N	north
nat.	national
NBC	National Building Code
NEC	National Electric Code
NFPA	National Fire Protection Association
NIST	National Institute of Standards andTechnology
no.	number
NRC	noise reduction coefficient
o.d.	outside diameter
OSB	oriented strand board
OSHA	Occupational Safety and Health Administration
oz.	ounce
p	page
P.E.	professional engineer

PA	public address system
Pa	pascal
pcf	pounds per cubic foot
PERT	project evaluation and review technique
PH	phase
PMT	photo mechanical transfer
P.O.	purchase order
ppm	parts per million
psf	pounds per square foot
psi	pounds per square inch
PUD	planned unit development
PVA	polyvinyl acetate
PVC	polyvinyl chloride
r or R	radius
R.I.B.A.	Royal Institute of British Architects
rad	radian
RCI	roof condition index
ref.	reference
reqd.	required
RFP	request for proposal
RH	relative humidity
Rh	Rockwell hardness
ROI	return on investment
ROW	right-of-way
S.W.G.	standard wire gage
S4S	surfaced four sides
SBC	Standard Building Code
sec.	second
Sh. Pl.	shear plate
SMC	sheet-metal screw
soc.	society
spec.	specification
sq.	square
STC	sound transmission class
stds.	standards
struc.	structural
T & G	tongue-and-groove
tbkl.	turnbuckle
thrd.	threaded rod
U	coefficient of heat transfer
UBC	Uniform Building Code
UHF	ultrahigh frequency

UL	Underwriters Laboratories
USG	United States Gage
uv	ultraviolet
V	volt
VAC	volts alternating current
VCP	visual comfort probability
VDT	video display terminal
VHF	very high frequency
VOC	volatile organic compound
vs.	versus
W or w	watt
wd.	wood
WF	wide flange
wk.	week
WORM	write once read many
wt.	weight
yd.	yard

Abbreviations used on drawings listed by term

Above	ABV
Above finished floor	AFF
Above finished grade	AFG
Above finished slab	AFS
Above grade	AG
Above ground level	AGL
Above raised floor	ARF
Above suspended ceiling	ASC
Abrasive	ABRSV
Absolute	ABS
Access door	AD
Access floor	AF
Access panel	AP
Acid proof	AP
Acid resistant	ACID RES
Acid resistant pipe	ACID RES P
Acid resistant vent	ACID RES V
Acid resistant waste	ACID RES W
Acid vent	AV
Acid waste	AW
Acoustical	ACOUS
Acoustical insulation	ACOUS INSUL
Acoustical panel	ACOUS PNL
Acoustical plaster	ACOUS PLAS
Acoustical plaster ceiling	APC
Acoustical tile	ACOUS TILE
Acoustical wall treatment	ACWT
Acrylonitrile butadiene styrene	ABS
Actual	ACT
Adapter	ADPTR
Addendum	ADD
Addition	ADD
Adhesive	ADH
Adjacent	ADJ
Adjustable	ADJ
Aggregate	AGGR
Aggregate base course	ABC
Ahead	AHD
Air conditioning	AC
Air conditioning unit	ACU

Air cooled condensing unit	ACCU
Air handling unit	AHU
Air moving device	AMD
Air supply unit	ASU
Air vent	AV
Alarm	ALM
Alarm annunciator panel	AAP
All weather	A/W
Allowance	ALLOW
Alloy	ALY
Alteration	ALTRN
Alternate	ALT
Alternate number	ALT NO
Alternating current	AC
Aluminum	AL
Ambient	AMB
American Lumber Standard	ALS
American National Standards Institute	ANSI
American wire gage	AWG
Ammeter	AMM
Amount	AMT
Ampere	AMP
Ampere hour	AMP HR
Ampere hour meter	AHM
Amplifier	AMPL
Amplitude modulation	AM
Analog	ANLG
Anchor	AHR
Anchor bolt	AB
Anneal	ANL
Annunciator	ANN
Anodized	ANOD
Antenna	ANT
Apartment	APT
Apparatus	APPAR
Appendix	APPX
Approved	APPD
Approximately	APPROX
Aquastat	AQST
Architect	ARCH
Architect-Engineer	A-E
Architectural projected window	APW

Architectural terra cotta	ATC
Area	A
Area drain	AD
Artificial	ART
As required	AR
Asphalt	ASPH
Asphaltic concrete	AC
Assembly	ASSY
Association	ASSN
Asymmetrical	ASYM
Attachment	ATCH
Audio frequency	AF
Audio visual	AV
Automatic	AUTO
Automatic air damper	AAD
Automatic door closer	ADC
Automatic door seal	ADS
Automatic frequency control	AFC
Automatic sprinkler	AS
Automatic sprinkler drain	ASD
Automatic sprinkler riser	ASR
Automatic transfer switch	ATS
Auxiliary power unit	APU
Auxiliary switch	ASW
Avenue	AVE
Average	AVG
Azimuth	AZ
Back to back	B/B
Back of curb	BC
Back water valve	BWV
Backdraft damper	BDD
Backflow preventer	BFP
Baffle	BAF
Balance	BAL
Balancing damper	BAL DMPR
Balancing valve	BAL V
Balcony	BALC
Ball bearing	BBRG
Ball valve	BV
Ballast	BLST
Balled and burlapped	B & B
Base board radiation	BBRR

Base line	BL
Base plate	BP
Baseboard	BB
Basement	BSMT
Beam	BM
Bearing	BRG
Bearing plate	BRG PL
Bed joint	BJT
Bedroom	BR
Bell and flange	B & F
Bell and spigot	B & S
Bell end	BE
Below	BLW
Below ceiling	BLW CLG
Below finish floor	BLW FFLR
Bench mark	BM
Bend radius	BR
Between	BETW
Bevel	BEV
Beveled plate glass	BPG
Bituminous	BITUM
Black iron	BI
Block	BLK
Blocking	BLKG
Blower	BLO
Board	BD
Boiler	BLR
Boiler feed booster pump	BFBP
Book shelves	BK SH
Booster	BSTR
Both faces	BF
Both sides	BS
Both ways	BW
Bottom	BOT
Bottom face	BF
Boulevard	BLVD
Bracing	BRCG
Bracket	BRKT
Brass	BRS
Breaker	BRKR
Brick	BRK
Bridging	BRDG

Bridging joist	BRDG JST
Bright annealed	BA
British thermal unit	BTU
British thermal units per hour	BTUH
Bronze	BRZ
Brown and Sharpe gage	B & S
Building	BLDG
Building line	BL
Built-up	BU
Built-up roof	BUR
Bulkhead	BLKHD
Bulletin board	BB
Burglar alarm	BA
Butt weld	BW
Butterfly check valve	BCV
Butterfly valve	BFV
Cabinet	CAB
Cabinet heater	CAB H
Cabinet unit heater	CUH
Cable television	CTV
Calking	CLKG
Camber	CAM
Candlepower	CP
Canvas	CANV
Capacity	CAP
Carpet	CARP
Cased opening	CO
Casement	CSMT
Casework	CSWK
Casing	CSG
Casing bead	CSB
Cast iron	CI
Cast iron pipe	CIP
Cast iron radiator	CIR
Cast iron soil pipe	CISP
Cast steel	CSTL
Cast stone	CS
Catalog	CAT
Catch basin	CB
Catwalk	CATW
Cavity	CAV
Ceiling	CLG

Ceiling diffuser	CLG DIFF
Ceiling grille	CG
Ceiling height	CLG HT
Ceiling register	CLG REG
Cement	CEM
Cement mortar	CEM MORT
Cement plaster	CEM PLAS
Center to center	C TO C
Center line	CL
Centimeter	CM
Ceramic	CER
Ceramic tile	CER TILE
Chalkboard	CH BD
Chamfer	CHAM
Change order	CO
Channel	CHAN
Check	CHK
Check valve	CHKV
Chemical	CHEM
Chilled and heating water return	CHHWR
Chilled and heating water supply	CHHWS
Chilled water	CHW
Chilled water primary pump	CHWPP
Chilled water pump	CHWP
Chilled water recirculating pumb	CHWRP
Chilled water return	CHWR
Chilled water supply	CHWS
Chiller	CH
Chimney	CHIM
Chlorinated polyethylene	CPE
Chlorinated polyvinyl chloride	CPVC
Chlorosulfonated polyethylene	CSPE
Chrome plated	CHR PL
Circle	CIR
Circuit	CKT
Circuit breaker	CKT BKR
Circular	CIRC
Circulating hot water	CHW
Circulating water pump	CWP
Circumference	CIRC
Circumference	CRCMF
Clamp	CLP

Classroom	CLRM
Cleanout	CO
Clear	CLR
Closed circuit television	CCTV
Closet	CLO
Closure	CLOS
Coated	CTD
Coaxial cable	COAX
Coefficient	COEF
Cold-rolled	CR
Cold-rolled steel	CRS
Cold water	CW
Column	COL
Column line	CLL
Combination	COMB
Combination towel dispenser & receptacle	CTD & R
Common	COM
Communication	COMM
Compartment	COMPT
Composite	CMPST
Composition	COMP
Compressible	CPRS
Compressor	CPRSR
Concrete masonry unit	CMU
Concrete	CONC
Concrete equipment base	CEB
Concrete floor	CONC FL
Concrete pipe	CP
Concrete splash block	CSB
Condenser water pump	CWP
Condenser water return	CWR
Condenser water supply	CWS
Condensor	COND
Conduit	CND
Conference	CONF
Connection	CONN
Construction	CONSTR
Construction joint	CJ
Continuous	CONT
Contract limit line	CLL
Contractor	CONTR
Contractor furnished equipment	CFE

Control joint	CLJ
Control panel	CP
Control valve	CV
Convector	CONV
Cool white	CW
Cool white deluxe	CWX
Cooling tower	CT
Cooling tower return	CTR
Cooling tower supply	CTS
Coordinate	COORD
Corner	CNR
Corner bead	COR BD
Corner guard	CG
Corridor	CORR
Corrugated	CORR
Corrugated metal pipe	CMP
Counter	CNTR
Counter-clockwise	CCW
Counterflashing	CFLG
Countersunk	CSK
Cover	COV
Cover plate	COV PL
Cross arm	X ARM
Cross section	X SECT
Crown	CRN
Cubicle	CUB
Curb and gutter	C & G
Cycle	CY
Cylinder	CYL
Cylinder lock	CYL L
Damper	DMPR
Dampproof course	DPC
Dampproofing	DMPF
Datum	DAT
Dead load	DL
Degree	DEG
Deluxe white	DW
Demolition	DEMO
Department	DEPT
Detail	DET
Detector	DET
Diagonal	DIAG

Diameter	DIAM
Diesel fuel	DF
Difference	DIFF
Diffuser	DIFF
Dimension	DIM
Dimmer control panel	DCP
Dining room	DR
Direct current	DC
Direct expansion	DX
Dishwasher	DW
Distance	DIST
Distribution panel	DISTR PNL
Ditto	DO
Division	DIV
Domestic water heater	DWH
Door closer	DCL
Door frame	DFR
Door louver	DLV
Door stop	DST
Double	DBL
Double acting	DBL ACT
Double acting door	DAD
Double glazing	DBL GLZ
Double hung	DH
Double joist	DJ
Double pole, double throw	DPDT
Double pole, single throw	DPST
Dowel	DWL
Down	DN
Downspout	DS
Drain tile	DT
Drain valve	DV
Drain, waste & vent	DWV
Drawer	DWR
Drawing	DWG
Drinking fountain	DF
Drive	DR
Drop manhole	DMH
Drop siding	D/S
Drum trap	DT
Dry bulb	DB
Dry standpipe	DSP

Dry well	DRW
Duct access panel	DAP
Duct covering insulation	DCI
Duct liner insulation	DLI
Dumbwaiter	DWTR
Duplex	DX
Duplicate	DUP
Dutch door	DD
Each face	EF
Each way	EW
Eased edges	EE
Easement	ESMT
Easement line	EL
East	E
Eccentric	ECC
Economizor	ECON
Effluent	EFL
Electrical	ELEC
Electrical cabinet	ECAB
Electrical hand dryer	EHD
Electrical heating unit	EHP
Electrical metalic tubing	EMT
Electrical outlet	EO
Electrical panel	EP
Electrical water cooler	EWC
Electrical water heater	EWH
Elevation	EL
Elevator	ELEV
Emergency	EMER
Emergency shower	EMER SHR
Emergency switch panel	ESP
Enamel	ENAM
Enclosure	ENCL
Energy	ENGY
Engine	ENG
Engineer	ENGR
Entrance	ENTR
Equally spaced	EQL SP
Equipment	EQUIP
Equipment drain	EDR
Equivalent	EQUIV
Erection	ERECT

Escalator	ESCAL
Estimate	EST
Ethylene propylene diene monomer	EPDM
Evaporate	EVAP
Evaporative cooling unit	ECU
Excavate	EXC
Exchanger	EXCH
Exhaust	EXH
Exhaust air	EXH A
Exhaust duct	EXH DT
Exhaust fan	EXH FN
Exhaust grille	EXH GR
Exhaust hood	EXH HD
Exhaust register	EXH RG
Existing	EXST
Existing grade	EXST GR
Expansion	EXP
Expansion bolt	EXP BT
Expansion joint	EXP JT
Explosion proof	EPRF
Extension	EXTN
Exterior	EXT
Exterior insulation and finish system	EIFS
Extra heavy	X HVY
Extrusion	EXTR
Fabric wall covering	FWC
Fabricate	FAB
Face of concrete	FOC
Face of finish	FOF
Face of masonry	FOM
Face of studs	FOS
Face to face	F/F
Fan coil unit	FCU
Far side	FS
Fastener	FSTNR
Federal Specification	FS
Feeder	FDR
Feedwater	FDW
Feet board measure	FBM
Feet per minute	FPM
Feet per second	FPS
Female	FEM

Female pipe thread	FPT
Fence	FN
Fiberboard	FBD
Fiberglass	FGL
Finish	FIN
Finish floor	FIN FL
Finish grade	FIN GR
Finned tube convector	FTC
Finned tube radiator	FTR
Fire alarm	FA
Fire alarm control panel	FACP
Fire brick	F BRK
Fire damper	FDMPR
Fire department connection	DFC
Fire department valve	FDV
Fire extinguisher	FEXT
Fire extinguisher cabinet	FEC
Fire hose cabinet	FHC
Fire hose rack	FHR
Fire hydrant	FHY
Fire protection water supply	FPW
Fire rating	FR
Fire sprinkler head	FSH
Fire standpipe	FSP
Fire water pump	FWP
Fireplace	FPL
Fireproofing	FPRF
Fixture	FXTR
Flange	FLG
Flared	FLRD
Flashing	FL
Flat bar	FB
Flat head machine screw	FHMS
Flat head wood screw	FHWS
Flexible connector	FLEX C
Float glass	FLT GL
Floor	FLR
Floor cleanout	FCO
Floor drain	FD
Floor finish	FLR FIN
Floor plate	FLR PL
Floor register	FLR REG

Floor sink	FLR SK
Flooring	FLG
Flow line	FLL
Flow switch	FLSW
Fluorescent	FLUOR
Folding	FLDG
Footcandle	FC
Footing	FTG
Foundation	FDN
Frame	FR
Framed mirror	FR MIR
Frequency	FREQ
Frequency modulation	FM
Fresh air intake	FAI
From floor above	FFA
From floor below	FFB
Front	FRT
Fuel oil	FO
Full size	FS
Full height partition	FHP
Furnace	FUR
Furniture	FURN
Furring	FURR
Future	FUT
Gage	GA
Gallon	GAL
Gallons per day	GPD
Gallons per hour	GPH
Gallons per minute	GPM
Gallons per second	GPS
Galvanized	GALV
Galvanized iron	GI
Galvanized iron pipe	CIP
Galvanized steel	GALVS
Garage	GAR
Gas	G
Gas vent through roof	GVTR
Gas water heater	GWH
Gasket	GSKT
Gate valve	GTV
General	GENL
General contractor	GC

Generator	GEN
Glass	GL
Glass block	GLB
Glaze, Glazing	GLZ
Glazed	GLZD
Glazed concrete masonry unit	GLZ CMU
Glazed facing unit	GFU
Globe valve	GLV
Glued laminated	GLU LAM
Gooseneck	GSNK
Government	GOVT
Grab bar	GB
Grade	GR
Grade beam	GR BM
Grade line	GR LN
Gravel	GVL
Gravity roof ventilator	GRV
Gravity vent	GV
Grease trap	GT
Grille	GRL
Ground	GND
Ground fault interrupter	GFI
Grout	GT
Guard rail	GDR
Gutter	GUT
Gutter drain	GD
Gypsum	GYP
Gypsum board	GYP BD
Gypsum plaster	GYP PLAS
Hand dryer	HD
Handrail	HNDRL
Hanger	HGR
Hardboard	HDBD
Hardware	HDW
Hardwood	HDWD
Head	HD
Head joint	HD JT
Header	HDR
Heat	HT
Heat absorbing glass	HAGL
Heat exchanger	HEX
Heat recovery unit	HRU

Heat transfer coefficient	U
Heater	HTR
Heating	HTG
Heating, ventilating and air conditioning	HVAC
Heating water return	HTWR
Heating water supply	HTWS
Heavy	HVY
Heavy duty	HD
Height	HGT
Hertz	HZ
Hexagonal	HEX
High	H
High intensity discharge	HID
High output	HO
High point	HPT
High pressure	HP
High pressure boiler	HPB
High pressure gas	HPG
High pressure return	HPR
High pressure steam	HPS
High strength	HS
High strength bolt	HSB
High velocity diffuser	HVD
High velocity terminal	HVT
Highway	HWY
Hold-open	HO
Hollow concrete masonry unit	HCMU
Hollow core	HC
Hollow metal	HM
Hollow metal door	HMD
Hollow metal frame	HMF
Horizontal	HORIZ
Horsepower	HP
Hose bibb	HB
Hose cabinet	HC
Hose valve	HV
Hospital	HOSP
Hot and cold water	H & CW
Hot water	HW
Hot water boiler	HWB
Hot water circulating pump	HWCP
Hot water coil	HWC

Hot water pump	HWP
Hot water return	HWR
Hot water supply	HWS
Hot water circulating	HWC
Hour	HR
House	HSE
Humidistat	HSTAT
Hydrant	HYD
Hydraulic	HYDR
Impregnate	IMPRG
Incandescent	INCAND
Incinerator	INCIN
Include	INCL
Indicator	IND
Indirect waste	IW
Inlet	INL
Inlet manhole	IMH
Inside diameter	ID
Inside face	IF
Instantaneous water heater	IWH
Insulate	INS
Insulated panel	INSUL PNL
Insulation	INSUL
Intake fan	IF
Intercommunication	INTERCOM
Interior	INTR
Interior telephone cabinet	ITC
Invert	INV
Invert elevation	INV EL
Inverted roof membrane assembly	IRMA
Iron pipe	IP
Iron pipe size	IPS
Irrigation water	IW
Isometric	ISO
Janitor	JAN
Janitor's closet	JC
Joint	JT
Joist	JST
Junction	JCT
Junction box	JB
Junior	JR
Keene's cement plaster	KCP

Keyway	KWY
Kick plate	KPL
Kiln dried	KD
Kilogram	KG
Kilovolt	KV
Kilovolt ampere	KVA
Kilovolt-ampere hour meter	KVAHM
Kilowatt	KW
Kilowatt-hour	KWH
Kilowatt-hour meter	KWAM
Kip	K
Kips per linear foot	KLF
Kips per squre foot	KSF
Kitchen	KIT
Knee brace	KB
Knock down	KD
Knockout	KO
Knockout panel	KOP
Laboratory	LAB
Ladder	LAD
Lag bolt	LB
Lamination	LAM
Landing	LDG
Large	LRG
Lateral	LATL
Lath and plaster	L & P
Latitude	LAT
Laundry	LAU
Lavatory	LAV
Leader	LDR
Left	L
Left hand	LH
Left hand reverse	LHR
Length	LG
Length overall	LOA
Level	LVL
Library	LIB
Light	LT
Light pole	LP
Lighting	LTG
Lighting panel	LTG PNL
Lightproof	LP

Lightweight	LT WT
Lightweight concrete	LWC
Lightweight concrete masonry unit	LCMU
Linear	LIN
Linear ceiling diffuser	LCD
Linear diffuser	LD
Linear foot	LF
Lintel	LNTL
Liquefied petroleum	LP
Live load	LL
Living room	LR
Load bearing	LD BRG
Locker	LKR
Locker room	LKR RM
Long leg horizontal	LLH
Long leg vertical	LLV
Longitudinal	LONG
Loudspeaker	LS
Louver	LVR
Louvered roof vent	LRV
Low point	LPT
Low pressure	LP
Low pressure boiler	LPB
Low pressure condensate return	LPCR
Low voltage	LV
Lumber	LBR
Machine	MACH
Machine bolt	MB
Machine room	MACH RM
Maintenance	MAINT
Make-up air unit	MAU
Manfacturing	MFG
Manhole	MH
Manual	MAN
Manual volume damper	MVD
Marble	MARB
Mark	MK
Masonry	MAS
Masonry opening	MO
Master antenna television system	MATV
Master bedroom	MBR
Material	MATL

Maximum	MAX
Maximum overall length	MOL
Mechanical	MECH
Mechanical equipment room	MER
Medicine cabinet	MC
Medium	MED
Medium density overlay	MDO
Meeting	MTG
Membrane	MEMB
Metal	MET
Metal lath	ML
Meter	M
Mezzanine	MEZZ
Mile	MI
Mill run	MR
Million gallons per day	MGD
Millwork	MLWK
Minimum	MIN
Minute	MIN
Mirror	MIR
Miscellaneous	MISC
Mixing box	MB
Mixture	MIX
Module	MOD
Molding	MLDG
Monitor	MON
Monument	MON
Mop service basin	MSB
Mop/broom holder	MBH
Mortar	MTR
Motor	MOT
Motor control center	MCC
Motor generator	MG
Motor operated damper	MOD
Motor starter panel	MSP
Mounted	MTD
Mounting	MTG
Movable	MVBL
Mullion	MULL
Multi-zone	MZ
Multiple	MULT
Nameplate	NPL

National Electric Code	NEC
National Fire Protection Association	NFPA
Natural	NAT
Near face	NF
Near side	NS
Negative	NEG
Neutral	NEUT
Nipple	NIP
Nipple	NPL
No paint	NP
Noise criterion	NC
Noise reduction	NR
Noise reduction coefficient	NRC
Nominal	NOM
North	N
Not applicable	MA
Not in contract	NIC
Not to scale	NTS
Number	NO
Obscure	OBS
Obscure glass	OGL
Obscure wire glass	OWGL
Office	OFF
Oil circuit breaker	OCB
On center	OC
One thousand foot pounds	KIP FT
Opening	OPNG
Opposite	OPP
Optional	OPT
Original	ORIG
Ounce	OZ
Out to out	O/O
Outside air	OA
Outside air damper	OAD
Outside air intake	OIA
Outside diameter	OD
Outside dimension	OD
Outside face	OF
Outside radius	OR
Overall	OA
Overflow	OVFL
Overflow roof drain	ORD

Overhead	OVHD
Owner furnished-contractor installed	OFCI
Owner furnished-owner installed	OFOI
Oxygen	OXY
Paint	PNT
Painted	PTD
Pair	PR
Panel	PNL
Panic bar	PB
Paper cup dispenser	PCD
Paper towel dispenser	PTD
Paper towel receptacle	PTR
Parallel	PAR
Parging	PARG
Parking	PRKG
Parkway	PKWY
Particleboard	PBD
Partition	PTN
Passenger	PASS
Pavement	PVMT
Paving	PVG
Pedestal	PED
Pegboard	PGBD
Perforated	PERF
Perimeter	PERIM
Permanent	PERM
Perpendicular	PERP
Phase	PH
Phillip's head screw	PHS
Piece	PC
Plaster	PLAS
Plastic laminate	PLAM
Plate	PL
Plate washer	PW
Platform	PLAT
Plumbing	PLMB
Plywood	PLYWD
Pneumatic	PNEU
Point of intersection	PI
Point of tangency	PT
Polished	POL
Polyethylene	POLY

Polyvinyl chloride	PVC
Portable	PORT
Portland cement	PC
Portland cement plaster	PCP
Pound	LB
Pounds per cubic foot	PCF
Pounds per linear foot	PLF
Pounds per square foot	PSF
Pounds per square inch	PSI
Power	PWR
Power panel	PP
Power roof exhauster	PRE
Power roof ventilator	PRV
Power wall exhauster	PWE
Precast	PRCST
Prefabricated	PREFAB
Prefinished	PREFIN
Preliminary	PRELIM
Pressure gage	PG
Pressure reducing valve	PRV
Pressure relief valve	PRV
Prestressed concrete	PS CONC
Project	PROJ
Property	PROP
Property line	PL
Public address	PA
Pull box	PB
Pull chain	PC
Purse shelf	PSH
Pushbutton	PB
Quality	QUAL
Quantity	QTY
Quarry tile	QT
Quarter	QTR
Rabbet	RAB
Radiator	RAD
Radius	R
Radius	RAD
Railing	RLG
Railroad	RR
Rain water conductor	RWC
Rain water leader	RWL

Rapid start	RS
Receptacle	RCPT
Recessed	REC
Recirculate	RECIRC
Rectangular	RECT
Reducer	RDC
Reference	REF
Refrigerator	REFR
Register	REG
Reinforced concrete	RC
Reinforced, reinforcing	REINF
Relative humidity	RH
Relief	RLF
Relief valve	RV
Remote control	RC
Removeable	REM
Repair	REP
Replace	REPL
Required	REQD
Resilient	RESIL
Return	RET
Return air fan	RA FAN
Return air grille	RA GR
Reverse	RVS
Revolutions per minute	RPM
Right hand	RH
Right hand reverse	RHR
Right-of-way	ROW
Riser	R
Road	RD
Roof drain	RD
Roof vent	RV
Roofing	RFG
Room	RM
Rough opening	RO
Round	RND
Round head machine screw	RHMS
Round head wood screw	RHWS
Rubber	RBR
Safety	SAF
Safety valve	SV
Sanitary	SAN

Sanitary napkin dispenser	SND
Sanitary napkin receptacle	SNR
Sanitary sewer	SS
Sanitary vent	V
Schedule	SCHED
Screen	SCRN
Section	SECT
Separate	SEP
Service	SERV
Service sink	SSK
Sewer	SEW
Sheating	SHTHG
Sheet	SH
Sheet metal	SM
Sheet metal screw	SMS
Shelving	SHV
Shoulder	SHLDR
Shower	SHR
Shut off valve	SOV
Signal	SIG
Similar	SIM
Single	SGL
Single phase	1PH
Single pole	SP
Single pole, double throw	SPDT
Single pole, single throw	SPST
Sink	SK
Sleeve	SLV
Sliding	SL
Sliding door	SLD
Sliding glass door	SGD
Slip joint	SJ
Slope	SLP
Soap dispenser	SD
Soil pipe	SP
Solid concrete masonry unit	SCMU
Solid core	SC
Sound transmission class	STC
South	S
Space	SP
Speaker	SPKR
Special	SPL

Specification	SPEC
Splash block	SB
Split ring	SR
Sprinkler	SPKLR
Square	SQ
Square foot	SQ FT
Square inch	SQ IN
Square kilometer	SQ KM
Square meter	SQ M
Square yard	SQ YD
Stainless steel	SST
Standard	STD
Standard wire gage	SWG
Standpipe	SP
Station	STA
Steam	STM
Steam supply	SS
Steel	STL
Steel joist	STL JST
Steel plate	STL PL
Stiffener	STIF
Stirrup	STIR
Stock	STK
Storage	STOR
Storm drain	SD
Straight	STR
Street	ST
Strike	STR
Structural	STRUCT
Structural clay tile	SCT
Styrene butadiene rubber	SBR
Substitute	SUB
Supply	SPLY
Supply air	SA
Supply air grille	SAG
Supply diffuser	SD
Supply fan	SF
Surface	SURF
Surfaced four sides	S4S
Surfaced two sides	S2S
Suspended	SUSP
Suspended ceiling	SUSP CLG

Suspended unit heater	SUH
Switch	SW
Switchboard	SWBD
Switchgear	SWGR
Symmetrical	SYMM
Synthetic	SYN
System	SYS
Tackboard	TK BD
Tangent	TAN
Tee	T
Telephone	TEL
Television	TV
Temperature	TEMP
Temperature control panel	TCP
Temperature control valve	TCV
Tempered	TMPD
Tempered glass	TMPD GL
Temporary	TEMP
Terminal	TERM
Terra cotta	TC
Terrazzo	TER
Thermal	THERM
Thermal resistance	R
Thermostat	T
Thickness	THK
Thousand	M
Thousand board feet	MBF
Thousand circular mils	MCM
Thousand cubic feet	MCF
Thousand foot pounds	KIP FT
Thread	THD
Three phase	3PH
Threshold	THRES
Through	THRU
Through bolt	TB
To floor above	TFA
To floor below	TFB
Toilet paper holder	TPH
Tolerance	TOL
Tongue and groove	T & G
Top and bottom	T & B
Top of beam	TB

Top of concrete	TC
Top of curb	TC
Top of finished floor	TFF
Top of footing	TF
Top of joist	TJ
Top of pavement	TP
Top of slab	TSL
Top of steel	TST
Top of wall	TW
Total	TOT
Towel bar	TB
Towel dispenser	TD
Towel dispenser/receptacle	TDR
Transformer	TRANS
Transparent	TRANS
Tread	T
Trench drain	TD
Tubing	TUB
Turnbuckle	TRNBKL
Typical	TYP
Ultra high frequency	UHF
Ultraviolet	UV
Under floor duct	UFD
Underground	UGND
Underwriters Laboratories Inc.	UL
Unexcavated	UNEX
Unfinished	UNFIN
Uniform	UNIF
Uninterruptible power supply	UPS
Unit heater	UH
Unit ventilator	UV
United States gage	USG
Unless otherwise noted	UON
Utility	UTIL
Vacuum	VAC
Vacuum breaker	VB
Valve box	VB
Vapor proof	VAP PRF
Vapor retarder	VR
Variable air volume	VAV
Vehicle	VEH
Velocity	VEL

Veneer	VNR
Vent pipe	VP
Vent through roof	VTR
Ventilator	VENT
Vertical	VERT
Vertical grain	VG
Very high frequency	VHF
Very high output	VHO
Vestibule	VEST
Video display terminal	VDT
Vinyl	VIN
Vinyl base	VB
Vinyl faced acoustic tile	VFAT
Vinyl tile	VT
Vinyl wall covering	VWC
Vitreous	VIT
Vitrified clay tile	VCT
Volt	V
Volt ampere	VA
Volts, alternating current	VAC
Volume	VOL
Volume damper	VD
Wainscot	WSCT
Wall cleanout	WCO
Wall hung	WH
Wall hydrant	WH
Wall to wall	W/W
Warehouse	WHSE
Warm white	WW
Warm white deluxe	WWX
Waste	W
Waste disposer	WDSP
Waste receptacle	WR
Wastewater	WW
Water closet	WC
Water cooling coil	WCC
Water hammer arrester	WHA
Water heater	WH
Water resistant	WR
Waterproof	WP
Waterproofing	WPG
Watt	W

Weatherstripping	WS
Weight	WT
Welded	WLD
Welded base	WB
Welded wire fabric	WWF
West	W
Wet standpipe	WSP
Wide flange	WF
Width	WD
Window	WDW
Wire glass	WGL
With	W/
Without	W/O
Wood	WD
Working point	WP
Wrought iron	WI
Wrought washer	WW
Yard	YD

Abbreviations used on drawings listed by abbreviation

1PH	Single phase
3PH	Three phase
A	Area
AAD	Automatic air damper
AAP	Alarm annunciator panel
AB	Anchor bolt
ABC	Aggregate base course
ABRSV	Abrasive
ABS	Absolute
ABS	Acrylonitrile butadiene styrene
ABV	Above
AC	Air conditioning
AC	Alternating current
AC	Asphaltic concrete
ACCU	Air cooled condensing unit
ACID RES	Acid resistant
ACID RES P	Acid resistant pipe
ACID RES V	Acid resistant vent
ACID RES W	Acid resistant waste
ACOUS	Acoustical
ACOUS INSUL	Acoustical insulation
ACOUS PLAS	Acoustical plaster
ACOUS PNL	Acoustical panel
ACOUS TILE	Acoustical tile
ACT	Actual
ACU	Air conditioning unit
ACWT	Acoustical wall treatment
AD	Access door
AD	Area drain
ADC	Automatic door closer
ADD	Addendum
ADD	Addition
ADH	Adhesive
ADJ	Adjustable
ADJ	Adjacent
ADPTR	Adapter
ADS	Automatic door seal
A-E	Architect-Engineer
AF	Access floor
AF	Audio frequency

AFC	Automatic frequency control
AFF	Above finished floor
AFG	Above finished grade
AFS	Above finished slab
AG	Above grade
AGGR	Aggregate
AGL	Above ground level
AHD	Ahead
AHM	Ampere hour meter
AHR	Anchor
AHU	Air handling unit
AL	Aluminum
ALLOW	Allowance
ALM	Alarm
ALS	American Lumber Standard
ALT	Alternate
ALT NO	Alternate number
ALTRN	Alteration
ALY	Alloy
AM	Amplitude modulation
AMB	Ambient
AMD	Air moving device
AMM	Ammeter
AMP	Ampere
AMP HR	Ampere hour
AMPL	Amplifier
AMT	Amount
ANL	Anneal
ANLG	Analog
ANN	Annunciator
ANOD	Anodized
ANSI	American National Standards Institute
ANT	Antenna
AP	Access panel
AP	Acid proof
APC	Acoustical plaster ceiling
APPAR	Apparatus
APPD	Approved
APPROX	Approximately
APPX	Appendix
APT	Apartment

APU	Auxiliary power unit
APW	Architectural projected window
AQST	Aquastat
AR	As required
ARCH	Architect
ARF	Above raised floor
ART	Artificial
AS	Automatic sprinkler
ASC	Above suspended ceiling
ASD	Automatic sprinkler drain
ASPH	Asphalt
ASR	Automatic sprinkler riser
ASSN	Association
ASSY	Assembly
ASU	Air supply unit
ASW	Auxiliary switch
ASYM	Asymmetrical
ATC	Architectural terra cotta
ATCH	Attachment
ATS	Automatic transfer switch
AUTO	Automatic
AV	Acid vent
AV	Air vent
AV	Audio visual
AVE	Avenue
AVG	Average
AW	Acid waste
A/W	All weather
AWG	American wire gage
AZ	Azimuth
BA	Bright annealed
BA	Burglar alarm
BAF	Baffle
BAL	Balance
BAL DMPR	Balancing damper
BAL V	Balancing valve
BALC	Balcony
BB	Baseboard
BB	Bulletin board
B/B	Back to back
B & B	Balled and Burlapped
BBRG	Ball bearing

BBRR	Base board radiation
BC	Back of curb
BCV	Butterfly check valve
BD	Board
BDD	Backdraft damper
BE	Bell end
BETW	Between
BEV	Bevel
BF	Both faces
BF	Bottom face
B & F	Bell and flange
BFBP	Boiler feed booster pump
BFP	Backflow preventer
BFV	Butterfly valve
BI	Black iron
BITUM	Bituminous
BJT	Bed joint
BK SH	Book shelves
BL	Base line
BL	Building line
BLDG	Building
BLK	Block
BLKG	Blocking
BLKHD	Bulkhead
BLO	Blower
BLR	Boiler
BLST	Ballast
BLVD	Boulevard
BLW	Below
BLW CLG	Below ceiling
BLW FFLR	Below finish floor
BM	Beam
BM	Bench mark
BOT	Bottom
BP	Base plate
BPG	Beveled plate glass
BR	Bedroom
BR	Bend radius
BRCG	Bracing
BRDG	Bridging
BRDG JST	Bridging joist
BRG	Bearing

BRG PL	Bearing plate
BRK	Brick
BRKR	Breaker
BRKT	Bracket
BRS	Brass
BRZ	Bronze
BS	Both sides
B & S	Bell and spigot
B & S	Brown and Sharpe gage
BSMT	Basement
BSTR	Booster
BTU	British thermal unit
BTUH	British thermal units per hour
BU	Built-up
BUR	Built-up roof
BV	Ball valve
BW	Both ways
BW	Butt weld
BWV	Back water valve
CAB	Cabinet
CAB H	Cabinet heater
CAM	Camber
CANV	Canvas
CAP	Capacity
CARP	Carpet
CAT	Catalog
CATW	Catwalk
CAV	Cavity
CB	Catch basin
CCTV	Closed circuit television
CCW	Counter-clockwise
CEB	Concrete equipment base
CEM	Cement
CEM MORT	Cement mortar
CEM PLAS	Cement plaster
CER	Ceramic
CER TILE	Ceramic tile
CFE	Contractor furnished equipment
CFLG	Counterflashing
CG	Ceiling grille
CG	Corner guard
C & G	Curb and gutter

CH	Chiller
CH BD	Chalkboard
CHAM	Chamfer
CHAN	Channel
CHEM	Chemical
CHHWR	Chilled and heating water return
CHHWS	Chilled and heating water supply
CHIM	Chimney
CHK	Check
CHKV	Check valve
CHR PL	Chrome plated
CHW	Chilled water
CHW	Circulating hot water
CHWP	Chilled water pump
CHWPP	Chilled water primary pump
CHWR	Chilled water return
CHWRP	Chilled water recirculating pump
CHWS	Chilled water supply
CI	Cast iron
CIP	Cast iron pipe
CIP	Galvanized iron pipe
CIR	Cast iron radiator
CIR	Circle
CIRC	Circular
CIRC	Circumference
CISP	Cast iron soil pipe
CJ	Construction joint
CKT	Circuit
CKT BKR	Circuit breaker
CL	Center line
CLG	Ceiling
CLG DIFF	Ceiling diffuser
CLG HT	Ceiling height
CLG REG	Ceiling register
CLJ	Control joint
CLKG	Calking
CLL	Column line
CLL	Contract limit line
CLO	Closet
CLOS	Closure
CLP	Clamp
CLR	Clear

CLRM	Classroom
CM	Centimeter
CMP	Corrugated metal pipe
CMPST	Composite
CMU	Concrete masonry unit
CND	Conduit
CNR	Corner
CNTR	Counter
CO	Change order
CO	Cased opening
CO	Cleanout
COAX	Coaxial cable
COEF	Coefficient
COL	Column
COM	Common
COMB	Combination
COMM	Communication
COMP	Composition
COMPT	Compartment
CONC	Concrete
CONC FL	Concrete floor
COND	Condensor
CONF	Conference
CONN	Connection
CONSTR	Construction
CONT	Continuous
CONTR	Contractor
CONV	Convector
COORD	Coordinate
COR BD	Corner bead
CORR	Corridor
CORR	Corrugated
COV	Cover
COV PL	Cover plate
CP	Candlepower
CP	Concrete pipe
CP	Control panel
CPE	Chlorinated polyethylene
CPRS	Compressible
CPRSR	Compressor
CPVC	Chlorinated polyvinyl chloride
CR	Cold-rolled

CRCMF	Circumference
CRN	Crown
CRS	Cold-rolled steel
CS	Cast stone
CSB	Casing bead
CSB	Concrete splash block
CSG	Casing
CSK	Countersunk
CSMT	Casement
CSPE	Chlorosulfonated polyethylene
CSTL	Cast steel
CSWK	Casework
C TO C	Center to center
CT	Cooling tower
CTD	Coated
CTD & R	Combination towel dispenser & receptacle
CTR	Cooling tower return
CTS	Cooling tower supply
CTV	Cable television
CUB	Cubicle
CUH	Cabinet unit heater
CV	Control valve
CW	Cold water
CW	Cool white
CWP	Circulating water pump
CWP	Condenser water pump
CWR	Condenser water return
CWS	Condenser water supply
CWX	Cool white deluxe
CY	Cycle
CYL	Cylinder
CYL L	Cylinder lock
DAD	Double acting door
DAP	Duct access panel
DAT	Datum
DB	Dry bulb
DBL	Double
DBL ACT	Double acting
DBL GLZ	Double glazing
DC	Direct current
DCI	Duct covering insulation

DCL	Door closer
DCP	Dimmer control panel
DD	Dutch door
DEG	Degree
DEMO	Demolition
DEPT	Department
DET	Detail
DET	Detector
DF	Diesel fuel
DF	Drinking fountain
DFC	Fire department connection
DFR	Door frame
DH	Double hung
DIAG	Diagonal
DIAM	Diameter
DIFF	Difference
DIFF	Diffuser
DIM	Dimension
DIST	Distance
DISTR PNL	Distribution panel
DIV	Division
DJ	Double joist
DL	Dead load
DLI	Duct liner insulation
DLV	Door louver
DMH	Drop manhole
DMPF	Dampproofing
DMPR	Damper
DN	Down
DO	Ditto
DPC	Dampproof course
DPDT	Double pole, double throw
DPST	Double pole, single throw
DR	Dining room
DR	Drive
DRW	Dry well
DS	Downspout
D/S	Drop siding
DSP	Dry standpipe
DST	Door stop
DT	Drum trap
DT	Drain tile

DUP	Duplicate
DV	Drain valve
DW	Deluxe white
DW	Dishwasher
DWG	Drawing
DWH	Domestic water heater
DWL	Dowel
DWR	Drawer
DWTR	Dumbwaiter
DWV	Drain, waste & vent
DX	Direct expansion
DX	Duplex
E	East
ECAB	Electrical cabinet
ECC	Eccentric
ECON	Economizo
ECU	Evaporative cooling unit
EDR	Equipment drain
EE	Eased edges
EF	Each face
EFL	Effluent
EHD	Electrical hand dryer
EHP	Electrical heating unit
EIFS	Exterior insulation and finish system
EL	Easement line
EL	Elevation
ELEC	Electrical
ELEV	Elevator
EMER	Emergency
EMER SHR	Emergency shower
EMT	Electrical metallic tubing
ENAM	Enamel
ENCL	Enclosure
ENG	Engine
ENGR	Engineer
ENGY	Energy
ENTR	Entrance
EO	Electrical outlet
EPDM	Ethylene propylene diene monomer
EPRF	Explosion proof

EQL SP	Equally spaced
EQUIP	Equipment
EQUIV	Equivalent
ERECT	Erection
ESCAL	Escalator
ESMT	Easement
ESP	Emergency switch panel
EST	Estimate
EVAP	Evaporate
EW	Each way
EWC	Electrical water cooler
EWH	Electrical water heater
EXC	Excavate
EXCH	Exchanger
EXH	Exhaust
EXH A	Exhaust air
EXH DT	Exhaust duct
EXH FN	Exhaust fan
EXH GR	Exhaust grille
EXH HD	Exhaust hood
EXH RG	Exhaust register
EXP	Expansion
EXP BT	Expansion bolt
EXP JT	Expansion joint
EXST	Existing
EXST GR	Existing grade
EXT	Exterior
EXTN	Extension
EXTR	Extrusion
FA	Fire alarm
FAB	Fabricate
FACP	Fire alarm control panel
FAI	Fresh air intake
F BRK	Fire brick
FB	Flat bar
FBD	Fiberboard
FBM	Feet board measure
FC	Footcandle
FCO	Floor cleanout
FCU	Fan coil unit
FD	Floor drain
FDMPR	Fire damper

FDN	Foundation
FDR	Feeder
FDV	Fire department valve
FDW	Feedwater
FEC	Fire extinguisher cabinet
FEM	Female
FEXT	Fire extinguisher
F/F	Face to face
FFA	From floor above
FFB	From floor below
FGL	Fiberglass
FHC	Fire hose cabinet
FHMS	Flat head machine screw
FHP	Full height partition
FHR	Fire hose rack
FHWS	Flat head wood screw
FHY	Fire hydrant
FIN	Finish
FIN FL	Finish floor
FIN GR	Finish grade
FL	Flashing
FLDG	Folding
FLEX C	Flexible connector
FLG	Flooring
FLG	Flange
FLL	Flow line
FLR	Floor
FLR FIN	Floor finish
FLR PL	Floor plate
FLR REG	Floor register
FLR SK	Floor sink
FLRD	Flared
FLSW	Flow switch
FLT GL	Float glass
FLUOR	Fluorescent
FM	Frequency modulation
FN	Fence
FO	Fuel oil
FOC	Face of concrete
FOF	Face of finish
FOM	Face of masonry
FOS	Face of studs

FPL	Fireplace
FPM	Feet per minute
FPRF	Fireproofing
FPS	Feet per second
FPT	Female pipe thread
FPW	Fire protection water supply
FR	Fire rating
FR	Frame
FR MIR	Framed mirror
FREQ	Frequency
FRT	Front
FS	Federal Specification
FS	Far side
FS	Full size
FSH	Fire sprinkler head
FSP	Fire standpipe
FSTNR	Fastener
FTC	Finned tube convector
FTG	Footing
FTR	Finned tube radiator
FUR	Furnace
FURN	Furniture
FURR	Furring
FUT	Future
FWC	Fabric wall covering
FWP	Fire water pump
FXTR	Fixture
G	Gas
GA	Gage
GAL	Gallon
GALV	Galvanized
GALVS	Galvanized steel
GAR	Garage
GB	Grab bar
GC	General contractor
GD	Gutter drain
GDR	Guard rail
GEN	Generator
GENL	General
GFI	Ground fault interrupter
GFU	Glazed facing unit
GI	Galvanized iron

GL	Glass
GLB	Glass block
GLU LAM	Glued laminated
GLV	Globe valve
GLZ	Glaze, Glazing
GLZ CMU	Glazed concrete masonry unit
GLZD	Glazed
GND	Ground
GOVT	Government
GPD	Gallons per day
GPH	Gallons per hour
GPM	Gallons per minute
GPS	Gallons per second
GR	Grade
GR BM	Grade beam
GR LN	Grade line
GRL	Grille
GRV	Gravity roof ventilator
GSKT	Gasket
GSNK	Gooseneck
GT	Grease trap
GT	Grout
GTV	Gate valve
GUT	Gutter
GV	Gravity vent
GVL	Gravel
GVTR	Gas vent through roof
GWH	Gas water heater
GYP	Gypsum
GYP BD	Gypsum board
GYP PLAS	Gypsum plaster
H	High
HAGL	Heat absorbing glass
HB	Hose bibb
HC	Hollow core
HC	Hose cabinet
HCMU	Hollow concrete masonry unit
H & CW	Hot and cold water
HD	Hand dryer
HD	Heavy duty
HD	Head
HD JT	Head joint

HDBD	Hardboard
HDR	Header
HDW	Hardware
HDWD	Hardwood
HEX	Heat exchanger
HEX	Hexagonal
HGR	Hanger
HGT	Height
HID	High intensity discharge
HM	Hollow metal
HMD	Hollow metal door
HMF	Hollow metal frame
HNDRL	Handrail
HO	High output
HO	Hold-open
HORIZ	Horizontal
HOSP	Hospital
HP	High pressure
HP	Horsepower
HPB	High pressure boiler
HPG	High pressure gas
HPR	High pressure return
HPS	High pressure steam
HPT	High point
HR	Hour
HRU	Heat recovery unit
HS	High strength
HSB	High strength bolt
HSE	House
HSTAT	Humidistat
HT	Heat
HTG	Heating
HTR	Heater
HTWR	Heating water return
HTWS	Heating water supply
HV	Hose valve
HVAC	Heating, ventilating, and air conditioning
HVD	High velocity diffuser
HVT	High velocity terminal
HVY	Heavy
HW	Hot water

HWB	Hot water boiler
HWC	Hot water coil
HWC	Hot water, circulating
HWCP	Hot water circulating pump
HWP	Hot water pump
HWR	Hot water return
HWS	Hot water supply
HWY	Highway
HYD	Hydrant
HYDR	Hydraulic
HZ	Hertz
ID	Inside diameter
IF	Inside face
IF	Intake fan
IMH	Inlet manhole
IMPRG	Impregnate
INCAND	Incandescent
INCIN	Incinerator
INCL	Include
IND	Indicator
INL	Inlet
INS	Insulate
INSUL	Insulation
INSUL PNL	Insulated panel
INTERCOM	Intercommunication
INTR	Interior
INV	Invert
INV EL	Invert elevation
IP	Iron pipe
IPS	Iron pipe size
IRMA	Inverted roof membrane assembly
ISO	Isometric
ITC	Interior telephone cabinet
IW	Indirect waste
IW	Irrigation water
IWH	Instantaneous water heater
JAN	Janitor
JB	Junction box
JC	Janitor's closet
JCT	Junction
JR	Junior

JST	Joist
JT	Joint
K	Kip
KB	Knee brace
KCP	Keene's cement plaster
KD	Kiln dried
KD	Knock down
KG	Kilogram
KIP FT	One thousand foot pounds
KIT	Kitchen
KLF	Kips per linear foot
KO	Knockout
KOP	Knockout panel
KPL	Kick plate
KSF	Kips per square foot
KV	Kilovolt
KVA	Kilovolt ampere
KVAHM	Kilovolt-ampere hour meter
KW	Kilowatt
KWAM	Kilowatt-hour meter
KWH	Kilowatt-hour
KWY	Keyway
L	Left
LAB	Laboratory
LAD	Ladder
LAM	Lamination
LAT	Latitude
LATL	Lateral
LAU	Laundry
LAV	Lavatory
LB	Lag bolt
LB	Pound
LBR	Lumber
LCD	Linear ceiling diffuser
LCMU	Lightweight concrete masonry unit
LD	Linear diffuser
LD BRG	Load bearing
LDG	Landing
LDR	Leader
LF	Linear foot
LG	Length
LH	Left hand

LHR	Left hand reverse
LIB	Library
LIN	Linear
LKR	Locker
LKR RM	Locker room
LL	Live load
LLH	Long leg horizontal
LLV	Long leg vertical
LNTL	Lintel
LOA	Length overall
LONG	Longitudinal
LP	Light pole
LP	Lightproof
LP	Liquefied petroleum
LP	Low pressure
L & P	Lath and plaster
LPB	Low pressure boiler
LPCR	Low pressure condensate return
LPT	Low point
LR	Living room
LRG	Large
LRV	Louvered roof vent
LS	Loudspeaker
LT	Light
LT WT	Lightweight
LTG	Lighting
LTG PNL	Lighting panel
LV	Low voltage
LVL	Level
LVR	Louver
LWC	Lightweight concrete
M	Meter
M	Thousand
MA	Not applicable
MACH	Machine
MACH RM	Machine room
MAINT	Maintenance
MAN	Manual
MARB	Marble
MAS	Masonry
MATL	Material
MATV	Master antenna television system

MAU	Make-up air unit
MAX	Maximum
MB	Machine bolt
MB	Mixing box
MBF	Thousand board feet
MBH	Mop/broom holder
MBR	Master bedroom
MC	Medicine cabinet
MCC	Motor control center
MCF	Thousand cubic feet
MCM	Thousand circular mils
MDO	Medium density overlay
MECH	Mechanical
MED	Medium
MEMB	Membrane
MER	Mechanical equipment room
MET	Metal
MEZZ	Mezzanine
MFG	Manfacturing
MG	Motor generator
MGD	Million gallons per day
MH	Manhole
MI	Mile
MIN	Minimum
MIN	Minute
MIR	Mirror
MISC	Miscellaneous
MIX	Mixture
MK	Mark
ML	Metal lath
MLDG	Molding
MLWK	Millwork
MO	Masonry opening
MOD	Module
MOD	Motor operated damper
MOL	Maximum overall length
MON	Monitor
MON	Monument
MOT	Motor
MR	Mill run
MSB	Mop service basin
MSP	Motor starter panel

MTD	Mounted
MTG	Meeting
MTG	Mounting
MTR	Mortar
MULL	Mullion
MULT	Multiple
MVBL	Movable
MVD	Manual volume damper
MZ	Multi-zone
N	North
NAT	Natural
NC	Noise criterion
NEC	National Electric Code
NEG	Negative
NEUT	Neutral
NF	Near face
NFPA	National Fire Protection Association
NIC	Not in contract
NIP	Nipple
NO	Number
NOM	Nominal
NP	No paint
NPL	Nipple
NPL	Nameplate
NR	Noise reduction
NRC	Noise reduction coefficient
NS	Near side
NTS	Not to scale
OA	Outside air
OA	Overall
OAD	Outside air damper
OBS	Obscure
OC	On center
OCB	Oil circuit breaker
OD	Outside diameter
OD	Outside dimension
OF	Outside face
OFCI	Owner furnished-contractor installed
OFF	Office
OFOI	Owner furnished-owner installed

OGL	Obscure glass
OIA	Outside air intake
O/O	Out to out
OPNG	Opening
OPP	Opposite
OPT	Optional
OR	Outside radius
ORD	Overflow roof drain
ORIG	Original
OVFL	Overflow
OVHD	Overhead
OWGL	Obscure wire glass
OXY	Oxygen
OZ	Ounce
PA	Public address
PAR	Parallel
PARG	Parging
PASS	Passenger
PB	Panic bar
PB	Pull box
PB	Pushbutton
PBD	Particleboard
PC	Piece
PC	Portland cement
PC	Pull chain
PCD	Paper cup dispenser
PCF	Pounds per cubic foot
PCP	Portland cement plaster
PED	Pedestal
PERF	Perforated
PERIM	Perimeter
PERM	Permanent
PERP	Perpendicular
PG	Pressure gage
PGBD	Pegboard
PH	Phase
PHS	Phillip's head screw
PI	Point of intersection
PKWY	Parkway
PL	Plate
PL	Property line
PLAM	Plastic laminate

PLAS	Plaster
PLAT	Platform
PLF	Pounds per linear foot
PLMB	Plumbing
PLYWD	Plywood
PNEU	Pneumatic
PNL	Panel
PNT	Paint
POL	Polished
POLY	Polyethylene
PORT	Portable
PORT CEM	Portland cement
PP	Power panel
PR	Pair
PRCST	Precast
PRE	Power roof exhauster
PREFAB	Prefabricated
PREFIN	Prefinished
PRELIM	Preliminary
PRKG	Parking
PROJ	Project
PROP	Property
PRV	Power roof ventilator
PRV	Pressure reducing valve
PRV	Pressure relief valve
PS CONC	Prestressed concrete
PSF	Pounds per square foot
PSH	Purse shelf
PSI	Pounds per square inch
PT	Point of tangency
PTD	Painted
PTD	Paper towel dispenser
PTN	Partition
PTR	Paper towel receptacle
PVC	Polyvinyl chloride
PVG	Paving
PVMT	Pavement
PW	Plate washer
PWE	Power wall exhauster
PWR	Power
QT	Quarry tile
QTR	Quarter

QTY	Quantity
QUAL	Quality
R	Radius
R	Riser
R	Thermal resistance
RA FAN	Return air fan
RA GR	Return air grille
RAB	Rabbet
RAD	Radiator
RAD	Radius
RBR	Rubber
RC	Reinforced concrete
RC	Remote control
RCPT	Receptacle
RD	Road
RD	Roof drain
RDC	Reducer
REC	Recessed
RECIRC	Recirculate
RECT	Rectangular
REF	Reference
REFR	Refrigerator
REG	Register
REINF	Reinforced, reinforcing
REM	Removeable
REP	Repair
REPL	Replace
REQD	Required
RESIL	Resilient
RET	Return
RFG	Roofing
RH	Relative humidity
RH	Right hand
RHMS	Round head machine screw
RHR	Right hand reverse
RHWS	Round head wood scret
RLF	Relief
RLG	Railing
RM	Room
RND	Round
RO	Rough opening
ROW	Right-of-way

RPM	Revolutions per minute
RR	Railroad
RS	Rapid start
RV	Relief valve
RV	Roof vent
RVS	Reverse
RWC	Rain water conductor
RWL	Rain water leader
S	South
S2S	Surfaced two sides
S4S	Surfaced four sides
SA	Supply air
SAF	Safety
SAG	Supply air grille
SAN	Sanitary
SB	Splash block
SBR	Styrene butadiene rubber
SC	Solid core
SCHED	Schedule
SCMU	Solid concrete masonry unit
SCRN	Screen
SCT	Structural clay tile
SD	Soap dispenser
SD	Storm drain
SD	Supply diffuser
SECT	Section
SEP	Separate
SERV	Service
SEW	Sewer
SF	Supply fan
SGD	Sliding glass door
SGL	Single
SH	Sheet
SHLDR	Shoulder
SHR	Shower
SHTHG	Sheating
SHV	Shelving
SIG	Signal
SIM	Similar
SJ	Slip joint
SK	Sink
SL	Sliding

SLD	Sliding door
SLP	Slope
SLV	Sleeve
SM	Sheet metal
SMS	Sheet metal screw
SND	Sanitary napkin dispenser
SNR	Sanitary napkin receptacle
SOV	Shut off valve
SP	Single pole
SP	Standpipe
SP	Space
SP	Soil pipe
SPDT	Single pole, double throw
SPEC	Specification
SPKLR	Sprinkler
SPKR	Speaker
SPL	Special
SPLY	Supply
SPST	Single pole, single throw
SQ	Square
SQ FT	Square foot
SQ IN	Square inch
SQ KM	Square kilometer
SQ M	Square meter
SQ YD	Square yard
SR	Split ring
SS	Sanitary sewer
SS	Steam supply
SSK	Service sink
SST	Stainless steel
ST	Street
STA	Station
STC	Sound transmission class
STD	Standard
STIF	Stiffener
STIR	Stirrup
STK	Stock
STL	Steel
STL JST	Steel joist
STL PL	Steel plate
STM	Steam
STOR	Storage

STR	Straight
STR	Strike
STRUCT	Structural
SUB	Substitute
SUH	Suspended unit heater
SURF	Surface
SUSP	Suspended
SUSP CLG	Suspended ceiling
SV	Safety valve
SW	Switch
SWBD	Switchboard
SWG	Standard wire gage
SWGR	Switchgear
SYMM	Symmetrical
SYN	Synthetic
SYS	System
T	Tee
T	Thermostat
T	Tread
TAN	Tangent
TB	Top of beam
TB	Towel bar
TB	Through bolt
T & B	Top and bottom
TC	Top of concrete
TC	Top of curb
TC	Terra cotta
TCP	Temperature control panel
TCV	Temperature control valve
TD	Towel dispenser
TD	Trench drain
TDR	Towel dispenser/receptacle
TEL	Telephone
TEMP	Temperature
TEMP	Temporary
TER	Terrazzo
TERM	Terminal
TF	Top of footing
TFA	To floor above
TFB	To floor below
TFF	Top of finished floor
T & G	Tongue and groove

THD	Thread
THERM	Thermal
THK	Thickness
THRES	Threshold
THRU	Through
TJ	Top of joist
TK BD	Tackboard
TMPD	Tempered
TMPD GL	Tempered glass
TOL	Tolerance
TOT	Total
TP	Top of pavement
TPH	Toilet paper holder
TRANS	Transformer
TRANS	Transparent
TRNBKL	Turnbuckle
TSL	Top of slab
TST	Top of steel
TUB	Tubing
TV	Television
TW	Top of wall
TYP	Typical
U	Heat transfer coefficient
UFD	Under floor duct
UGND	Underground
UH	Unit heater
UHF	Ultra high frequency
UL	Underwriters Laboratories, Inc.
UNEX	Unexcavated
UNFIN	Unfinished
UNIF	Uniform
UON	Unless otherwise noted
UPS	Uninterruptible power supply
USG	United States gage
UTIL	Utility
UV	Ultraviolet
UV	Unit ventilator
V	Sanitary vent
V	Volt
VA	Volt ampere
VAC	Vacuum
VAC	Volts, alternating current

VAP PRF	Vapor proof
VAV	Variable air volume
VB	Vacuum breaker
VB	Valve box
VB	Vinyl base
VCT	Vitrified clay tile
VD	Volume damper
VDT	Video display terminal
VEH	Vehicle
VEL	Velocity
VENT	Ventilator
VERT	Vertical
VEST	Vestibule
VFAT	Vinyl faced acoustic tile
VG	Vertical grain
VHF	Very high frequency
VHO	Very high output
VIN	Vinyl
VIT	Vitreous
VNR	Veneer
VOL	Volume
VP	Vent pipe
VR	Vapor retarder
VT	Vinyl tile
VTR	Vent through roof
VWC	Vinyl wall covering
W	Waste
W	Watt
W	West
W/	With
WB	Welded base
WC	Water closet
WCC	Water cooling coil
WCO	Wall cleanout
WD	Width
WD	Wood
WDSP	Waste disposer
WDW	Window
WF	Wide flange
WGL	Wire glass
WH	Wall hung
WH	Wall hydrant

WH	Water heater
WHA	Water hammer arrester
WHSE	Warehouse
WI	Wrought iron
WLD	Welded
W/O	Without
WP	Working point
WP	Waterproof
WPG	Waterproofing
WR	Waste receptacle
WR	Water resistant
WS	Weatherstripping
WSCT	Wainscot
WSP	Wet standpipe
WT	Weight
WW	Wrought washer
WW	Warm white
WW	Wastewater
W/W	Wall to wall
WWF	Welded wire fabric
WWX	Warm white deluxe
X ARM	Cross arm
X HVY	Extra heavy
X SECT	Cross section
YD	Yard

Drawing terminology

ACCESS DOOR	Used for small, prefabricated doors not on the door schedule.
ACCESS FLOOR	Not *computer floor* or *pedestal floor*.
ACCESS PANEL	A removable part of the finish.
ACCORDION	Not *accordian*.
ACOUSTICAL PANEL	Not *acoustic*.
ACOUSTICAL SEALANT	Not *calking*; use COMPRESSIBLE FOAM TAPE or other appropriate term if the material is not a sealant.
ACOUSTICAL TILE	Standard ceiling board materials.
acoustical underlayment	Use SOUND DEADENING BOARD.
ACRYLIC SHEET	Not *Plexiglas* or other trade name.
ADHESIVE	Not *cement, glue, paste,* or *mastic* unless the adhesive is commonly called glue.
AGGREGATE BASE COURSE	Not *crushed rock* or *gravel*.
ALTERATION	Not *remodel*.
ALTERNATE	Used to describe a pricing or bidding option referred to in the project manual. When the owner has a choice of selecting one priced item over another based on cost it is an alternate. When the contractor is given a choice of methods use the word OPTION.
ANCHOR BOLT	Not used to describe an EXPANSION BOLT.
ANODIZED	Not *alumilite, duranodic,* or *kalcolor*.
apply	Use INSTALL.
asbestos cement	Use MINERAL FIBER.
ASPHALT CONCRETE	Not *asphalt paving* or *bituminous concrete*.
asphalt roofing	Use BUILT-UP ROOFING.
BACKER ROD	Do not use *Ethafoam* or other trade names.

BACKING	Material used behind a finished surface to provide a solid base for attachment of some item on the surface of the finish.
bar joists	Use STEEL JOISTS.
BASE FLASHING	Flashing bonded to a roof membrane.
BATT INSULATION	Not *bat*, or *Fiberglas* or other trade name. Use for roll type insulation placed between studs or joists. See BLANKET INSULATION.
bituminous	Do not use.
blackboard	Use CHALKBOARD.
BLANKET INSULATION	Use for roll type insulation installed over a suspended ceiling or attached to a flat wall surface, either laid loose or secured with clips or pins. See BATT INSULATION.
borrowed lite (or light)	Use GLAZED OPENING.
BUILDING PAPER	Heavy, durable paper used to improve weather protection and act as a vapor barrier.
BUILT-UP ROOF	Not *tar and gravel* or *asphalt roof.*
bulkhead	Do not use.
bulletin board	Use TACKBOARD.
butyl membrane	Use WATERPROOFING.
CALK, CALKING	Not *caulk*. Use only for non-elastomeric joint fillers, usually indoors. See SEALANT and ACOUSTICAL SEALANT.
CASEWORK	Not *case* or *cabinetwork*. See MILLWORK.
CASING BEAD	Used for a plaster stop, not for gypsum wallboard. Use CORNERBEAD or METAL TRIM for gypsum wallboard construction.
CELLULAR INSULATION	Not *Styrofoam* or other trade name.
Celotex™	Use MINERAL BOARD INSULATION.

CEMENT	Use when referring to portland cement.
CEMENT FIBER PANEL	Not *Tectum* or other trade name.
CERAMIC TILE	Not *ceramic mosaic tile, wall tile,* or similar terms.
CHALKBOARD	Not *blackboard*.
chipboard	Use PARTICLEBOARD.
COLD JOINT	Used to signify where material (most commonly concrete) on one side of a joint will be set before the other side is installed with no bonding required.
COLUMN	Not *post*.
computer floor	Use ACCESS FLOOR.
concrete block	Use CONCRETE UNIT MASONRY or the abbreviation CMU.
CONCRETE MASONRY UNIT	Not concrete block or conc. blk. Concrete unit masonry is often used when spelled out and in specifications while CMU is typically used as the abbreviation.
CONSTRUCTION JOINT	Used to signify where a joint is placed in order to sequence construction and where structural continuity or bonding is required.
CONTROL JOINT	A joint tooled or cut to control cracking.
corkboard	Use TACKBOARD.
CORNERBEAD	Metal or plastic reinforcement used for outside corners of gypsum wallboard. Do not use CASING BEAD.
Cor-Ten™	Use WEATHERING STEEL.
COUNTERFLASHING	Used over BASE FLASHING to protect the space between the base flashing and the vertical surface.
DADO	A groove cut within a piece of material, commonly wood. If the groove is cut at the edge of the material it is a RABBET.

DAMPPROOFING	Used to identify a material intended for stopping vapor transmission but not to stop water under pressure. See WATERPROOFING.
DELETE	Use OMIT for something to be left out.
DOWNSPOUT	A conduit for rainwater if it is fabricated from sheet metal. See also LEADER.
DRAWING	Use drawing instead of *sheet*.
dryvit™	Use EXTERIOR INSULATION AND FINISH SYSTEM.
drywall	Use GYPSUM WALLBOARD or the abbreviation GYP BD.
earth	Use SOIL or TOPSOIL.
ELASTOMERIC	Describes a material that can expand and contract without rupture. Used as an adjective with SEALANT, membrane, and flashing
EXPANSION BOLT	Do not use *Wej-it*, *Kwik Bolt* or other trade name.
EXPANSION JOINT	Describes a joint intended to accommodate movement. Do not confuse with CONTROL JOINT or CONSTRUCTION JOINT.
EXPANSION SHIELD	Describes a device used with a separate screw or bolt. Do not confuse with ANCHOR BOLT.
EXTERIOR INSULATION AND FINISH SYSTEM	Do not use *Dryvit* or other proprietary names.
FASCIA	Not *facia*.
felt	Use BUILDING PAPER for sheathing or PLY for individual layers of built-up roofing.
FIBER GLASS	Do not use *Fiberglas* or *glass fiber*.
FIREPROOFING PLASTER	Do not use *perlite*, *vermiculite*, or a trade name.
flakeboard	Use PARTICLEBOARD.
FOOTING	Not *footer*.
Formica™	Use PLASTIC LAMINATE.

free access floor	Use ACCESS FLOOR.
FURR	Not *fur*.
FURRED CEILING	A ceiling that is secondarily attached to a floor or roof above with furring strips. Does not include SUSPENDED ACOUSTICAL CEILING.
FURRING	Do not use *furing* or *stripping*.
FURRING CHANNEL	Cold-rolled steel channel. Use *hat channel* for standard light gage hat-shaped furring. See METAL FURRING.
GAGE	Do not use *gauge* or *guage*.
GLASS STOP	Do not use *glazing bead* or similar terms.
GLAZED OPENING	Do not use *borrowed light* or *sidelite*.
glue	Use ADHESIVE.
GROOVE	For wood, use DADO or RABBET if the groove is perpendicular to the grain.
GROUT	Do not use trade names.
GUARDRAIL	Identifies protective railing around walkways and other openings. See HANDRAIL.
GYPSUM BLOCK	Not *Pyrobar* or other trade name.
GYPSUM WALLBOARD	Do not use *drywall*, *sheetrock*, or other trade names.
HANDRAIL	Typically used for stairway railings which can be gripped by people using the stairway. See GUARDRAIL.
HANGER	Used for any member attached to an overhead structure that supports other construction items or assemblies.
HARDBOARD	Do not use *masonite*, or other trade name.
HARDWOOD	Used to call out category of wood from deciduous trees without specifically naming the species of the wood.

hat channel	Use METAL FURRING and show a hat shaped channel. Do not use FURRING CHANNEL.
HEAT-REDUCING GLASS	Do not use *Solarbronze* or other trade names.
HOISTWAY	Do not use *shaft*.
HOISTWAY BEAM	Do not use *separator beam*.
HOLLOW METAL	Used to describe steel doors and frames. Do not use for metals other than steel.
INSTALL	Do not use *apply, place,* or similar words. For items furnished and installed, use PROVIDE.
INSULATING CONCRETE	Do not use *vermiculite concrete* or similar terms.
INSULATING GLASS	Do not use *Thermopane* or other trade name.
JOINT BACKER	Material used behind a sealant.
JOINT FILLER	Material which fills the entire joint. More commonly, SEALANT or joint sealant is used.
kick space	Use TOE SPACE.
kwik bolt™	Use EXPANSION BOLT.
laminated plastic	Use PLASTIC LAMINATE.
LEADER	Rain water conduit made from pipe or tubing. See DOWN-SPOUT.
LIGHTGAGE FRAMING	Metal studs and joists 20 gage or heavier which are primarily used for loadbearing applications. For non-loadbearing lighter gage studs use METAL STUD.
LIGHTWEIGHT AGGREGATE CONCRETE	Concrete with lightweight aggregates not intended to provide insulation.
masonite	Use HARDBOARD.
MASONRY WALL REINFORCEMENT	Do not use *Dur-O-Wall* or other trade names.
mastic	Use ADHESIVE.
METAL FRAME	Describes pressed steel frames used in doors and frames.

METAL FURRING	Used to described hat-shaped, 25-gage steel channels. Do not use *hat channel*.
METAL LATH	Do not use *diamond mesh, chicken wire*, or similar terms.
METALLIC WATERPROOFING	Do not use *ferrous waterproofing* or similar terms.
METAL STUD	Used to describe 22 gage or lighter studs used for non-load-bearing partitions and similar framing. See LIGHTGAGE FRAMING.
METAL TRIM	Used to describe various types of edge trim used for gypsum wall-board. Use CORNERBEAD for outside corner reinforcement. Do not use CASING BEAD.
MINERAL BOARD INSULATION	Do not use *Celotex* or other trade names.
MINERAL FIBER	Replaces asbestos in name and material.
MIRROR GLASS	Do not use *one-way glass*.
moisture barrier	Use DAMPPROOFING or VAPOR BARRIER.
OMIT	Use to intentionally leave something out. See also DELETE.
open-web joists	Use STEEL JOISTS.
OPTION	Use only where there is a choice for the contractor.
PANELING	Used for interior finish sheet material.
PANELS	Used for exterior or interior sheet material.
PARTICLEBOARD	Do not use *chipboard, flakeboard*, or trade names.
PARTITION	Used for non-loadbearing interior walls. For loadbearing types use WALL.
PATCH	Used to call out a repair of finish or material to match surrounding existing material.
pedestal floor	Use ACCESS FLOOR.

per code	Do not use. Be specific about the particular requirement.
PLACE (concrete)	Do not use *pour*.
PLASTER	Use for any of the various types of materials composed of portland cement, lime, sand, gypsum, and water.
plaster stop	Use CASING BEAD.
PLASTIC LAMINATE	Do not use *laminated plastic* or trade names such as *Formica*.
plastic membrane	Use VAPOR BARRIER.
Plexiglas	Use ACRYLIC SHEET
PLIES	Do not use *plys*.
PLYWOOD	Call out separate types if required.
PRECAST CONCRETE PANELS	Do not use *architectural precast*, *exposed aggregate panels*, or similar terms.
PROTECTIVE BOARDS	Used to describe boards intended as protection for insulation, membranes, and similar materials from construction operations or placement of other materials.
PROVIDE	Used to mean supply *and* install.
QUARRY TILE	Use for actual quarry tile floor paving. Use CERAMIC TILE for walls and floor if appropriate.
RABBET	A groove cut at the edge of a piece of material, commonly wood. If the groove is cut in the middle of the material it is a DADO.
RAILING	The term HANDRAIL is preferred for the gripping rail of a stairway and the term GUARDRAIL for a protective railing around an opening. Do not use *rail* or *balustrade*.
rainwater leader	Use LEADER if the item is made of pipe or tubing and use DOWNSPOUT if made from sheet metal.

rebate	Use RABBET.
RECORD DRAWING	Used to indicate revised drawings showing construction changes. Use AS-BUILT DRAWINGS for drawings prepared by the contractor showing actual construction conditions.
REFINISH	Used to describe putting a finish back into its original condition. Do not use *remodel, refurbish, renew,* or similar terms.
RELOCATE	Used to mean to move from one place and install in another.
remodel	Use ALTERATION.
REPLACE	Used to call out a substitute of one item for another.
RESILIENT BASE	Do not use *vinyl base* or *rubber base.*
resilient flooring	Be more specific by using RESILIENT TILE, SHEET FLOORING, or SEEMLESS FLOORING.
RESILIENT TILE	Do not use *VAT, vinyl tile,* or *linoleum.*
RIGID INSULATION	Do not use *foam insulation, board insulation,* or *cellular insulation.*
ROOF HATCH	Do not use *scuttle.* If the opening is intended as a vent for smoke, use SMOKE VENT.
RUNNER CHANNEL	Use for the standard 1 1/2″ cold rolled steel channel.
SCREED	Strip of material used to maintain the thickness of an applied material such as plaster.
SCRIBE STRIP	Used to describe a piece of material trimmed to fit between one assembly (usually wood cabinets) and an adjoining surface.
SEALANT	Used for elastomeric materials for interior or exterior joints subject to movement. See also ACOUSTICAL SEALANT.

SEAMLESS FLOORING	Used to describe sheet material forming a homogeneous floor after joints are field welded or sealed.
SECTION	Used to refer to a drawing showing a cut through an object.
SELF-EDGE	Used to describe the application to the edge of plywood or particleboard of plastic laminate having the same color and pattern as the face surface.
separator beams	Use HOISTWAY BEAMS.
SERVICE SINK	Do not use *slop sink* or *janitor's sink*.
SHEATHING	Covering placed over exterior framing used for structural purposes and as a base for applying exterior finish.
SHEET	Do not use to describe a drawing. It should be used to call out thin construction material.
SHEET FLOORING	Used to describe resilient flooring installed in lengths of wide sections.
SHEET METAL	Generally used as a generic description for non-structural steel fabrications. Call out other materials, such as brass or aluminum, if necessary to avoid confusion.
sidelite	Use GLAZED OPENING.
SMOKE VENT	Used to call out a hatch specifically for the purpose of venting smoke.
SOIL	Do not use *earth*.
sound calking	Use ACOUSTICAL SEALANT.
SOUND DEADENING BOARD	Use for materials specifically designed for this purpose.
SPRAYED FIREPROOFING	Used to designate one of several types of materials sprayed directly to structural elements.
STEEL BEAM	Do not use *I-beam*.

STEEL JOISTS	Do not use *open-web steel joists* or *bar joists*.
STONE	Use the generic term on drawings and define more specifically in the specifications unless there are several different types adjacent to each other.
STORY	Do not use *storey*.
stripping	Use FURRING.
structural studs	Use LIGHTGAGE FRAMING.
stucco	Use CEMENT PLASTER.
STUD	An upright framing member placed in series with others.
SUBFLOORING	Used for layer of supporting flooring under the finish floor.
SUSPENDED ACOUSTICAL CEILING	Standard acoustical ceiling suspended from the structure above with wires.
Styrofoam™	Use CELLULAR INSULATION
TACKBOARD	Do not use *bulletin board, corkboard*, or similar terms.
TEMPERED GLASS	Do not use *Herculite* or other trade names.
Thermopane™	Use INSULATING GLASS
THROUGH	THRU commonly used as the abbreviated form.
TOE BOARD	Used to call out a protective edge which is raised above the floor level at balconies, landings, and other openings.
TOE SPACE	Used to describe the recessed area below base cabinets.
TOPSOIL	Used on landscape drawings. See also SOIL.
TYPE X GYP BD	Do not use *code drywall* or similar terms.
TYPICAL	Used to indicate that the called-out item or descriptive note is representative of similar conditions throughout the project.
UNDERLAY	Used for roofing felt applied below shingles.

UNDERLAYMENT	Used for the smooth sheet material commonly placed over subflooring to provide a surface for the application of carpet, resilient tile, and similar finishes.
VAPOR BARRIER	Do not use *visqueen, plastic film* or *waterproofing*.
visqueen™	Use VAPOR BARRIER.
WAINSCOT	Decorative or protective finish on the lower portion of an interior wall where it differs from the finish above.
WALL	Used for loadbearing separation between spaces. Use PARTITION for non-loadbearing separation.
wallboard	Use GYPSUM WALLBOARD.
WATERPROOFING	Used to call out materials designed to resist the passage of water under a static head. See also DAMPPROOFING.
WEATHERING STEEL	Do not use *Cor-Ten*, or other trade names.
wej-it™	Use EXPANSION BOLT.
WIRED GLASS	Do not use *wire glass*.
WOOD	Used for solid stock softwood. See also HARDWOOD.

Masterformat list of section numbers and headings

Bidding requirements, Contract forms, and Conditions of the contract

00010	Pre-bid information
00100	Instructions to bidders
00200	Information available to bidders
00300	Bid forms
00400	Supplements to bid forms
00500	Agreement forms
00600	Bonds and certificates
00700	General conditions
00800	Supplementary conditions
00900	Addenda

Division 1—General Requirements

01010	Summary of the work
01020	Allowances
01025	Measurement and payment
01030	Alternates/Alternatives
01035	Modification procedures
01040	Coordination
01050	Field engineering
01060	Regulatory requirements
01070	Identification systems
01090	References
01100	Special project procedures
01200	Project meetings
01300	Submittals
01400	Quality control
01500	Construction facilities and temporary controls
01600	Material and equipment
01650	Facility startup/Commissioning
01700	Contract closeout
01800	Maintenance

Division 2—Sitework

02010	Subsurface investigation
02050	Demolition
02100	Site preparation
02140	Dewatering
02150	Shoring and underpinning
02160	Excavation support systems
02170	Cofferdams
02200	Earthwork
02300	Tunneling
02350	Piles and caissons
02450	Railroad work
02480	Marine work
02500	Paving and surfacing
02600	Utility piping materials
02660	Water distribution
02680	Fuel and steam distribution
02700	Sewerage and drainage
02760	Restoration of underground pipe
02770	Ponds and reservoirs
02780	Power and communications
02800	Site improvements
02900	Landscaping

Division 3—Concrete

03100	Concrete formwork
03200	Concrete reinforcement
03250	Concrete accessories
03300	Cast-in-place concrete
03370	Concrete curing
03400	Precast concrete
03500	Cementitious decks and toppings
03600	Grout
03700	Concrete restoration and cleaning
03800	Mass concrete

Division 4—Masonry

04100	Mortar and masonry grout
04150	Masonry accessories
04200	Unit masonry
04400	Stone
04500	Masonry restoration and cleaning
04550	Refractories
04600	Corrosion resistant masonry
04700	Simulated masonry

Division 5—Metals

05010	Metal materials
05030	Metal coatings
05050	Metal fastening
05100	Structural metal framing
05200	Metal joists
05300	Metal decking
05400	Cold formed metal framing
05500	Metal fabrications
05580	Sheet metal fabrications
05700	Ornamental metal
05800	Expansion control
05900	Hydraulic structures

Division 6—Wood and Plastics

06050	Fasteners and adhesives
06100	Rough carpentry
06130	Heavy timber construction
06150	Wood and metal systems
06170	Prefabricated structural wood
06200	Finish carpentry
06300	Wood treatment
06400	Architectural woodwork
06500	Structural plastics
06600	Plastic fabrications
06650	Solid polymer fabrications

Division 7—Thermal and Moisture Protection

07100	Waterproofing
07150	Dampproofing
07180	Water repellents
07190	Vapor retarders
07195	Air barriers
07200	Insulation
07240	Exterior insulation and finish systems
07250	Fireproofing
07270	Firestopping
07300	Shingles and roofing tiles
07400	Manufactured roofing and siding
07480	Exterior wall assemblies
07500	Membrane roofing
07570	Traffic coatings
07600	Flashing and sheet metal
07700	Roof specialties and accessories
07800	Skylights
07900	Joint sealers

Division 8—Doors and Windows

08100	Metal doors and frames
08200	Wood and plastic doors
08250	Door opening assemblies
08300	Special doors
08400	Entrances and storefronts
08500	Metal windows
08600	Wood and plastic windows
08650	Special windows
08700	Hardware
08800	Glazing
08900	Glazed curtain walls

Division 9—Finishes

09100	Metal support systems
09200	Lath and plaster

09250	Gypsum board
09300	Tile
09400	Terrazzo
09450	Stone facing
09500	Acoustical treatment
09540	Special wall surfaces
09545	Special ceiling surfaces
09550	Wood flooring
09600	Stone flooring
09630	Unit masonry flooring
09650	Resilient flooring
09680	Carpet
09700	Special flooring
09780	Floor treatment
09800	Special coatings
09900	Painting
09950	Wall coverings

Division 10—Specialties

10100	Visual display boards
10150	Compartments and cubicles
10200	Louvers and vents
10240	Grilles and screens
10250	Service wall systems
10260	Wall and corner guards
10270	Access flooring
10290	Pest control
10300	Fireplaces and stoves
10340	Manufactured exterior specialties
10350	Flagpoles
10400	Identifying devices
10450	Pedestrian control devices
10500	Lockers
10520	Fire protection specialties
10530	Protective covers
10550	Postal specialties

10600	Partitions
10650	Operable partitions
10670	Storage shelving
10700	Exterior protection devices for openings
10750	Telephone specialties
10800	Toilet and bath accessories
10880	Scales
10900	Wardrobe and closet specialties

Division 11—Equipment

11010	Maintenance equipment
11020	Security and vault equipment
11030	Teller and service equipment
11040	Ecclesiastical equipment
11050	Library equipment
11060	Theater and stage equipment
11070	Instrumental equipment
11080	Registration equipment
11090	Checkroom equipment
11100	Mercantile equipment
11110	Commercial laundry and dry cleaning equipment
11120	Vending equipment
11130	Audio-visual equipment
11140	Vehicle service equipment
11150	Parking control equipment
11160	Loading dock equipment
11170	Solid waste handling equipment
11190	Detention equipment
11200	Water supply and treatment equipment
11280	Hydraulic gates and valves
11300	Fluid waste treatment and disposal equipment
11400	Food service equipment
11450	Residential equipment
11460	Unit kitchens
11470	Darkroom equipment
11480	Athletic, recreational, and therapeutic equipment

11500	Industrial and process equipment
11600	Laboratory equipment
11650	Planetarium equipment
11660	Observatory equipment
11680	Office equipment
11700	Medical equipment
11780	Mortuary equipment
11850	Navigation equipment
11870	Agricultural equipment

Division 12—Furnishings

12050	Fabrics
12100	Artwork
12300	Manufactured casework
12500	Window treatment
12600	Furniture and accessories
12670	Rugs and mats
12700	Multiple seating
12800	Interior plants and planters

Division 13—Special Construction

13010	Air supported structures
13020	Integrated assemblies
13030	Special purpose rooms
13080	Sound, vibration, and seismic control
13090	Radiation protection
13100	Nuclear reactors
13120	Pre-engineered structures
13150	Aquatic facilities
13175	Ice rinks
13180	Site constructed incinerators
13185	Kennels and animal shelters
13200	Liquid and gas storage tanks
13220	Filter underdrains and media
13230	Digester covers and appurtenances
13240	Oxygenation systems

13260	Sludge conditioning systems
13300	Utility control systems
13400	Industrial and process control systems
13500	Recording instrumentation
13550	Transportation control instrumentation
13600	Solar energy systems
13700	Wind energy systems
13750	Cogeneration systems
13800	Building automation systems
13900	Fire suppression and supervisory systems
13950	Special security construction

Division 14—Conveying Systems

14100	Dumbwaiters
14200	Elevators
14300	Escalators and moving walks
14400	Lifts
14500	Material handling systems
14600	Hoists and cranes
14700	Turntables
14800	Scaffolding
14900	Transportation systems

Division 15—Mechanical

15050	Basic mechanical materials and methods
15250	Mechanical insulation
15300	Fire protection
15400	Plumbing
15500	Heating, ventilating, and air conditioning
15550	Heat generation
15650	Refrigeration
15750	Heat transfer
15850	Air handling
15880	Air distribution
15950	Controls
15990	Testing, adjusting, and balancing

Division 16—Electrical

16050	Basic electrical materials and methods
16200	Power generation—built-up systems
16300	Medium voltage distribution
16400	Service and distribution
16500	Lighting
16600	Special systems
16700	Communications
16850	Electric resistance heating
16900	Controls
16950	Testing

Trade associations

Acoustical Society of America ASA
50 Sunnyside Blvd.
Woodbury, NY 11797
(516) 349-7800

Adhesive and Sealant Council, Inc. ASC
1627 K Street NW, Suite 1000
Washington, DC 20006
(202) 452-1500

Advisory Council on Historic Preservation ACHP
1100 Pennsylvania Ave. NW
Washington, DC 20004
(202) 786-0503

Air Diffusion Council ADC
230 North Michigan Ave.
Chicago, IL 60601
(312) 372-9800

Aluminum Association AA
900 19th St. NW, Suite 300
Washington, DC 20006
(202) 862-5100

American Arbitration Association AAA
140 West 51st Street
New York, NY 10020
(212) 484-4000

American Architectural Manufacturers Association AAMA
2700 River Road, Suite 118
Des Plaines, IL 60018
(708) 699-7310

American Association of Healthcare Consultants AAHC
11208 Waples Mill Road,
Suite 109
Fairfax, VA 22203
(703) 691-2242

American Association of Homes for the Aging AAHA
1129 20th Street N.W.,
Suite 400
Washington, DC 20036
(202) 296-5960

American Association of Museums AAM
1225 Eye Street N.W.,
Suite 200
Washington, DC 20005
(202) 289-1818

American Concrete Institute ACI
P.O. Box 19150, Redford
Station
Detroit, MI 48219
(313) 532-2600

American Concrete Pavement Association ACPA
3800 N. Wilke Road, Suite 490
Arlington Hts., IL 60004
(312) 394-5577

American Consulting Engineers Council ACEC
1015 15th Street NW
Washington, DC 20005
(202) 347-7474

American Design Drafting Association ADDA
5522 Norbeck Road
Rockville, MD 20853
(301) 460-6875

American Galvanizers Association AGA
1101 Connecticut Ave. N.W.
Washington, DC 20036-4303
(202) 857-1119

American Hardboard Association AHA
520 N. Hicks Road
Palatine, IL 60067
(312) 934-8800

American Hardware Manufacturers Association AHMA
931 N. Plum Grove Road
Schaumburg, IL 60173-4796
(708) 605-1025

American Hospital Association AHA
840 North Lake Shore Drive
Chicago, IL 60611
(312) 280-6000

American Institute of Architects AIA
1735 New York Avenue NW
Washington, DC 20006
(202) 626-7300

American Institute of Steel Construction AISC
400 N. Michigan Ave., 8th fl.
Chicago, IL 60611
(312) 670-2400

American Institute of Timber Construction AITC
11818 SE Mill Plain Blvd.
Vancouver, WA 98684
(206) 254-9132

American Insurance Association AIA
1130 Connecticut Ave N.W.
Ste. 1000
Washington, DC 20036
(202) 828-7100

American Iron and Steel Institute AISI
1133 15th St. NW, Suite 300
Washington, DC 20005
(202) 452-7100

American Library Association ALA
50 E. Huron St.
Chicago, IL 60611
(312) 944-6780

American Lighting Institute ALI
435 North Michigan Avenue,
Chicago, IL 60611
(312) 644-0828

American Lumber Standards Committee ALSC
P.O. Box 210
Germantown, MD 20874
(301) 972-1700

American National Standards Institute ANSI
1430 Broadway
New York, NY 10018
(212) 354-3300

American Parquet Association APA
2900 First Commercial Building
Little Rock, AR 72201
(501) 375-5561

American Planning Association APA
1776 Massachusetts Ave. N.W.
Washington, DC 20036
(202) 872-0611

American Plywood Association APA
P.O. Box 11700
Tacoma, WA 98411-0700
(206) 565-6600

American Public Transit Association APTA
1201 New York Ave. NW, Suite 400
Washington, DC 20005
(202) 898-4000

American Society for Industrial Security ASIS
1655 N. Fort Meyer Drive, Ste. 1200
Arlington, VA 22209
(703) 522-5800

American Society for Nondestructive Testing ASNT
4153 Arlingate Plaza, Caller #28518
Columbus, OH 43228
(614) 274-6003

American Society for Testing and Materials ASTM
1916 Race Street
Philadelphia, PA 19103
(215) 299-5400

American Society of Civil Engineers ASCE
345 E. 47th Street
New York, NY 10017
(212) 705-7496

American Society of Golf Course Architects ASGCA
221 North LaSalle St.
Chicago, IL 60601
(312) 372-7090

American Society of Heating, Refrigerating & Air Conditioning Engineers ASHRAE
1791 Tullie Circle N.E.
Atlanta, GA 30329
(404) 636-8400

American Society of Home Inspectors ASHI
3299 K St., NW, 7th Fl.
Washington, DC 20007
(202) 842-3096

American Society of Interior Designers ASID
608 Massachusetts Ave. N.E.
Washington, DC 20002
(202) 546-3480

American Society of Landscape Architects ASLA
4401 Connecticut Ave. NW
Washington, DC 20008
(202) 466-7730

American Society of
Mechanical Engineers ASME
345 E. 47th Street
New York, NY 10017
(212) 705-7722

American Society of
Plumbing Engineers ASPE
3617 Thousand Oaks Blvd.
Westlake, CA 91362
(805) 495-7120

American Society of Sanitary
Engineering ASSE
P.O. Box 40362
Bay Village, OH 44140
(216) 835-3040

American Solar Energy
Society ASES
2400 Central Avenue, Suite B1
Boulder, CO 80301
(303) 443-3130

American Textile Manufac-
turers Institute ATMI
1801 K Street, Suite 900
Washington, DC 20006
(202) 862-0500

American Underground-
Space Association AUA
University of Minnesota
511 11th Ave. South
Minneapolis, MN 55415
(612) 339-5403

American Welding Society
AWS
550 Le Jeune Rd NW
Miami, FL 33135
(305) 443-9353

American Wind Energy
Association AWEA
1730 North Lynn St., Suite 610
Arlington, VA 22209
(703) 276-8334

American Wood Council AWC
1250 Connecticut Ave. NW,
Ste. 230
Washington, DC 20036
(202) 833-1595

American Wood Preservers
Association AWPA
P.O. Box 849
Stevensville, MD 21666
(301) 643-4163

American Wood Preservers
Bureau AWPB
P.O. Box 5283
Springfield, VA 22150
(703) 339-6660

American Wood Preservers
Institute AWPI
1945 Old Gallows Rd., Ste. 550
Vienna, VA 22182
(703) 893-4005

Architectural and
Transportation Barriers
Compliance Board ATBCB
1111 18th St. NW, Suite 501
Washington, DC 20036-3894
(202) 653-7834

Architectural Anodizers
Council AAC
1227 W. Wrightwood Ave.
Chicago, IL 60614
(312) 871-2550

Architectural Precast Association APA
825 East 64th Street
Indianapolis, IN 46220
(317) 251-1214

Architectural Spray and Coaters Association ASCA
230 W. Wells, Suite 311
Milwaukee, WI 53203
(414) 273-3430

Architectural Woodwork Institute AWI
2310 South Walter Reed Drive
Arlington, VA 22206
(703) 671-9100

Asbestos Information Association of North America AIANA
1745 Jefferson Davis Hwy.
Arlington, VA 22202
(703) 979-1150

Asphalt Institute AI
Research Park Drive
Lexington, KY 40512-4052
(606) 288-4960

Asphalt Roofing Manufacturers Association ARMA
6288 Montrose Road
Rockville, MD 20852
(301) 231-9050

Associated Builders and Contractors, Inc. ABC
729 15th Street NW
Washington, DC 20005
(202) 637-8800

Associated General Contractors of America AGC
1957 E Street NW
Washington, DC 20006
(202) 393-2040

Association for Computing Machinery, SIGGRAPH ACMS
11 West 42nd St., 3rd. Floor
New York, NY 10036
(212) 869-7440

Association of Architectural Librarians AAL
1735 New York Avenue N.W.
Washington, DC 20006
(202) 626-7499

Association of Collegiate Schools of Architecture ACSA
1735 New York Ave N.W.
Washington, DC 20006
(202) 785-2324

Association of Energy Engineers AEE
4025 Pleasantdale Road
Suite 420
Atlanta, GA 30340
(404) 447-5083

Association of Specialists in Cleaning and Restoration ASCR
10830 Annapolis Jct. Rd.
Suite. 312
Annapolis Jct., MD 20701
(301) 604-4411

Association of Wall and Ceiling Industries International AWCII
1600 Cameron Street, Suite 200
Alexandria, VA 22314
(703) 684-2924

Association of Women in Architecture AWA
7440 University Drive
St. Louis, MO 63130
(314) 621-3484

Better Fabrics Testing Bureau, Inc. BFTB
101 W. 31st Street
New York, NY 10001
(212) 868-7090

Brick Institute of America BIA
11490 Commerce Park Drive
Ste. 300
Reston, VA 22091
(703) 620-0010

Builders Hardware Manufacturers Association BHMA
355 Lexington Ave, 17th Fl.
New York, NY 10017
(212) 661-4261

Building Officials and Code Administrators International BOCA
4051 West Flossmoor Road
Country Club Hills, IL 60478
(708) 799-2300

Building Owners and Managers Association BOMA
1201 New York Ave. NW
Suite 300
Washington, DC 20005
(202) 289-7000

Building Research Board BRB
2101 Constitution Ave. NW
Washington, DC 20418
(202) 334-3376

Building Seismic Safety Council BSSC
1015 15th Street NW
Washington, DC 20005
(202) 347-5710

Building Stone Institute BSI
420 Lexington Avenue
New York, NY 10017
(212) 490-2530

Building Systems Institute, c/o Thomas Associates BSI
1230 Keith Building
Cleveland, OH 44115-2180
(216) 241-7333

Business and Institutional Furniture Manufacturers Assoc. BIFMA
2335 Burton, S.E.
Grand Rapids, MI 49506
(616) 243-1681

California Redwood Association CRA
405 Enfrente Drive, Suite 200
Nevato, CA 94949
(415) 382-0662

**Carpet and Rug Institute
CRI**
310 Holiday Drive,
P.O.Box 2048
Dalton, GA 30722
(404) 278-3176

Cast Stone Institute CSI
Pavilions at Greentree
St. Hwy. 70
Marlton, NJ 08053
(609) 858-0271

**Cedar Shake and Shingle
Bureau CSSB**
515 116th Ave. N.E., Suite 275
Bellevue, WA 98004
(206) 453-1323

**Ceilings and Interior Systems
Construction Association
CISCA**
104 Wilmot Road, Suite 201
Deerfield, IL 60015-5195
(315) 940-8800

**Center for Fire Research,
Room A 247, Building 224
CRF**
National Institute. of
Standards and Technology
Gaithersburg, MD 20899
(301) 975-6850

**Ceramic Tile Institute of
America CTIOA**
700 N. Virgil Avenue
Los Angeles, CA 90029
(213) 660-1911

**Chemical Fabrics and Film
Association CFFA**
c/o Thomas Associates
1230 Keith Building
Cleveland, OH 44115
(216) 241-7333

**Color Association of the
United States CAUS**
343 Lexington Avenue
New York, NY 10016
(212) 683-9531

**Color Marketing Group
CMG**
4001 N. Ninth Street, Suite 102
Arlington, VA 22203
(703) 528-7666

**Concrete Reinforcing Steel
Institute CRS**
933 N. Plum Grove Road,
Room 215
Schaumburg, IL 60173
(312) 517-1200

**Construction Management
Association of America
CMAA**
12355 Sunrise Valley Drive,
Suite 640
Reston, VA 22091
(703) 391-1200

**Construction Specifications
Institute CSI**
601 Madison Street
Alexandria, VA 22314-1791
(703) 684-0300

Copper and Brass Fabricators Council, Inc. CBFC
1050 17th Street NW, Suite 440
Washington, DC 20036
(202) 833-8575

Copper Development Association CDA
2 Greenwich Office Park
Box 1840
Greenwich, CT 06836
(203) 625-8210

Council of American Building Officials CABO
5203 Leesburg Pike, Suite 708
Falls Church, VA 22041
(703) 931-4533

Council of Educational Facility Planners, International CEFPI
941 Chathan Lane, Suite 217
Columbus, OH 43221
(614) 292-6446

Council on Tall Buildings and Urban Habitat CTBUH
Building 13, Lehigh Univ.
Bethleham, PA 18015
(215) 861-3515

Cultured Marble Institute CMI
435 N. Michigan Ave., Ste. 1717
Chicago, IL 60611
(312) 644-0828

Decorative Laminate Products Association DLPA
600 S. Federal Street, Suite 400
Chicago, IL 60605
(312) 922-6222

Deep Foundations Institute DFI
P.O. Box 281
Sparta, NJ 07871
(201) 729-9679

Design and Construction Quality Institute DCQI
1015 15th Street N.W., Ste. 802
Washington, DC 20005
(202) 347-7474

Door and Hardware Institute DHI
7711 Old Springhouse Road
McLean, VA 22102
(703) 556-3990

Downtown Research and Development Center DRDC
1133 Broadway, Suite 1407
New York, NY 10010
(212) 206-7979

Educational Facilities Laboratories EFL
1255 23rd Street, N.W.
Suite 400
Washington, DC 20037
(202) 862-1900

Environmental Design Research Association EDRA
P.O. Box 24083
Oklahoma City, OK 73124
(405) 232-2655

Exterior Insulation Manufacturers Association EIMA
30 Holley Street
Wakefield, RI 02879
(401) 782-3687

Factory Mutual Research
Organization FMRO
1151 Boston-Providence
Turnpike
Norwood, MA 02062
(617) 762-4300

Federation of Societies for
Coating Technology FSCT
1315 S. Walnut Street, Ste. 830
Philadelphia, PA 19107
(215) 545-1506

Fine Hardwood Veneer
Association FHVA
5603 West Raymond, Suite O
Indianapolis, IN 46241
(317) 244-3311

Flat Glass Marketing
Association FGMA
3310 Harrison Street
Topeka, KS 66611
(913) 266-7013

Foodservice Consultants
Society International FCS
12345 30th Ave N.E., Suite A
Seattle, WA 98125-5405
(206) 367-3274

Forest Products Laboratory
FPL
1 Gifford Pinchot Drive
Madison, WI 53705-2398
(608) 231-9200

Forest Products Research
Society FPRS
2801 Marshal Court
Madison, WI 53705
(608) 231-1361

Foundation for Interior
Design Education Research
FIDER
60 Monroe Center NW
Grand Rapids, MI 49503-2920
(616) 458-0400

Friends of Terra Cotta, Inc.,
c/o Susan Tunick FTC
771 West End Ave., #10E
New York, NY 10025
(212) 932-1750

Glass Tempering Association
GTA
3310 Harrison Street
Topeka, KS 66611
(913) 266-7064

Gypsum Association GA
810 First St. N.E., Suite 510
Washington, DC 20002
(202) 289-5440

Hardwood Manufacturers
Association HMA
2831 Airways Blvd., Suite. 205
Memphis, TN 38132
(901) 346-2222

Hardwood Plywood
Manufacturers Association
HPMA
1825 Michael Faraday Drive
Reston, VA 22090
(703) 435-2900

Hardwood Research Council
HRC
P.O. Box 34518
Memphis, TN 38184
(901) 377-1824

**Historic Preservation
Education Foundation HPEF**
1233 20th Street N. W.
Washington, DC 20038-7080
(202) 828-9616

Human Factors Society HFS
P.O. Box 1369
Santa Monica, CA 90406
(213) 394-1811

**Illuminating Engineering
Society of North America
IESNA**
345 East 47th Street, 9th Floor
New York, NY 10017
(212) 705-7926

**Indiana Limestone Institute
of America, Inc. ILI**
Stone City Bank Bldg., Ste. 400
Bedford, IN 47421
(812) 275-4426

**Industrial Designers Society
of America IDSA**
1142-E Walker Road
Great Falls, VA 22066
(703) 759-0100

**Industrial Fabrics
Association International
IFAI**
345 Cedar Street, Suite 800
St. Paul, MN 55101
(612) 222-2508

**Institute for Security Design
and Training ISD**
74 Warren Street
New York, NY 10007
(212) 732-6565

**Institute of Business
Designers IBD**
341 Merchandise Mart
Chicago, IL 60654-1104
(312) 467-1950

Institute of Store Planners ISP
25 N. Broadway
Tarrytown, NY 10591
(914) 332-1806

**Institute of Textile
Technology ITT**
P.O. Box 391
Charlottesville, VA 22902
(804) 296-5511

**Insulated Steel Door Systems
Institute ISDSI**
30200 Detroit Road
Cleveland, OH 44145-1967
(216) 889-0010

**Insulating Glass Certification
Council, c/o ETL Testing Labs
IGCC**
Industrial Park, Route 11
Box 2040
Cortland, NY 13045
(607) 753-6711

**Intelligent Building Institute
IBI**
2101 L Street NW, Suite 300
Washington, DC 20037
(202) 457-1988

**Interfaith Forum on Religion,
Art, and Architecture IFRAA**
1913 Architects Building
Philadelphia, PA 19103
(215) 568-0960

Interior Design Educators Council, Inc. IDEC
14252 Culver Drive, Suite A-311
Irvine, CA 92714
(714) 551-1622

Interior Plantscape Division Association of Landscape Contractors of America IPD
405 N. Washington Street
Suite 104
Falls Church, VA 22046
(703) 476-8550

International Association of Lighting Designers IALD
18 East 16th St, Suite 208
New York, NY 10003
(212) 206-1281

International Conference of Building Officials ICBO
5360 South Workmen Mill Road
Whittier, CA 90601
(213) 699-0541

International Facility Management Association IFMA
1 Greenway Plaza, 11th Floor
Houston, TX 77046
(713) 253-7525

International Hardwood Products Association IHPA
P.O. Box 1308
Alexandria, VA 22313
(703) 836-6696

International Institute for Lathing and Plastering IILP
820 Transfer Road
St. Paul, MN 55114
(612) 645-0208

International Institute of Plumbing and Mechanical Officials IAPMO
20001 Walnut Drive South
Walnut, CA 91789-2825
(714) 595-8449

International Intelligent Buildings Association IIBA
P.O. Box 683
East Brunswick, NJ 08816
(201) 249-4159

International Masonry Institute IMI
823 15th St. NW, Suite 1001
Washington, DC 20005
(202) 783-3908

International Reprographics Association IRGA
611 E. Butterfield Road, #104
Lombard, IL 60148
(312) 852-3055

International Society of Interior Designers ISID
433 South Spring Street
10th Floor
Los Angeles, CA 90013
(213) 680-4240

Italian Marble Center IMC
499 Park Avenue
New York, NY 10022
(212) 980-1500

Italian Tile Association ITA
305 Madison Avenue
Suite 3120
New York, NY 10165
(212) 661-0435

Italian Tile Center ITC
499 Park Avenue
New York, NY 10022
(212) 980-1500

**Jute Carpet Backing Council
JCBC**
30 Rockefeller Plaza 24th Floor
New York, NY 10112
(212) 408-5100

**Laminators Safety Glass
Association LSGA**
3310 Harrison
Topeka, KS 66611
(913) 266-7014

**Lighting Research Institute
LRI**
345 East 47th Street, 9th Floor
New York, NY 10017
(212) 705-7511

**Lightning Protection
Institute LPI**
P.O. Box 1039
Woodstock, IL 60098
(815) 337-0277

**Manufactured Housing
Institute MHI**
1745 Jefferson Davis Hwy.
Suite 511
Arlington, VA 22202
(703) 979-6620

**Maple Flooring Manufac-
turers Association MFMA**
60 Revere Drive, Suite 500
Northbrook, IL 60062
(312) 480-9138

**Marble Institute of America
MIA**
33505 State Street
Farmington, MI 48024
(313) 476-5558

Masonry Society, The TMS
2619 Spruce Street, Suite B
Boulder, CO 80302-3808
(303) 939-9700

**Metal Building Manufac-
turers Association MBMA**
1230 Keith Building
Cleveland, OH 44115
(216) 241-7333

**Metal Lath/Steel Framing
Association MLSFA**
600 S. Federal Street, Suite 400
Chicago, IL 60605
(312) 922-6222

**Mineral Insulation
Manufacturers Association
MIMA**
1420 King Street
Alexandria, VA 22314
(703) 684-0084

**National Asbestos Council,
Inc. NAC**
1777 Northeast Expresswa,
Suite 150
Atlanta, GA 30329
(404) 633-2622

412

National Association of
Architectural Metal
Manufacturers NAAMM
600 S. Federal Street, Suite 400
Chicago, IL 60605
(312) 922-6222

National Association of
Decorative Architectural
Finishes NADAF
112 N. Alfred Street
Alexandria, VA 22314
(703) 836-6504

National Association of
Home Builders of the U.S.
NAHB
15th and M Streets NW
Washington, DC 20005
(202) 822-0200

National Association of
Home Builders Research
Foundation NAHBRF
400 Prince Georges Blvd.
Upper Marlboro, MD 20772
(301) 249-4000

National Association of
Housing and Redevelopment
Officials NAHRO
1320 18th Street, NW
Washington, DC 20036
(202) 429-2960

National Association of
Industrial and Office Parks
NAIOP
1215 Jefferson Davis Hwy.
Suite. 100
Arlington, VA 22202
(703) 979-3400

National Association of
Plumbing-Heating-Cooling
Contractors NAPHCC
180 S. Washington Street
Falls Church, VA 22046
(703) 237-8100

National Association of Store
Fixture Manufacturers
NASFM
5975 West Sunrise Boulevard
Sunrise, FL 33313
(305) 587-9190

National Association of
Women in Construction
NAWIC
327 S. Adams
Fort Worth, TX 76104
(817) 877-5551

National Building Museum
NBM
Judiciary Square, N.W.
Washington, DC 20001
(202) 272-2448

National Burgler and Fire
Alarm Association NBFAA
7101 Wisconsin Ave. No. 1390
Bethesda, MD 20814
(202) 907-3202

National Clay Pipe Institute
NCPI
P.O. Box 759
Lake Geneva, WI 53147
(414) 248-9094

National Computer Graphics Association NCGA
2722 Merrilee Drive, Suite 200
Fairfax, VA 22031
(703) 698-9600

National Concrete Masonry Association NCMA
P.O. Box 781
Herndon, VA 22070-0781
(703) 435-4900

National Conference of States on Building Codes & Standards NCSBCS
481 Carlisle Drive
Herndon, VA 22070
(703) 437-0100

National Council for Interior Design Qualification NCIDQ
118 East 25th Street
New York, NY 10010
(212) 473-1188

National Council of Acoustical Consultants NCAC
66 Morris Avenue
Springfield, NJ 07081
(201) 379-1100

National Council of Architectural Registration Boards NCARB
1735 New York Avenue NW
Suite 700
Washington, DC 20006
(202) 783-6500

National Council on Disabilities NCD
800 Independence Ave. S.W.
Ste. 814
Washington, DC 20591
(202) 267-3846

National Dimension Manufacturers' Association NDMA
1000 Johnson Ferry Road,
Suite A-130
Marietta, GA 30068
(404) 565-6660

National Electrical Manufacturers Association NEMA
2101 L Street NW
Washington, DC 20037
(202) 457-8400

National Elevator Industry, Inc. NEII
185 Bridge Plaza, North
Ft. Lee, NJ 07024
(201) 944-3211

National Fire Protection Association NFPA
Battery March Park
P.O. Box 9101
Quincy, MA 02269-9101
(617) 770-3000

National Fire Sprinkler Assoc., Robin Hill Corporate Park NFSA
Route 22, Box 1000
Patterson, NY 12563
(914) 878-4200

National Forest Products
Association NFPA
1250 Connecticut Ave. N.W.
Suite 200
Washington, DC 20036
(202) 463-2700

National Glass Association
NGA
8200 Greensboro Drive
Suite 302
McLean, VA 22102
(703) 442-4890

National Hardwood Lumber
Association NHLA
P.O. Box 34518
Memphis, TN 38184-0518
(901) 377-1818

National Housing and
Rehabilitation Association
NHRA
1726 18th St. N.W.
Washington, DC 20009
(202) 328-9197

National Institute for
Architectural Education
NIAE
30 W. 22nd Street
5th & 6th Floor
New York, NY 10010
(212) 924-7000

National Institute of
Building Sciences NIBS
1201 L Street, Suite 400
Washington, DC 20005
(202) 289-7800

National Institute of
Standards and Technology
NIST
Administration Bldg.
Room A625
Gaithersburg, MD 20899
(301) 975-4040

National Insulation
Contractors Association
NICA
99 Canal Center Plaza
Suite 222
Alexandria, VA 22314
(703) 683-6422

National Kitchen and Bath
Association NKBA
124 Main Street
Hackettstown, NJ 07840
(201) 852-0033

National Kitchen Cabinet
Association NKCA
P.O. Box 6830
Falls Church, VA 22046
(703) 237-7580

National Lighting Bureau
NLB
2101 L Street N.W., Suite 300
Washington, DC 20037
(202) 457-8437

National Oak Flooring
Manufacturing Association
NOFMA
P.O. Box 3009
Memphis, TN 38173-0009
(901) 526-5016

National Ornamental and Miscellaneous Metals Association NOMMA
804-10 Main Street, Suite E
Forest Park, GA 30050
(404) 363-4009

National Paint and Coatings Association NPCA
1500 Rhode Island Ave. NW
Washington, DC 20005
(202) 462-6272

National Parking Association NPA
1112 16th Street, NW, Suite 300
Washington, DC 20036
(202) 296-4336

National Particleboard Association NPA
18928 Premier Ct.
Gaithersberg, MD 20879
(301) 670-0604

National Roof Deck Contractors Association NRDCA
600 South Federal St., Suite 400
Chicago, IL 60605
(312) 922-6222

National Roofing Consultants Association NRCA
10255 W. Higgins Road, Ste. 600
Rosemont, IL 60018
(708) 299-9070

National Roofing Contractors Association NRCA
6250 River Road, #8030
Rosemont, IL 60018
(708) 318-6722

National Sanitation Foundation NSF
P.O. Box 1468
Ann Arbor, MI 48106
(313) 769-8010

National Sash and Door Jobbers Association NSDJA
2400 East Devon Ave., Ste. 314
Des Plaines, IL 60018
(312) 299-3400

National Spa and Pool Institute NSPI
2111 Eisenhower Ave.
Alexandria, VA 22314
(703) 838-0083

National Stone Association NSA
1415 Elliott Place NW
Washington, DC 20007
(202) 342-1100

National Terrazzo and Mosaic Association NTMA
3166 Des Plaines Ave., Suite 132
Des Plaines, IL 60018
(312) 635-7744

National Tile Roofing Manufacturers Association NTRMA
3127 Los Feliz Boulevard
Los Angeles, CA 90039
(213) 660-4411

National Trust for Historic Preservation NTHP
1785 Massachusetts Ave. N.W.
Washington, DC 20036
(202) 673-4000

National Wood Flooring
Association NWFA
11046 Manchester Road
St. Louis, MO 63122
(314) 821-8654

National Wood Window and
Door Association NWWDA
1400 E. Touhy Ave., Suite G-54
Des Plaines, IL 60018
(312) 299-5200

Northeast Sustainable
Energy Association NSEA
23 Ames Street
Greenfield, MA 01301
(413) 774-6051

Northeastern Lumber Manu-
facturers Association NELMA
272 Tuttle Road
CumberlandCenter, ME 04021
(207) 829-6901

Office Planners and Users
Group OPUG
P.O. Box 11182
Philadelphia, PA 19136
(215) 335-9400

Office Technology Research
Group OTRG
Box 65
Pasadena, CA 91102
(818) 796-2675

Organization of Women
Architects and Design
Professionals OWA
Box 26570
San Francisco, CA 94126
(415) 751-0342

Painting and Decorating
Contractors of America
PDCA
3913 Old Lee Hwy., Suite 33B
Fairfax, VA 22038
(703) 359-0826

Partners for Livable Places
PLP
1429 21st Street NW
Washington, DC 20036
(202) 887-5990

Passive Solar Industries
Council PSIC
1090 Vermont Ave. N.W.
Suite 1200
Washington, DC 20005
(202) 371-0357

Passive Solar Institute PSI
P.O. Box 722
Bascom, OH 44809
(419) 937-2225

Perlite Institute PI
88 New Dorp Plaza
Staten Island, NY 10306-2994
(718) 351-5723

Plastics Institute of America,
Stevens Inst. of Technology
PIA
Castle Point Station
Hoboken, NJ 07030
(201) 420-5553

Plumbing and Drainage
Institute, c/o Sol Baker PDI
1106 W. 77th St. South Dr.
Indianapolis, IN 46260
(317) 251-6970

Plywood Research
Foundation PRF
P.O. Box 11700
Tacoma, WA 98401
(206) 565-6600

Polyisocyanurate Insulation
Manufacturers Association
PIMA
104 Wilmot Road, Suite 201
Deerfield, IL 60015-5195
(708) 940-8800

Polyurethane Manufacturers
Association PMA
Building C, Suite. 20
800 Roosevelt Rd.
Glen Ellyn, IL 60137
(312) 858-2670

Porcelain Enamel Institute PEI
1001 Connecticut Ave. N.W.
Suite 700
Washington, DC 20036
(202) 857-1134

Portland Cement Association
PCA
5420 Old Orchard Road
Skokie, IL 60077
(312) 966-6200

Post-Tensioning Institute
PTI
1717 W. Northern Ave., Ste. 218
Phoenix, AZ 85013
(602) 870-7540

Powder Coating Institute PCI
1800 Diagonal Road, Suite 370
Alexandria, VA 22314
(703) 684-1770

Prestressed Concrete
Institute PCI
175 W. Jackson Blvd., Ste. 1859
Chicago, IL 60604
(312) 786-0300

Professional Services
Management Association
PSMA
1213 Prince Street
Alexandria, VA 22314
(703) 684-3993

Professional Women in
Construction PWC
342 Madison Avenue, Ste. 453
New York, NY 10173
(212) 687-0610

Project Management Institute
PMI
P.O. Box 43
Drexel Hill, PA 19026-3190
(215) 622-1796

Redwood Inspection Service
RIS
405 Enfrente Drive, Suite 200
Novato, CA 94949
(415) 382-0662

Reinforced Concrete
Research Council RCRC
205 N. Mathews Avenue
Urbana, IL 61801
(217) 333-7384

Resilient Floor Covering
Institute RFCI
966 Hungerford Dr., Suite 12B
Rockville, MD 20850
(301) 340-8580

Roof Research Center
Martin Marietta Research RRC
Bldg. 3147, Mail Stop 6070
P.O. Box 200
Oak Ridge, TN 37831-6070
(615) 574-4345

Roofing Industry
Educational Institute RIEI
14 Inverness Drive East, Bldg. H
Englewood, CO 80112-5608
(303) 790-7200

Rubber Manufacturers
Association, Roofing
Products Div. RMA
1400 K Street NW, Suite 900
Washington, DC 20005
(202) 682-4815

Safe Buildings Alliance SBA
655 15th St. NW
Washington, DC 20005
(202) 879-5120

Safety Glazing Certification
Council SGCC
c/o ETL Testing Labs
Industrial Park, Route 11
Cortland, NY 13045
(607) 753-6711

Sealant and Waterproofing
Restoration Institute SWRI
3101 Broadway
Suite 300
Kansas City, MO 64111
(816) 561-8230

Sealed Insulating Glass
Manufacturers Association
SIGMA
111 East Wacker Drive Suite 600
Chicago, IL 60601
(312) 644-6610

Security Industry Association
SIA
2800 28th Street, Suite 101
Santa Monica, CA 90405
(213) 450-4141

Seismological Society of
America SSA
El Cerrito Plaza Prof. Bldg.
#201
El Cerrito, CA 94530
(415) 525-5474

Sheet Metal and Air Condi-
tioning Contractors National
Association SMACNA
P.O. Box 70
Merrifield, VA 22116
(703) 790-9890

Single Ply Roofing Institute
SPRI
104 Wilmot Road, Suite 201
Deerfield, IL 60015
(312) 940-8800

Society for Computer
Applications in Engineering,
Planning and Architecture
CEPA
Five Park Avenue
Gaithersburg, MD 20877
(301) 926-7070

Society for Marketing Professional Services SMPS
99 Canal Center Plaza, Ste. 320
Alexandria, VA 22314
(703) 549-6117

Society of American Registered Architects SARA
1245 S. Highland Avenue
Lombard, IL 60148
(312) 932-4622

Society of American Wood Preservers, Inc. SAWP
7297 Lee Highway, Unit P
Falls Church, VA 22042
(703) 237-0900

Society of Architectural Administrators, SAA
c/o Deborah Worth 11225 S E
6th Street, Building. C, Ste. 200
Bellevue, WA 98004
(206) 682-8151

Society of Architectural Historians SAH
1232 Pine Street
Philadelphia, PA 19107
(215) 735-0224

Society of the Plastics Industry, Inc. SPI
1275 K Street NW, Suite 400
Washington, DC 20005
(202) 371-5200

Society of Wood Science and Technology SWST
One Gifford Pinchot Drive
Madison, WI 53705
(608) 231-9347

Solar Energy Industries Association SEIA
1730 North Lynn Street, Ste. 610
Arlington, VA 22209
(703) 524-6100

Solar Energy Research Institute SERI
1617 Cole Boulevard
Golden, CO 80401
(303) 231-1000

Southern Building Code Congress International SBCCI
900 Montclair Road
Birmingham, AL 35213
(205) 591-1853

Southern Forest Products Association SFPA
P.O. Box 52468
New Orleans, LA 70152
(504) 443-4464

Southern Pine Inspection Bureau SPIB
4709 Scenic Highway
Pensacola, FL 32504
(904) 434-2611

Special Libraries Association SLA
1700 18th St N.W.
Washington, DC 20009
(202) 234-4700

Stained Glass Association of America SGAA
4050 Broadway, Suite 219
Kansas City, MO 64111
(816) 561-4404

Steel Deck Institute SDI
P.O. Box 9506
Canton, OH 44711
(216) 493-7886

Steel Door Institute SDI
30200 Detroit Road
Cleveland, OH 44145-1967
(216) 899-0010

Steel Joist Institute SJI
1205 48th Avenue North
Suite A
Myrtle Beach, SC 29577
(803) 449-0487

**Steel Window Institute
c/o Thomas Associates SWI**
1230 Keith Building
Cleveland, OH 44115
(216) 241-7333

**Systems Builders Association
SBA**
28 Lowry Drive
West Milton, OH 45383
(513) 698-4127

**Thermal Insulation
Manufacturers Association
TIMA**
29 Bank Street
Stamford, CT 06901
(203) 324-7533

Tile Council of America TCA
P.O. Box 326
Princeton, NJ 08542-0326
(609) 921-7050

**Tilt-Up Concrete Association
TCA**
P.O. Box 430
Horse Shoe, NC 28742
(704) 891-9578

Truss Plate Institute TPI
583 D'Onofrio Drive, Suite 200
Madison, WI 53719
(608) 833-5900

Underwriters Laboratories UL
333 Pfingsten Road
Northbrook, IL 60062
(312) 272-8800

Urban Land Institute ULI
1090 Vermont Ave., NW
Washington, DC 20005
(202) 289-8500

Vermiculite Association VA
600 South Federal Way
Suite 400
Chicago, IL 60605
(312) 922-6222

**Vinyl Window and Door
Institute VWDI**
355 Lexington Ave.
New York, NY 10017
(212) 351-5400

**Wallcovering Manufacturers
Association WMA**
355 Lexington Avenue
17th Floor
New York, NY 10017
(212) 661-4261

West Coast Lumber
Inspection Bureau WCLIB
P.O. Box 23145
Tigard, OR 97223
(503) 639-0651

Western Red Cedar Lumber
Association WRCLA
1500 Yeon Building
522 SW Fifth Avenue
Portland, OR 97204-2122
(503) 224-3930

Western Wood Products
Association WWPA
1500 Yeon Building
522 SW Fifth Avenue
Portland, OR 97204-2122
(503) 224-3930

Wire Reinforcement Institute
WRI
1760 Reston Pkwy., Suite 403
Reston, VA 22090
(703) 709-9207

Wood and Synthetic Flooring
Institute WSFI
4415 West Harrison Street
Suite 242C
Hillside, IL 60162
(708) 449-2933

Wood Moulding and
Millwork Producers
Association WMMPA
P.O. Box 25278
Portland, OR 97225
(503) 292-9288

Wood Products Information
Center/World Forestry
Institute WPIC
4033 S.W. Canyon Road
Portland, OR 97221
(503) 228-1367

Wood Truss Council of
America WTCA
111 East Wacker Drive
Suite 600
Chicago, IL 60601
(312) 644-6610

Wool Bureau WB
360 Lexington Avenue
New York, NY 10017
(212) 986-6222